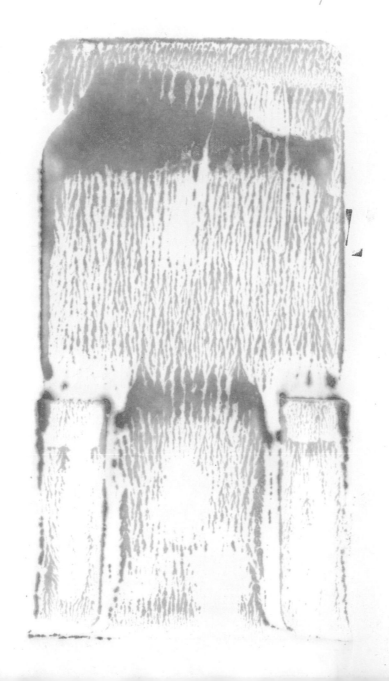

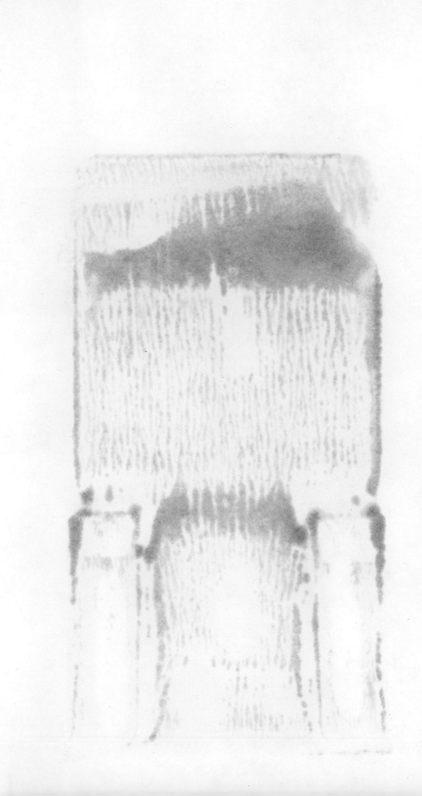

Designing and Decorating Interiors

Other Books by David B. Van Dommelen:

Design At Work: Its Forms and Functions
(with Edward Adams and George Pappas),
Center for Continuing Liberal Education,
The Pennsylvania State University, 1961.

Decorative Wall Hangings: Art with Fabric,
Funk and Wagnalls, New York, 1962.

Walls: Enrichment and Ornamentation,
Funk and Wagnalls, New York, 1965.

Designing and Decorating Interiors

DAVID B. VAN DOMMELEN

The Pennsylvania State University

John Wiley & Sons, Inc.   New York   London   Sydney

To my wife and children

■ PREFACE

The interior of a home often tells the story of the people who live there. When you notice line and form, texture and color, works of crafts and of fine arts, arrangements for beauty and for efficiency, you can begin to understand personalities of family members and the collective character of the family as a whole.

Designing and Decorating Interiors has been prepared to help you as a homemaker—and your family—to surround yourselves with beauty that reveals the real "you." This book will suggest creative uses of interior space that will help your family to live most fully according to its special individuality. The book should also help you convince your visitors that there is only *one* home such as yours.

The first part of this book, "Characteristics of Design for Interiors," presents basic principles of design so you can apply them to interior spaces. Here the aim is to sharpen your understanding of the many aesthetic and functional elements that make up a home setting and the varied ways these elements can be combined to give your home its most personally expressive meaning.

The second part, "Roots and Heritage," offers a brief history of design in furniture and architecture. It should make you more aware of dynamic contemporary trends by revealing important past events in the world of design.

In the third part, "Contemporary Designer," you will discover how modern designers and manufacturers bring products of good design to your doorstep. Some specific producers are mentioned, but the plan is not to rate one producer above another; rather, it is to show the contributions to twentieth-century design of craftsmen, architects, fine artists, and technicians. All are working together toward the common goal of enhancing your home.

Chapters such as "Fine Arts in the Home" and "The Contemporary Artist-Craftsman" discuss the accessories that can enrich your home with interesting objects. Chapters dealing with fabrics and with construction of furniture are offered to help every homemaker select wisely and well. The ideas and methods are inexpensive enough to fit virtually any family's budget; but some are costly, too. They are offered here to give you a broad view of the many directions you can take in giving individual attractiveness to each area of your home. They range all the way from the imaginative uses of weeds, rocks, and shells to unusual ways of displaying oil paintings and other works of art.

The last part of this book, "The Total Concept," brings together the many elements, small and large, that must be organized to make your complete house an attractive, individual, and useful space in which to live. The total plan of your home, efficient patterns of traffic, integration of the interior with the exterior, planning of outdoor areas, special-purpose rooms for family members with special interests, and development of multiple-purpose rooms are among the many problems discussed fully.

There is no ultimate answer to all the questions raised by interior space, but at least we know that some approaches lead to happier solutions than others. These are the approaches suggested here, in the belief that through looking and reading, making personal investigations and learning, you can discover how to combine your own creative impulses and needs with contemporary approaches to good design. The result? A home that will please and satisfy your whole family and each of its individual members in the years ahead!

University Park, Pennsylvania   David B. Van Dommelen
July, 1965

■ ACKNOWLEDGMENTS

Completion of this book was made possible through the help of many people. It is not possible to mention each one of them. However, I would like to thank Florence Knoll Bassett of Knoll Associates, Inc., and Jim Lucas, formerly of Herman Miller Inc., for reading parts of this manuscript; Richard L. Tooke of the Museum of Modern Art who spent many hours searching for photographs for this book; the companies that donated photographs; and the students who have contributed by answering questionnaires concerning the content and arrangement of this book. My special thanks to Sally Kaiser, Sandra Scholl, and James Watts, students in the Department of Family Housing and Home Art, of The Pennsylvania State University, for their drawings used in Chapter Eleven.

D.B.V.D.

■ CONTENTS

Part One: CHARACTERISTICS
OF DESIGN FOR INTERIORS

A uniform line effect is achieved in this room by the use of furniture of identical height. The line is broken by sculptures and plants just enough to add interest to the arrangement. (Photo: courtesy of Knoll Associates, Inc.)

The lines in this tree are very different from the line effect in the previous photograph. Here lines are active and unrestful.

Chapter 1 DESIGN GUIDES

Throughout the history of man and throughout all human activity, design has played an important part in the everyday environment of human beings. Man has devised many unique designs and motifs to decorate his living spaces and his clothing. These decorative motifs have changed from year to year as man has changed his outlook on the world. His sources of design have changed to some extent also, but in general his most influential source has been nature. From around the natural environment of man have come the stimulation and excitement of pattern and line, color and form, and shape and texture. Through his understanding of this exciting world surrounding him, man has built a vocabulary to aid him in assembling beauty.

An appreciation of beauty and good design cannot be learned easily and then put aside for use during some few moments when they are deemed necessary; instead, this appreciation must become an integral part of one's life, entering each part of every day and each activity that takes place. An awareness of good design becomes a part of the individual and his character—the way he feels, thinks, and sees his world. All the reading in design books and art books will not make one a designer if one is not ready to live the excitement described therein. Good design cannot be developed with a closed and unwilling mind; it can only grow when the individual is ready to investigate all the information available and then is willing creatively to experiment, look, live, and feel the things that make up design.

In order to have a better understanding of beauty and aesthetics in objects and design, we shall attempt to become familiar with some of the measuring devices used to determine the elements of which design is composed. In the vocabulary of design, many words and phrases have been developed to pinpoint certain fundamentals that seem essential to creating a successful composition or design. This composition or design could be a piece of architecture, a painting, or a rug. Any object, whether it is a clothing ensemble or a home, can be examined by using the basic design fundamentals.

Obviously, the individual working in fields of creative art must be familiar with design terminology, but we must always keep in mind that there is no better way to understand these terms than in their practical application. Little can be understood about color, for instance, unless the person working with color can actually put it together, mix it, and find excitement with it. Until he does this, his feeling for and knowledge of design problems is almost nothing.

The emotional content of design is by far one of the most important aspects of design and the one most consistently overlooked in the world of education. The creative painter or designer does not "research" each color combination he wishes to use in his project, but instead he feels it and explores it. When he has done this—and only then—will he know and fully comprehend what vast possibilities are available for him in creating. The libraries are full of meaningless studies in design problems, from the most ridiculous pulling apart of color to minute examinations of rhythm and line in clothing and furnishings. In the end these studies are useless, because the creative designer calls from within himself for meaningful and personal interpretation.

Each term used today in the vocabulary of design can be interpreted in many different ways. There are no longer traditional rules by which design must be measured. Books and authorities vary greatly in meanings and uses of terms. Many designers are closely tied to the elements and principles of design, while others seldom use the terms at all. In looking at the breakdown of design guides, the reader should remember that the author is not setting himself up as the last word in this area. Instead, he has carefully culled many sources and finally has attempted to pull together many ideas for a general over-all picture of the many definitions of words used in design.

Because we are concerned here with interiors, we shall think of these design guides in light of living spaces. While you read and investigate the terms that will become basic to your knowledge of interiors, you should also be aware that beauty is not necessarily formed by the use of these guides alone.

PRINCIPLES AND ELEMENTS

If we were called upon to break down all the working guides in formulating a design, two groups would emerge —*the elements* and *the principles*. Many people feel it is necessary to use these terms consistently in their traditional categories, while others hardly mention them and instead depend on less rigid vocabularies.

The elements of art or design are those basic things necessary to all the visual arts. Into this group fall *line*, *texture*, *form*, and *color*, as well as *pattern*, *light*, and *space*.

The principles, which are applied to the elements of design, are *balance*, *emphasis*, *rhythm*, and *proportion*.

The use of any or all of the above guides will not guarantee an aesthetic composition, but an understanding of these ingredients will *help* attain the goals toward which one works.

Line

Line is a basic design element that should be carefully considered when designing the interior spaces of a room or home. It has many properties and can do many things for a room or composition. Line is unlimited in its characteristics. It can be static and dead, a state represented by a line lying in a horizontal position, or line can be alive and full of movement. A line can portray emotion and excitement, rhythm and strength, decoration and unity.

In an interior, line can be a unifying factor or a destructive element in the over-all effect of a room. When too many lines of opposing nature predominate in a house, the result is a visual impression of chaos. It is therefore important to reduce line to a well-integrated plan. Rooms that have beamed ceilings, paneling on the walls, and too many different patterns are apt to present a disorganized picture.

Line should be continuous to produce an impression of the most unity. This does not mean there can never be a break in line, but the fewer breaks there are, the more organized the room will appear. Strong straight lines will help pull the room together, but at the same time may give the room a very rigid look. The addition of curved transitional lines will then soften the sheer, cold look. Of course, if one is looking for a very contemporary architectural appearance in a room, straight lines alone should be used.

Vertical lines on the interior or the exterior will add an appearance of height to the room or building, while horizontal lines will give a room an appearance of more length and less height.

In furniture arrangement, the effect of unity is increased when equal heights are present in the room. This adds to the feeling of a continuous line around the room. When large, oversized pieces of furniture are used next to small delicate pieces, the eye is carried away from a delicate piece to a massive one, and there is no gradual move-ment of the eye as it passes around the room. Instead, it jumps and stops and often sees little of importance. Furniture pieces should be scaled equally, so that the eye will move quietly across the room from one object to another. Lines should be related to each other and to the surrounding factors.

Texture

Texture is the surface characteristic of objects, furniture, and architectural planes. There are many types of textural surfaces, ranging from smooth to very rough. A

There is a nice harmony of textures in this room. The rough rug offers a contrast to the smooth, dull surface of the walls, and the shiny aluminum of the furniture adds a needed sparkle. Notice the grain of the door, which does not dominate the room but adds an interesting pattern to a rather quiet entrance. Even the trees outside contribute textural qualities to this room. (Photo: courtesy of Herman Miller Inc.)

careful balance is needed to make a room work well. The rougher the texture, the more light it will absorb; the smoother the surface of an object, the more light it will reflect. In rooms that are small and have few windows, smoother textures should be used so that more light is reflected into the room. Larger rooms with more windows and open spaces can utilize the rougher textures with more grace.

Texture refers to the tactile sensations as well as to the visual impressions that one receives. The tactile qualities are of great importance in the consideration of textiles for furniture. Certain textures are unpleasant to sit on, such as frieze, and others, like plastic, might be too cold in character to utilize in some situations.

The maintenance problems of textures should also be considered in the design of an interior. The smoother the surface, the more difficult it will be to keep it clean in appearance; each fingerprint and mark will show; on the other hand, the rougher the texture, the more easily will dirt be able to gather in its pores.

Textures utilized in an object can have a great effect on it, for textures are part of the structural components of an object; the wrong use of texture or material will reduce the object to a badly designed product.

A balance of textures should be used to create harmony in a room, just as a correct balance and scale of furniture must be planned.

Shape and Form

Shape and form are closely related areas. Shape is two-dimensional in character and can be considered as a flat plane. Form is three-dimensional, showing mass and volume. Form displaces space, while shape delineates the contour of an object.

There are three types of shape and form. The first of these is *representational* and presents a likeness of an object that is easily recognizable. Representational and realistic are two words that may be used interchangeably in discussing shape and form.

The second type of shape and form is *abstract*. This type of shape and form is derived from objects in nature or from other things that are familiar to us; however, they have been distorted, exaggerated, and reorganized, sometimes beyond recognition.

The third type of shape and form is called *nonobjective*. In this grouping we find geometric forms and biomorphic shapes. These do not have any relationship to any real object; however, we have attached names to many

In nature textures are important to the beauty of our visual world. Smooth surfaces and pebbly surfaces balance each other like music.

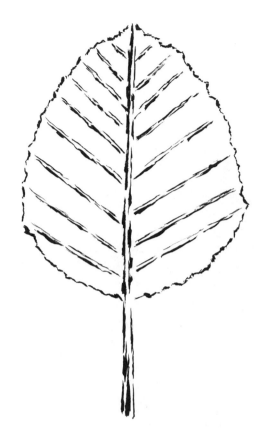

Representational: presenting a likeness that is recognizable and realistic.

Abstract: presenting an image that is derived from the familiar, but has been distorted and rearranged.

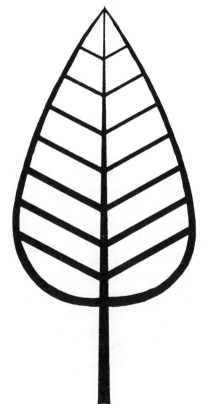

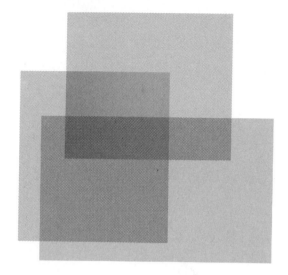

Geometric: a shape or form that is not associated with nature but is mathematical in character.

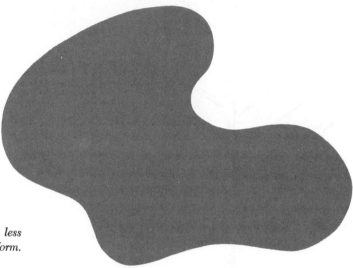

Biomorphic: irregular, free-form shape with less mathematical character than the geometric form. It is often found in nature.

of the shapes in this category. The "free-form" design is in this group, as are mathematical configurations.

All these shapes and forms are found in the home in some way or other. They can be seen as flat two-dimensional shapes or as three-dimensional forms. Plates, cylinders for lamp bases and drinking glasses, or bubble lamps become shapes when silhouetted against a background.

Shape and form play a dominant role in the interior of any home as well as on the exterior of the house or building. Shape and form unite with line to achieve certain effects in the over-all design of the room. Each manifests itself and either weakens or gives strength to the other. A long, low rectangular table or sofa will help create a line of unity in the whole room. When there are too many varie-

ties of shape and form in the room, confusion and chaos result. Of course, variety is necessary to give the room life, but it should be used cautiously.

Unity and Variety

A most important attribute in a room is unity within the living space. For unity, a room must have harmony or continuity. This can be achieved easily in diverse ways. The easiest way to accomplish it is by painting the walls all in the same color. Another way is by utilizing the same type of woods or identical styles of furniture. The unification of a room, then, is carried out by repeating certain elements. This repetition does not necessarily guarantee complete success, but it does help in tying a room together. The danger in seeking unity is the possibility of getting too much of it, thus making the room dull and uninteresting. Monotony can be found in many rooms, because the homeowner or housewife purchased a "set" of furniture or carried unity too far in some other way without injecting variety.

Variety will break the sameness of unity. This can be done by adding contrasting color to a room, by introducing varied types of furniture styles, by having several kinds of woods in the room, or by painting one wall in a room a different color. Variety can also be brought to a room by the types of objects and enrichment that are added. One must remember not to have too much variety, or the room will be cluttered and messy in appearance. When both unity and variety have been carefully balanced, the room will have harmony and continuity.

Balance

A major principle in all types of interiors and all kinds of compositions is balance. In a living space, the balance constantly changes. As people use a room, the balance within the room shifts; as light enters the room through the windows and apertures of the architecture, its effect alters the manner in which the viewer sees the space.

The simple architectural features of this room have been overpowered by too much variety. The interesting linear characteristics that were the main decorative elements of this room have been destroyed. Unity can be restored by removal of many objects on the wall and sofa. (Photo: courtesy of Douglas Fir Plywood Association.)

Unity and variety are always found beautifully balanced in nature. Unity is seen here in the rocks, and variety is observed in the different sizes and shapes.

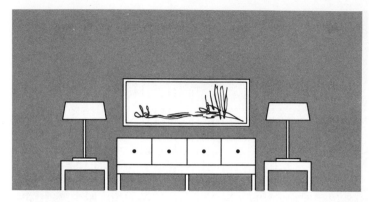

Symmetrical balance is usually rather limited and formal.

Asymmetrical balance is casual and is unlimited in its possibilities for arrangements.

A broken symmetrical design lends variety to the symmetrical balance. It also introduces a somewhat casual effect.

Balance in an interior changes with color, and a visual weight is the result. Darker colors will produce a heavier effect, while lighter colors will give the impression of a lighter weight.

There are three types of balance used in interiors.

Symmetrical Balance. Symmetry is formal in character. In this arrangement, the wall of a room is carefully balanced from a center-line point. Each element is repeated in pairs, one on each side of the center line. A line drawn through the middle of the composition would reveal identical scenes on each side of the line. Symmetrical balance is seen at its best in traditional architecture and in period rooms. Precise order is the result of symmetrical balance; it tends to be limited and unimaginative in its application.

Asymmetrical Balance. Asymmetry has much more freedom than does symmetrical balance; it is also called informal, occult, or active balance. This type of arrangement is casual and is therefore found more often in contemporary interiors and in modern architecture. This does not mean, however, that it may not be utilized in traditional settings. In this type of balance there is no obvious center line which divides the composition into two parts. Instead, the design is like a teeter-totter on which varied weights are carefully placed at certain distances from the balancing point. Each side of the balancing point is different, allowing for a great number of possible arrangements. There are few limitations on the various visual impacts that can be achieved by invention and imagination. Informal balance gives the designer much more freedom than does formal balance wherein everything has a predetermined placement. It usually is an exciting type of balance. Because occult balance is active, it has gained more favor in the last few years. Chapter 4 shows how the *de Stijl* members in Holland used asymmetrical design successfully.

Both the sculpture and the arrangement of table and chairs are examples of radial balance, based on a wheel-and-spoke design. The flowers on the table are given the part of the center core in this elegant setting of Eero Saarinen furniture. (Photo: courtesy of Knoll Associates, Inc.)

Radial Balance. The third type of balance is radial or circular in nature. All the elements of the design radiate from a center point or core. This type of design is based on the wheel. Although radial balance is not often used, it can be very effective and interesting in many places in the home. The most usual place to see radial balance is on a round dining table, with a floral arrangement in the center and individual place settings around the edge of the table. Another place where this form of balance is used is in conversational areas. Here the chairs are arranged in a circle, with a coffee table in the middle. A spacious room is needed for this type of arrangement, but its effectiveness is undoubtedly very great.

Emphasis

Emphasis is an important factor in all interiors. Emphasis could be called the focal point of a room or the center of interest. Not enough people consider emphasis when they are designing a room. It is important to have no more than one emphasized point in the room; with one focal point, there may be several areas that are subordinate to that point. Emphasis is achieved through contrasts in color, texture, and size. It is up to the designer to decide which part of a room is to be emphasized, the extent to which attention is to be called to it, and in what way it is to be emphasized. It should also be remembered that when people enter a room, the emphasis point might easily

SITUATION	EMPHASIS
Monochromatic blue living room with various values and intensities of blue.	A large orange and yellow painting over a sofa.
White-walled hallway.	End of hall—blank space covered with colorful patterned wallpaper.
Shelf arrangement of glass bottles.	One object with different texture and shape.
Pure contemporary room with prominent glass, metal and plastic.	Antique wood breakfront.

This black dot illustrates emphasis. It was probably the first thing you saw on the page.

change, and therefore it might be necessary to make the emphasis point stronger than the room seems to call for when there are no people within the space. There is no formula for the success of emphasis—each situation and each room will dictate different needs. Patterns of walls, rugs, and fabrics must be carefully balanced with each other as well as with colors used in the room. One object with too much color or too much pattern can very easily shift the focal point; dominant patterns and colors are therefore sometimes necessarily omitted for more successful effects. Furniture can be arranged to bring emphasis to a particular part of the room. Emphasis is completely a problem of dominance and subordination. There are endless ways to bring good emphasis into a room. The following ideas might be studied for examples.

Rhythm

Rhythm is the movement of the eye across a design. This can be achieved in several ways; *repetition* is one of them. The repetition of a line or shape carries the eye along the design from one line to the next. Alternating lines and shapes can be exciting and should be varied so that the design does not become too dull and monotonous. The consideration of unity and variety is essential in rhythm; unity helps in moving the eye across or along the design, while variety makes it a more interesting movement. In an interior, the repetition of chairs and objects would have the same effect as the repetition of a motif in a textile design. Another way to provide rhythm is by *continuous line,* which induces the eye to follow the line slowly, moving along its direction with continuity and determination. Occasionally a break may occur for interest, and continuity will depend on the strength of the line. *Progression* of sizes is another device to achieve rhythm. In this technique, the designer uses a variety of sizes of objects so placed as to pull the eye in the direction desired. Three objects slowly graduated in size and placed next to each other will force the eye to move up or down the design. A frequent fault in this approach to rhythm is a stereotyped placement of objects in a step arrangement. An example would be the placing of duck or flying-geese plaques on a wall. The big one is placed first, then the middle-sized one, and finally the smallest, each stepping down—a very unimaginative ar-

Rhythm develops through the repetition of one shape. The eyes move across the design in a slow, steady movement.

Continuous line is another device for creating rhythm and movement. The eyes follow the curves and twists of the line. The line could also be straight and rigid.

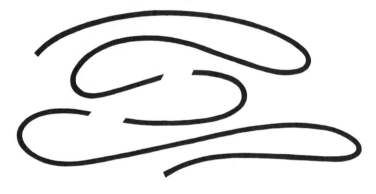

Rhythm is achieved in this fabric design through the progression of sizes of birds. The eye starts with either the smaller or larger birds and slowly moves up or down the drapery in quiet rhythm. (Photo: courtesy of Ben Rose.)

rangement, but one that points out progression through size to achieve rhythm.

Proportion

This is an extremely difficult design problem. There seems to be no definite rule or formula that can be used to define correctly the term proportion. Proportion is the consideration of weight and shape and division of an object. Several authors have dealt with complex mathematical computations to arrive at what might be considered good proportions, but probably the best way to learn the nature of good proportions is actual work with concrete problems in design. Proportion, like asymmetrical balance, requires close observation and many manipulations before it can be learned.

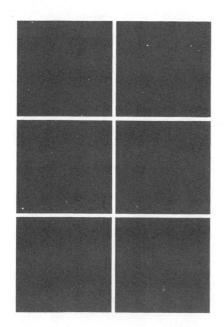

Objects and furnishings divided by the "Golden Oblong."

A device that is often employed in determining good proportion is the *Golden Oblong* or *Golden Section* used by the Greeks during early times. This form of proportion is based on a system of two–three, three–four, and so on, with the idea that a square is less interesting than an oblong. While this may be true, we should not reject the square as unaesthetic. Artists for hundreds of years have been using the rectangle for painting and at the same time incorporating the rules dictated by the ancient Greeks.

The following diagrams will give you a visual idea of how the Greek division of space works, and how this could be applied to objects within the home.

Color

Color is an important factor in giving character and personality to a room or to an object in a room. Color is a very personal consideration and must be handled as such by the designer when he begins to apply color to a living space. No interior is complete without some manipulation of color. Of course, color not only adds glow and sparkle to an interior but also presents various other aspects to the viewer. Psychological characteristics must be carefully considered in each room, for different colors will affect different people and activities in the room. Color will also reflect light or absorb light, producing darker or lighter spaces in the home.

There are many complex color theories used today by interior designers, lecturers, and physicists, for color can be approached in many ways. The scientists' approach to color varies greatly from the way the artist views color. We are, and should be, more concerned here with the artistic or aesthetic approach.

In the discussion of color, it is generally a practice to utilize one of the basic color theorist's studies. Some of these are extremely complex, while others can be readily understood without graphs and charts. The following discussion of color will be based on a modified Prang system.

One must first become aware of the many words used in describing color and its major characteristics. These

Wall unit divided by the "Golden Oblong."

words are part of the professional vocabulary of teachers of design, interiors, and related problems in design. We shall look at these words and their meanings in relationship to living spaces.

Hue. The classification of color or the name by which a color is known is hue. There are standard names for many colors, and there are more dramatic names for colors that industry uses. A name like red is not as romantic as "Lipstick Red," so the color institutes employ names that will sound more entrancing and will supposedly add glamour to the room or object being colored. Some of these names eventually become standard descriptions, such as "Forest Green," "Kelly Green," "Apple Green," and "Olive Green." With each name listed above, the reader receives a visual color image. Prang uses the initials of the hues such as R for Red and BG for Blue-Green.

Hues are primary, secondary, and intermediate. In the Prang System, 12 hues are found on the color wheel. The primary colors are those colors from which all other colors are mixed—red, yellow, and blue. By mixing two primary colors together, one obtains secondary colors. These are orange, green, and purple (violet). An intermediate color is obtained by mixing one primary and one secondary color together. An example is red-orange, produced by mixing red and orange.

Each of these hues has a cool or warm characteristic. The cool colors are those that would be found in the shade, such as greens, blues and purples; the warm colors are those that are found in the sunlight. These are red, orange and yellow. It is necessary to consider the temperature aspects of colors when using them in some rooms. A cold northern-exposure room can be warmed up and given more cheery qualities by using sunshine yellow or pumpkin orange; a very warm room with a southwest exposure can be cooled with use of green or blue. Temperature aspects of color also apply to the kitchen, where the heat from the range, the oven, and a great deal of activity will call for cooler colors rather than the warm colors so often found in kitchens.

Value. A color's value is its lightness or darkness. The lightness is achieved by adding white to any color, while the darkness is the result of mixing black with a color. For example, when white is added to red, a pink tint is achieved, while maroon is the result of adding black to red. When a proper value study is made, one discovers that there is a huge range of values for *this* color—from pure white through red to pure black. In an examination of a value study, the average person will discover several visual color changes (or steps) within the process.

The value of a color makes a great difference in the visual size of a room. The darker the color, the less spacious is the feeling; and the lighter the color, the larger the room appears. To exaggerate this point, imagine a room painted in pure white and one painted in pure black. The room with white walls will seem to enlarge to a spacious living room, and the black-walled room will close in on the inhabitant, causing a feeling of claustrophobia.

Intensity. The chroma, or intensity, of a color is the purity of a color or the strength of a color. The purer the color, or the more intense the color, the less another color is mixed with it. If we take red as an example again, and if we begin to add green, which is the complementary color of red, we will discover that the red will become less bright with each drop of green that is added, until it is a very dull color—almost a brown. If we were to take a tint of red, such as pink, and add a small amount of green to it, we would find that a rose color would result. To break down the intensity of any color, its complement is added. The complement of any color is found exactly across from it on the color wheel. Intensities can also be lowered and raised by various types of lights projected onto a color; thus the lighting arrangement in the room must be well planned.

Intensities, as well as values, are important in a room. One can imagine what a room would be like if all the intensities were the same. If the identical hue of red were used for the walls, draperies, carpet, sofa, and chairs, it would be a difficult room in which to live. Therefore, intensities must be varied to break down monotony.

Color Schemes

It is not necessary to use standardized color schemes when designing a room. In fact, the most exciting room is probably one that is put together with creativity and spontaneity. However, it is generally considered good to establish an understanding of the various types of schemes used. This is probably all right for the beginner who feels insecure when starting to design an interior. There are two groups of color schemes, the *related* and the *contrasting*. These are called "mechanical" color schemes (*Design For You*, Beitler & Lockhart, p. 120). Both have good points and can be used very effectively in interiors.

Related Color Schemes. Utilization of colors that have common characteristics is the distinctive quality of related color schemes. The colors used are very closely situated to each other on the color wheel and have one color in common.

Monochromatic. Color schemes using only one hue are monochromatic. The word monochromatic implies this in its structure—mono (one) and chromatic (color intensity). In this color scheme, the designer employs several or many values and intensities of one color. The range might be from white to black or from very pure color to very dull color. But in any case, only one family of color is incorporated. Often people think of the monochromatic as either brown or black in character, but any color can be used—blue, yellow, or red.

This type of scheme helps to give a more spacious feeling to a room and also provides more unity for the composition. It presents a quieter background for objects and people within the room and it gives the designer a reasonable chance of success. The drawback to this scheme is that it can easily become monotonous, and therefore we seldom see it used in its pure form. More often we see small accents of another color introduced for variety and for excitement. Often whites and blacks can be used rather nicely with this type of scheme to break the monotony.

Analogous. Color schemes utilizing colors that are situated next to each other on the color wheel are called analogous. Such a scheme generally uses one color as its major force, with the two neighboring colors as secondary forces. An example would be yellow, yellow-green, and green; all of these colors have yellow in them. Another example would be blue, blue-green, and blue-purple; each color has blue in it, thus relating it to each of the others. For simplicity it is best to use only three of the colors next to each other on the color wheel, although more can be used. The more colors that are used in an analogous scheme, the more confusing the room may become unless the designer is extremely able.

Of course, the analogous color scheme also incorporates various values and intensities, cool or warm colors. The analogous and the monochromatic schemes are more likely to be harmonious than are the contrasting schemes, which are based on extreme differences on the color wheel.

Accented Neutral. Color schemes that utilize a neutral color, such as brown, grey, or white, with an accent color for breaking the monotony, are known as accented neutral. The neutral scheme is a very good one, because it presents a room with a neutral background for both objects and people. The white neutral scheme became extremely popular in the 1960s because of its adaptability not only to contemporary rooms but also to many traditional-style interiors. It is a very versatile scheme that allows for easy color-accent changes by the simple process of altering pillow covers, slipcovers, and small objects. It also is good for homeowners who have large collections of art objects and who need neutral walls in order to exhibit a collection effectively.

Contrasting Color Schemes. Differences are the basis for contrasting schemes. Here the designer takes two colors which are extreme opposites in one way or another. One might be cool, and the other warm. In any event, the schemes rely on definite contrasts rather than on the close color relationship used in a monochromatic and an analogous scheme. In the contrast group, there can be

ROOM	EXPOSURE	WALLS	CEILINGS	FLOORS	DRAPERIES
Living	Southwest	Chalk white	Chalk white	Terra-cotta tile Large grey shag rug	White casement
Living	Southeast	3 walls sky blue 1 wall white	White	Blue and grey salt-and-pepper carpeting	Textured grey-blue linen
Living	North	Beige	Off-white	Light brown carpeting	Beige
Dining	North	Light pumpkin	Brown	Old oak	Off-white cotton
Dining	Southwest	White	White	Emerald-green carpeting	White and light green patterned
Dining	North	Dusty rose	Rose-tinted white	Rose carpeting	Rose, pink, and moss-green, textured
Hallway	North	Light mustard yellow	Off-white	Fieldstone	None
Hallway	South	Mauve	White	Concord grape carpeting	White casements on side windows
Bedroom	South	Walnut paneling	White	Beige rug	Brown and green patterned linen
Bedroom	Northeast	Apricot	Off-white	Champagne-yellow carpeting	Pale apricot rayon curtains
Bedroom	South	Light blue	White	Hardwood floor Burnt-orange area rugs	Light blue, white, and burnt-orange striped draperies
Kitchen	North	White	White	Green vinyl tile	Purple, green, and orange pattern
Kitchen	Southeast	Light pastel yellow	White	Yellow and burnt-orange tile	Yellow-green patterned

FURNITURE	UPHOLSTERY	ACCESSORIES	TYPE SCHEME	OVER-ALL EFFECT
Scandinavian teak	Orange and turquoise fabrics	Slate lamps Black throw pillows	Complementary	Modern, clean, spacious look
Walnut	Black-striped fabric on sofa Blueprint-blue chairs	Ceramic pieces Orange wall hanging	Monochromatic with accent	Airy and open effect
Teak White plastic chairs	Light brown and tan linen	Orange paintings Burnt-orange small objects	Neutral with accent	Quiet, warm, unified
White plastic chairs Teak table	None	White porcelain	Close to a monochromatic	Warm, close, and sophisticated
Mahogany chairs, table, and serving board	Emerald green	Gold and white china		Clean, neat, cold, formal
Fruitwood	Deep red	Pink china	Monochromatic almost complementary	Warm, soft, and feminine
Cherry bench and table	None	Antique copper	None—close to analogous	Casual and informal
White antiqued-wood settee	Champagne damask	None	Complementary	Formal, traditional
Walnut	Brown leather Green spread	Brown, green, and white		Masculine, warm, close, cosy
Off-white	Light orange	White and cream	Analogous	Feminine and soft
Walnut	Dark blue chairs and spread	Beige, blue, and orange	Complementary	Master bedroom, neither feminine nor very masculine
Cabinets light green	Orange chairs	Violet	Triad with secondary colors	Cheerful and colorful
White	Burnt orange	Yellow and orange	Analogous	Probably too warm for a kitchen

great variations from highly saturated color to very dull combinations. There is a great variety of possibilities in this group.

Complementary Schemes. Schemes relying on two colors found across from each other on the color wheel are complementary. Two examples would be blue and orange or yellow-green and red-violet. These colors need not be used in their pure form but can be used in many possible values and intensities. Thus there is a great variety in the complementary scheme. It can be developed from a monochromatic scheme accented with a complementary color or from an even balance of the two colors.

Double Complementary Schemes. Similar to the complementary, the double complementary scheme uses two (rather than one) sets of complementary colors. These two sets of complementary colors must be next to each other on the color wheel—for example, orange and yellow and their respective complements. There is little doubt that this type of color scheme could be rather chaotic if it is not worked out carefully. It is best to carry out many experiments with the double complementary until a completely satisfactory arrangement of colors has been reached.

Split Complementary Schemes. The designer takes one color and, instead of its complementary color, uses the two colors on each side of the complementary color, in a split complementary scheme. This offers more variety then the simple complementary scheme. An example of this would be yellow with red-violet and blue-violet. This color scheme also must be approached carefully, or the results can be disastrous.

Triad Schemes. Use of three colors that form a triangle on the color wheel creates a triad scheme. The colors are at equal distance from each other, such as red, blue, and yellow, for example. A group of artists who used this particular type of triad color scheme formed a group known as the *de Stijl* movement, about which you will read in a later chapter.

Creative Schemes

The creative scheme is by far the most exciting type of scheme, for it allows the designer complete freedom for experimentation. There is no mechanical scheme or set of rules with which he must work; instead, he can let his imagination carry the scheme to completion. This type of approach to color schemes is, of course, not a reliable one, unless the designer has had a great deal of experience with color and interiors. It is the manner in which most professional designers work with interiors. They seldom depend on a particular scheme, though this does not imply that the end result will never be identifiable as, perhaps, an analogous or monochromatic scheme. In a creative scheme, the designer might use highly intense colors of reds and pinks with oranges or magentas, or he might use a scheme of all blacks and whites. The room, its occupants, and its use will help dictate the nature of the environment he is creating. But most of all, the feeling of color will come to him from his emotional response to the interior he is planning.

Creating a Color Scheme. There are many approaches to creating a scheme for a room. The best way to proceed is by investigation and study. Gather as many colors as possible from all sources—magazines, advertisements, wallpaper samples, and fabric swatches. Begin to assemble them in some way that will be helpful to you for later references. Make lists of colors you and other members of the family like. Slowly a group of colors will begin to emerge as more suitable for the varying members of a household, and these colors can then be suited to particular rooms.

A very effective way of assembling a color scheme is to take a variety of color samples of fabric and yarn out into the garden or yard. Place them next to flowers and grasses until pleasing arrangements are reached. Nature is especially good for basic colors, and natural colors are easy for the beginner to understand. When pleasing groupings have been made, then a search can be started for colors in paints and materials to match those found in nature. It is not necessary actually to copy the color schemes found in the garden, but rather to study the many intensities and values and how they work together.

The accompanying chart will give you a general idea of some color combinations that could be used in various rooms in the home. These are merely suggestions; they do not represent ideals. From these you can continue to grow and experiment with newer and probably more personal combinations.

Other Aspects of Color

Ideas about color are stereotyped, just as are many other concepts in our society. Some colors are immediately associated with particular things or occasions because through the years we have continually seen them used in one way. An example of what is meant by this might be this question: what color does a baby boy wear? At once the reader thinks of a certain color. The same thing happens when you think of colors for Christmas. Two colors come into mind. The more creative and less stereotyped person will be able to think of more interesting colors, but the average person will always list the same colors: blue for the baby boy and green and red for Christmas. We also find ourselves thinking that certain colors can be used only in certain rooms. Or we may also think that certain color combinations cannot be used together. Blue and green have traditionally been thought of as a pair of colors that should never be put together. Only in contemporary design have we seen more experimentation taking place in color combinations. Stereotyped colors and combinations are difficult to erase.

The psychological aspects of colors are important in rooms and interiors. Psychology does not stop in the psychologists' offices but can be projected into living rooms and kitchens. Certain colors, because of their past associations, put up barriers for some of us. To some people black is a funereal color; these people would not use it in any part of a home. The more pure and warm a room's color, the more activity it will provoke in the person who is using the room. An example would be that a red room will heighten the productivity of a secretary, while a blue room will cause her output to drop. For this we can determine that a room to relax in should utilize cooler colors, while a room meant for greater activity might use more vivid colors. Colors do affect people, and it is, therefore, important to select the proper color for the proper room.

Colors will also make walls and ceiling appear to recede or drop. Warm colors appear closer, and cool colors seem farther away. A room that we wish to make appear larger should be painted in cool colors; a room we wish to make appear smaller should be painted in warmer colors.

Studies have been made to determine what colors flies and insects prefer; not that the fly goes around looking for a certain color, but they say that psychologically he is drawn to particular ones.

BIBLIOGRAPHY AND SUGGESTED READINGS

Anderson, Donald M., *Elements of Design,* Holt, Rinehart, and Winston, Inc., New York, 1961.

Beitler, Ethel Jane, and Bill Lockhart, *Design For You,* John Wiley and Sons, New York, 1961.

Bevlin, Marjorie Elliott, *Design Through Discovery,* Holt, Rinehart, and Winston, Inc., New York, 1963.

Emerson, Sybil, *Design, A Creative Approach,* International Textbook Co., Scranton, 1953.

Kepes, Gyorgy, *The New Landscape,* Paul Theobald and Co., Chicago, 1947.

Moholy-Nagy, Lazlo, *The New Vision,* Norton, New York, 1958.

Neutra, Richard, *Survival Through Design,* Oxford University Press, New York, 1954.

Scott, Robert G., *Design Fundamentals,* McGraw-Hill Book Co., New York, 1951.

Warner, Esther, *Art: An Everyday Experience,* Harper and Row, New York, 1963.

PART ONE: COMMENTS

With a basic vocabulary such as the one you have now acquired, you can begin to look at the past events that have led the designer into the twentieth century. The principles and elements of design were used in varying ways by designers of the nineteenth century and the early part of the twentieth. At times their applications harmonized with concepts you have read and discussed, while at other times they seemed to be at extreme opposites.

Because there is such a vast range of ideas of what is good design and bad design, the quality of design has fluctuated from one year to another. In addition, we must remember that trends and fads play an important role in our world of design.

The person interested in design can only understand what is happening today by understanding what has happened previously.

Part Two: ROOTS AND HERITAGE

Decorated objects from the isolated Eskimos of eastern Greenland include a throwing board, an eye shade, a pail, and a needle case of skin. To offset the barrenness of their surroundings, the eastern Greenland Eskimos enriched their tools and household equipment with delicate ivory carvings depicting their struggle for existence. (Photo: National Museum, Copenhagen.)

Masks from the Nunivak Eskimos were collected by Knud Rasmussen from 1921 to 1924 during his Fifth Thule Expedition. Made of walrus ivory and other materials, these masks were used for ceremonial dances and rituals. The ornamentation was purposeful and meaningful. (Photo: National Museum, Copenhagen.)

Chapter 2 THE TRIUMVIRATE: DESIGNER, CRAFTSMAN, AND CONSUMER

The designer, the craftsman, and the consumer have been a unified force of energy throughout history. This triumvirate has worked together and has been interdependent in the production and consumption of all goods marketed for use by the family and the community. At every level of civilization and at each stratified layer of society, it has existed as a necessary creative group producing the objects that made life in a community a more successful and meaningful experience.

The objects designed and developed by man were the outgrowth of his daily activities, needs, and attitudes toward his world. He was led by internal and external forces of survival and not necessarily by the desire for money or the mere satisfaction of his curiosity. He was oriented to the particular problems of his time and to the imperative need to exist in his society, which was often harsh and difficult.

At times, this relationship has been good, and manifested itself in stronger ways than at other times in history. In some societies this triumvirate has been powerful and has contributed greatly to the design of man's household objects and architecture; and in other eras during the history of man, it has played a very subservient role and has been unable to make worthy additions to the philosophy of design.

Before the devastating effects of the machine were felt, the designer, the craftsman, and the consumer were often one and the same person. We know that each individual could not manufacture everything his activities required, but we also know that each person, as a community member, could remain extremely close to the production of his needs. From his own experience, he could judge honestly the integrity and standards used on goods being designed for his use. This relationship is seldom seen in our present world of manufacturing. Too often the designer, the craftsman, and the consumer live in their own separate worlds and understand little of one another. Because of this gap in understanding, the consumer, beginning in the late nineteenth century, was faced with a huge amount of goods on the market, which he bought only because he was persuaded that he needed them; his situation was not at all unlike the consumer's situation today as the result of television advertising. The artist-craftsman was faced with a world taken over to a large extent by industrialization.

THE TRIUMVIRATE AT ITS BEST

When this triumvirate of the designer, the craftsman, and the consumer worked well together, the results of its labors were worthwhile. There was a sense of good utilitarian design. In examining the successful times of this trio, we find that the household objects then produced fitted the needs of the community and of the individual who requested a particular item. Because this triumvirate

was often really one man, the consumer who needed a tool for his work was also the designer who planned the needed piece of equipment—and to carry this even further, he was, as well, the person who produced the object, using the materials that suited the purpose for which the object was intended. In many societies this closeness vanished when the members of the triumvirate were separated. The understanding, the intelligence, and the utilitarian qualities were lost to ornateness and overembellishment.

Excellent examples of the good aspects of this triumvirate at work can be found in the very primitive cultures of our world. In these cultures and societies, there was a need for utilitarian objects that answered a particular use and purpose; and only after this function was fulfilled was the ornamental aspect considered. And even when ornamentation *was* included on a piece, it too had a purpose. In many of these communities, the more elaborate design had a very significant religious intent; it was not placed on a tool or household item merely to mar and scar the surface of the material, as we see done in more "civilized" societies. When ornamentation was applied to the surface of an object, it fit the contours and shape with understanding and meaningful application.

The Eskimo Triumvirate

The Eskimos of the far north are among the many peoples who have contributed a significant quantity of designed objects that reflect the unification of the designer, the craftsman, and the consumer. The Eskimo knew exactly what tools and household goods he needed, and he also was very aware of the shapes and forms in which they should be created for most efficient use. His pieces were simple, relatively unornamented, extremely functional, and answered his direct needs. The objects he designed were designed solely to be used by himself and his family for those jobs that had to be done to enable him to exist in his rugged world. The Eskimo's home life and his activity patterns were reflected in the simplicity of his tools; they were uncomplicated and plain and seldom highly embellished with design. Occasionally, however, the Eskimo decorated his utensils with small, delicate, incised drawings. These were drawn in thin lines on the objects made of bone from the animals he killed for food. Some of these objects he ornamented with simple carved forms repeated over and over. The designs were usually related to his everyday activities and sometimes told about the spirits and mysterious forces that he believed guided his actions and life. These were certainly more meaningful decorations than the flowers and scrolls we so often see used today.

The Triumvirate in Cultures of Africa and the South Seas

The cultures of Africa and the South Sea Islands also produced objects that were created with relative simplicity in design elements and yet tell us a great deal about the lives and activities of the creators. This is something that we, as Americans, cannot boast, for our belongings are so mechanically and senselessly created that they portray little of our beliefs. Seldom have our philosophical ideologies crept into our creative work. The African's and South Sea Islander's designs are closely associated with religious and spiritual beliefs. The objects these people design, from their huts to their ceremonial pieces, are all heavily laden with religious significance. The creator and the piece made by him are closely associated with each other. The piece manifests the individual's needs, his philosophy, and his religious aspirations.

A large ritual board in open lace carving from New Guinea is typical of boards often used as interior walls of ceremonial houses. The native craftsmen had a real understanding of the needs of the community. (Photo: by Friedrich Hewicker. Collection of Bremen Museum.)

A ceremonial "kwoi" from New Guinea was considered a carrier of supernatural powers and was hung between the skulls of human heads. The ornamentation is not superficial, but represents the religious needs of a society. (Photo: by Friedrich Hewicker. Collection of Hamburg Museum.)

Carved section of a house post of the Maori in New Zealand. (Photo: courtesy of Smithsonian Institution.)

A wooden door from Dahomey, Africa, where many natives accepted carving commissions for their fellow natives, shows that the craftsmen retained an understanding of the needs of their clients, even though they were manufacturing in a business sense. (Collection of the University Museum, Philadelphia.)

A wooden mask from Baulé illustrates the elegant sophistication and simplification of many African craft objects. (The Wurtzburger Collection, Baltimore Museum of Art.)

The Shaker Community

An interesting nonprimitive society in which the triumvirate was at its best was a subculture existing in the nineteenth century in the United States. The Shakers were highly religious and adapted their philosophy to the creative objects they made for their homes and their fields.

". . . Their leader, 'Mother Ann' Lee, reached the colonies from England in 1774, with her own mystical version of the Protestant faith. Mother Ann insisted on strict communal life, with all property held in common, equality of the sexes combined with absolute celibacy, and simplicity and directness in all things. 'Be hand-minded,' she would urge. 'Put your hands to work and your hearts to God.' Soon there were nineteen self-contained communities scattered through New England, New York, Kentucky and Indiana. Every Shaker practiced a craft with particular diligence, producing everything except babies. They have now almost died out for lack of new recruits.

"The Shakers at their height were sternly anti-esthetic, considering beauty a snare. Yet their interest to the world is emphatically esthetic. The Shaker Museum at Old Chatham, New York, founded [in 1950] in recognition of the Shaker's unique contribution to American culture, already gets close to 9,000 visitors a season, sends them away charmed by the clean, consecrated ingenuity of Shaker crafts. Some 8,000 objects, crammed into the museum's six sizeable buildings, show that despite themselves the Shakers created and lived in beauty.

"The Shakers distrusted the ornamental; they avoided both 'carpenter Gothic' and the Victorian arabesques. Their furniture is functional to a **T**, and yet their tools are subtly shaped to charm the eye and hand. . . .

"In their dedicated isolation, Shaker communities hit on a host of new forms and techniques that have become commonplace. Before the Civil War, Shakers invented a flat broom, a wheel-driven washing machine, a circular saw, a tiltback chair (on ball-and-sockets) and, a century

The simple elegance of these boxes is not unlike that of the masks from Africa. Utilitarian shapes and honest use of materials are trade-marks of all Shaker objects. Notice the beautiful craftsmanship in the structure of the boxes. (Photo: Shaker Museum, Old Chatham, New York.)

The interior of a Shaker room shows the interest of this group of people in keeping their furnishings unadorned, simple, and honest. The design of these pieces illustrates the triumvirate (designer, craftsman, consumer) at its best. (Photo: Shaker Museum, Old Chatham, New York.)

before its use in medicine, electric shock therapy, using a primitive static-electricity generator.

"As with much modern design, even the best Shaker products are sometimes a bit chill. But their meaning of severity and grace is unparalleled" (*Time*, October 19, 1959, Courtesy of *Time;* copyright *Time Inc.* 1959).

It was in cultures such as the Shaker groups that the triumvirate was kept alive in its purest form, producing objects of utilitarian value which answered those needs demanded by the family.

THE DISINTEGRATION OF THE TRIUMVIRATE

During the Middle Ages, town guilds were powerful and active, and the church fostered designing for architecture, art objects, and even objects of daily use. There existed a common spiritual atmosphere between the consumer and the craftsman-designer; and because their goals were so closely related, communication of ideas was easily achieved. Through the efforts of these craftsmen the spires and windows of cathedrals rose above the cities, glorifying the religious ideals of which all men were fully aware. Of the fate of craftsmen, Lewis Mumford wrote:

"With the rise of the merchant class [in America], the industrial guild began to weaken, as it had weakened in Europe during the Renaissance. For about a hundred years the carpenter-builder continued to remain on the scene, and work in his forthright and painstaking and honest manner; but in the middle of the eighteenth century he was joined, for the first time, by the professional architect, the first one being probably Peter Harrison, who designed the Redwood Library, which still stands in Newport. Under competition with architects and amateurs of taste, the carpenter-builder lost his position as an independent craftsman, building intelligently for his equals; he was forced to meet the swift, corrosive influence brought in from foreign lands by men who had visited the ports of the world; and he must set his sails in order to catch the new winds of fashion" (*Sticks & Stones*, Lewis Mumford, p. 37).

When we look into the furnishings and art objects that resulted from artistic accomplishments in the seventeenth and eighteenth centuries in Europe, we find that they were highly ornate and had very little functional association with the individual except to add luxury and frills to his life. Because of their extreme riches and abundant leisure time, the prominent wealthy classes spent their money on trimmings to elaborate their homes beyond utilitarian needs. Thus it came about that, as Thorstein Veblen noted, even though " . . . among objects of use the simple and unadorned article is aesthetically the best . . . ," among the leisured wealthy ". . . most objects alleged to be beautiful, and doing duty as such, show considerable ingenuity of design and are calculated to puzzle the beholder—to bewilder him with irrelevant suggestions and hints of the improbable—at the same time that they give evidence of an expenditure of labor in excess of what would give them their fullest efficiency for their ostensible economic end" (*The Theory Of The Leisure Class*, Thorstein Veblen, p. 152). The royalty and nobility merely commissioned craftsmen to design for them, and the craftsmen continued to add the curves and rosettes of luxury until the pieces they designed had little association with the materials used. The furniture did, however, illustrate characteristics of the rich, that is, their decadence and their deep interest in exaggerated comfort. The palaces of Europe are full of furniture designed with little understanding of the rapport between the designer, the craftsman, and the consumer. As the machine age came into being, the gap of misunderstanding grew larger and larger, until the consumers in the middle and lower classes, as well as in the upper classes, from the late nineteenth century until now were compelled to buy objects produced by manufacturers who had no thought for the usefulness or design of the items.

The consumer had no choice, for there were few articles on the market reflecting good design components.

The growing popularity of the machine and its increasing potential in production were paralleled by a sudden compulsion to invent. In the middle of the eighteenth century, in England, persons in all areas of society were affected by this urge to create, while a similar surge swept across the United States. In all parts of Europe, men joined the restless pursuit of designing mechanical contrivances to exploit almost every human pursuit that can be imagined. Patent files full of the records of this invention vogue attest the variety and array of devices which played an important role in the evolution of our complex contemporary civilization. The arts suffered irreparable damage during this time, as creative vitality was diverted into this new mechanical experimentation. In America, especially, an indigenous art failed to materialize during a time when native abilities were so ripe for development.

By the end of the nineteenth century the market was flooded with monstrously designed home furnishings, and the people purchased them because the products were available.

This happened not only to the furnishings to be placed into homes but also to the architecture that was to surround the furnishings. The craftsman was slowly pushed aside and replaced, and other forces took over the production of these objects to be incorporated into everyday life. The businessman and factory owner became the designers; their only interest was to make money. They did not care about standards of design or integrity; they had knowledge of neither.

The consumer goods produced during this time were highly overdecorated, ugly, misconceived objects that were suited for no one's taste. When Frank Lloyd Wright, the architect, was in need of building materials for his houses at the beginning of his career, he found, according to James Marston Fitch, that:
". . . 'simple things . . . were nowhere at hand. A piece of wood without a moulding was an anomaly; a plain wooden

*The contrast between this Victorian mansion and
the Shaker interior is extreme. Although this architecture may be fascinating and "fun" to look at,
there is little question that it exhibits ostentatious
ornamentation for its own sake, reflecting the style
of its period. It is known as the Carson mansion.
(Photo: courtesy of Eureka Chamber of Com-
merce, California.)*

The excessive ornamentation that appeared in products made by the machine led to the Gothic "wedding-cake" style in houses, typified by this famous one in Maine. The wood decoration is laid over the surface of the box-shaped house for no logical reason. (Photo: courtesy of State of Maine, Department of Economic Development.)

slat instead of a turned baluster a joke; the omission of the merchantable 'grille' a crime; plain fabric for hangings or floor coverings were nowhere to be found in stock.' Ornament had destroyed material; content was lost in bankrupt form'' (*Architecture And The Esthetics Of Plenty*, James Marston Fitch, p. 106).

As the tempo of mass production and industrialization accelerated, it was evident that this relationship of the designer, the craftsman, and the consumer would fall into disrepute. Products that once would have been based on human factors as well as material value, on close personal relationship between those designing them and those wanting them, were now impersonally manufactured in volume. Punching, pressing, stamping, and casting were only a few of the new methods used to pour forth products from the factories into the hands of the public. The public had little or no understanding of evaluation. Its integrity was static, based on outmoded standards.

The smaller the cost of an object, the more of it was produced. Homes began to be filled with tawdry products, and gross imitations of materials took the place of the honest approach to designing objects. This overproduction aided in the adulteration and obliteration of materials, and a sense of decay and cheapness crept into the world of art objects and utilitarian household design. The craftsman was pushed into the background, submerged in dishonest manufacturing.

With this degeneration and disintegration of design, industry, manufacturing, and consumer tastes, it was imperative that some new ideology be introduced to clear away the chaos that existed by the middle of the nineteenth century and inject an honest vitality in its place. This invigoration was to come in the form of Art Nouveau, with its stimulating philosophies.

BIBLIOGRAPHY AND SUGGESTED READINGS

Andrews, Edward D. & Faith, *Shaker Furniture*, Dover Publications, Inc., New York, 1950.

Christensen, Erwin O., *Primitive Art*, Thomas Y. Crowell Co., New York, 1955.

Fitch, James Marston, *Architecture And The Esthetics Of Plenty*, Columbia University Press, New York, 1961.

Giedion, Sigfried, *Mechanization Takes Command*, Oxford University Press, New York, 1948.

Mumford, Lewis, *Art And Technics*, Columbia University Press, New York, 1952.

Mumford, Lewis, *Sticks & Stones*, Dover Publications, Inc., New York, 1955.

Mumford, Lewis, *Technics And Civilization*, Harcourt, Brace, and Co., New York, 1934.

Neutra, Richard, *Survival Through Design*, Oxford University Press, New York, 1954.

Schaefer-Simmern, Henry, *Eskimo-Plastik aus Kanada*, Friedr. Lometsch-Verlag, Kassel, 1958.

Tischner, Herbert, *Oceanic Art*, Pantheon Books, New York, 1954.

Veblen, Thorstein, *Theory Of The Leisure Class*, Modern Library, Viking Press, New York, 1934.

Spandrel of cast iron, painted grey was designed about 1898 by Louis Henry Sullivan; the model of it is by Kristian Schneider. This is typical of the architectural embellishment that Sullivan used on his buildings. (Collection, The Museum of Modern Art, New York. Gift of Dubin and Dubin, Architects, Chicago.)

An asymmetrical desk is a forerunner of the L-shaped desk of today. It was designed by Guimard in African and olive ash woods, about 1903. (Collection, The Museum of Modern Art, New York. Gift of Mme. Hector Guimard.)

Chapter **3** ART NOUVEAU

In the latter part of the nineteenth century, a movement arose with many new concepts that began to set the stage for the ideas and technology of the twentieth century, replacing the old and traditional design philosophies. The movement that created such a turmoil was called Art Nouveau. Its name has been attributed to different sources of inspiration, but probably came from S. Bing, in Paris, who ran a small shop dealing in the objects created by the artists and craftsmen of this movement. The shop was called *Maison de l'Art Nouveau.*

WILLIAM MORRIS: ARTS AND CRAFTS MOVEMENT

Just prior to the emergence of Art Nouveau, there was an art movement for which William Morris can be held directly responsible. He was an Englishman who felt the need for a revival and stimulation of the arts and crafts. He found that the age of industry had completely taken over the world of the artist and the craftsman, with the result that the market was flooded with cheap imitative materials, brash, gaudy, and irresponsibly designed. The craftsmen and designers had retreated into their garrets and studios, unable to fight the wave of machine-manufactured objects.

Morris's idea was to arouse in the artists and the craftsmen a new force of creative expression that would bring forth an art "for the people and by the people" (*Pioneers of Modern Design*, Nikolaus Pevsner, p. 10). He was revolted by the machine, and his movement of Arts and Crafts was gauged to revive craftsmanship rather than to improve design in industry. Even though industrialization was reaching new heights in England, Morris rejected its advantages.

In 1851 the eyes of the world were turned on the Crystal Palace, designed by Joseph Paxton, an enormous building that utilized iron and glass in revolutionary ways. The presence of this structure in the first international exhibition ever to be held marked the full arrival of the age of industrial and technical advancement. The radical new uses of glass, iron, and other metals undoubtedly opened up whole new areas of architectural concepts. Yet even with this kind of innovative achievement in industry and in architecture, Morris still clung to his belief of the necessity of a renaissance in the field of objects handcrafted without the aid of machine methods.

Morris's design concepts in the area of crafts may seem, at first glimpse by a contemporary person, to be nothing but the same old Victorian clutter; but on the second look, one sees a logical composition and a real understanding of nature that was not apparent before. His work, in comparison with the work being done before his time, was certainly more simple. His ornamentation was prophetic of what the future in design held for new generations; yet it managed to cling to the traditions of the past. His work recalled the medieval scene, and the objects he designed in his shop were highly reminiscent of the Gothic era. So important was his influence that he has been called:

"... the true prophet of the twentieth century, the father of the Modern Movement. We owe it to him that an ordinary man's dwelling-house has once more become a worthy object of the architect's thought, and a chair, a wallpaper, or a vase a worthy object of the artist's imagination" (*Pioneers of Modern Design*, Nikolaus Pevsner, p. 9).

Morris established a firm for designing, peopled with followers and students interested in promoting his philosophy. Walter Crane and C. R. Ashbee were both members of Morris's company, engaged in designing for the new ideology.

This group was not alone in its disgust with industrialization. The famous critic John Ruskin was also an antimachinery advocate, and his inspired writing helped the Arts and Crafts Movement stay alive longer than had been expected. However, the movement was doomed to failure. J. M. Richards explained, "Their limitation was that they could not visualize a new architecture that was not a return to that of some past age" (*Modern Architecture*, p. 68). But William Morris's work later led indirectly to the design movement that took hold in Europe and became known as Art Nouveau.

HENRI VAN DE VELDE: ART NOUVEAU

S. Giedion claims in *Space, Time and Architecture* that Brussels, Belgium, was the center of contemporary art from 1880 to 1890, and rightly so, because during that decade the Belgian galleries, shops, exhibition halls, and display stores were showing the world some of the most avant-garde work of the time. Exhibitions featured such artists as Van Gogh, Cezanne, and Seurat, to name only a few. These artists were not Belgian, but this was the only place where many could find hanging space for their work. Many outstanding publications of art were also displayed in Belgium to let the world know of the new language being presented by the artists, designers, and architects.

And it was in Belgium that Henri van de Velde took the lead in establishing the movement of Art Nouveau. (At one time van de Velde was a fellow student of Van Gogh.) The major contribution van de Velde made to this group was his interest in revitalizing the machine as a tool for the designer. He depended on industry, in exact opposition to Morris's concepts, and attempted to bring about an understanding between the artist and the manufacturer. Until this time, the manufacturer had completely ignored the artist and had proceeded with production without considering the aesthetics of the product. There

were many protagonists of the usefulness of the machine and the possibilities of less ornamentation and more honesty in materials. Pevsner lists two Austrians, Otto Wagner and Adolf Loos, two Americans, Louis Sullivan and Frank Lloyd Wright, and one Belgian, Henri van de Velde, in his *Pioneers of Modern Design*. He even adds Oscar Wilde as a praiser of beauty in the machine.

Like Morris's Arts and Crafts Movement, the Art Nouveau was short-lived, but for a different reason. While Morris went back into medieval times for his inspiration, Art Nouveau designers were antitraditional. Because theirs was an art that was antimovement, it was soon replaced with another ideology, but only after it had established the concept that looking to the future and to new ideas is a quality needed to make an art meaningful.

Art Nouveau was responsible for many unusual structures and home furnishings, and the forms of the period were completely new in relation to the traditional designs of the past. The new concept presented by Art Nouveau was a completely surface-oriented ideology. No structural change was introduced in the new idiom. Instead, the characteristics were of undulating lines and curvilinear shapes, dancing across the objects. Buds and flowers were emphasized in large sizes, almost out of proportion, incorporating the whiplash and other distorted shapes of nature. All these were the identifying marks of the artists of Art Nouveau. This is how Arthur Drexler and Greta Daniel described it:

"Like the painting of Van Gogh, Gauguin, and Lautrec, Art Nouveau was influenced by curvilinear patterns of Japanese prints at the time popular in Europe and America. The sinuous whiplash curve became Art Nou-

The entrance gate to the Paris subway station was designed by Hector Guimard around 1900. Utilizing the flower as the form, this cast-iron gate is painted green and has amber glass fixtures. (Collection, The Museum of Modern Art, New York. Gift of Régie Autonome des Transports Parisiens.)

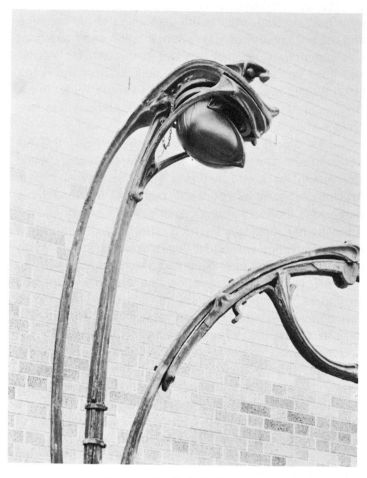

This is a detail of the light fixture at the entrance to the Paris subway station. (Collection, The Museum of Modern Art, New York. Gift of Régie Àutonome des Transports Parisiens.)

veau's typical contour, embracing everything from poster design to architecture with forms reminiscent of plants and flowers" (*Twentieth Century Design*, p. 12).

Toulouse-Lautrec instilled in his graphic work the same undulating lines, slowly and rhythmically turning and twisting around the contours of his figures dancing in the cafes of Paris. Aristide Maillot, who once worked in tapestries, incorporated the Art Nouveau flavor in his sculptures, bringing his work to the attention of the new movement.

Art Nouveau Architecture

This active Art Nouveau movement produced a huge array of artists, designers, craftsmen, and architects, all of them experimenting in freedom and enjoying the release from traditionally imposed standards. One of the first architects to embrace Art Nouveau was Victor Horta in Brussels. His work was typical of the curved shapes and ornamental designs of the 1890s. The culmination of Art Nouveau architecture, however, was the work of Antoni Gaudi. He was Spanish and worked independently of the

Jewel box designed by Charles Knox and executed by William Craythorne around 1900. Made of silver, mother-of-pearl, turquoise, and enamel, it has a very contemporary appearance. (Collection, The Museum of Modern Art, New York. Gift of the family of Mrs. John D. Rockefeller, Jr.)

rest of the movement, but he probably said the most in the movement's language. Henry-Russel Hitchcock wrote:

"The architecture of Gaudi certainly makes a powerful impression on even the most casual observer—an impression quite as likely to be unfavorable as favorable. His buildings are not easy to understand. . . . The art of Gaudi is so rich, so varied, so impossible to reduce to a simple formula, that he will always be to some extent an architect's architect" (*Gaudi*, p. 12).

His work is like a heavily decorated wedding cake, which looks as though it should be eaten rather than lived in; yet it is vastly interesting in the materials, textures,

The façade of Casa Batllo designed by Antoni Gaudi from 1905 to 1907. (Photo: courtesy of The Museum of Modern Art, New York.)

Bronze umbrella stand (c. 1902), side chair (c. 1912) of cherry, and desk chair (c. 1905) were designed by Hector Guimard. Carefully planned joints help make the various pieces appear to have the flowing lines of plants. Although he sometimes designed with asymmetrical elements, these pieces are symmetrical. Guimard designed this group of furniture for his own house in Paris. (Collection, The Museum of Modern Art, New York. Gifts of Mme. Hector Guimard.)

and forms utilized. The buildings are encrusted with stones and mosaics—eclectic structures that are almost surrealistic in feeling. His buildings show a real understanding of nature, and materials are used with imaginative creativity. The furnishings he designed were as creatively conceived as the buildings into which he put them. Certainly he contributed to the complete edifice—inside and out. While his was an architectural world, it involved many other aspects of design that influenced the period in which he lived. His buildings still stand in Spain as monuments to his genius.

Besides the architects of the Art Nouveau, there were many artists and furniture designers who were actively engaged in contributing to the over-all picture of the movement. Among these designers, Hector Guimard, a Frenchman, was particularly active. His work is typical of the movement, using plant shapes and flower forms that twist and curve on the surface of the piece. Guimard's designing included the light fixtures of the entrance gates over the subway in Paris. These bulbous shapes hang in perilous buds, which seem overweight and ungainly.

Art Nouveau in America

America was not left behind in this movement of design. Although the people mainly responsible for Art Nouveau were in Europe, there were artists and architects in the United States who were very active. One such designer was Louis Tiffany, who developed an irridescent glass that sparkled in beautiful colors. Tiffany named his new glass "favrile"; many of his pieces are extremely fragile and delicate, designed as flower forms with thin stems and wide, flaring tops.

An American who used Art Nouveau forms in architecture was Louis Sullivan. Although his buildings are basically plain and structural, he apparently was unable to complete a building without adding some embellishment. One of his best examples is the Carson, Pirie & Scott building in Chicago. The top floors line the building in horizontal strips of huge windows, while the street floor is

Iron decoration on interior column was designed by Antoni Gaudi for Palau Guell between 1885 and 1888. This ornamentation is an excellent example of the use of flower and plant forms characteristic of the movement called Art Nouveau. (Photo: courtesy of The Museum of Modern Art, New York.)

The gate lodge of Park Guell is rich in texture and pattern. It was designed by Antoni Gaudi from 1900 to 1914. (Photo: courtesy of The Museum of Modern Art, New York.)

The finial of the tower of the Sagrada Familia in Barcelona, Spain, is shown here. Gaudi designed this rich mosaic tower from 1903 to 1926. (Photo: courtesy of The Museum of Modern Art, New York.)

heavily encrusted with cast iron decoration. And yet Sullivan once wrote in one of his publications that "ornament is mentally a luxury, not a necessary," and that "it would be greatly for our esthetic good, if we should refrain entirely from the use of ornament for a period of years, in order that our thought might concentrate acutely upon the production of buildings well formed and comely in the nude" (*Pioneers of Modern Design,* Nikolaus Pevsner, p. 13).

Thonet and Bentwood

Bentwood was introduced in the nineteenth century and took the furniture field by storm. The person primarily responsible for this revolution in wood was Michael Thonet. In 1856, Thonet developed a process by which wood was steamed and could then be bent into softly curved pieces;

this made it possible to eliminate joints and other complicated contours formerly necessary in furniture design. His furniture was manufactured in huge quantities and was considered almost a necessity in many parts of the world. The American ice-cream parlor used his chairs almost exclusively. And now this process and some of the designs that he created are being used again. Although he accomplished his work during the beginning of the Art Nouveau movement, it does not seem to belong with the overdecorated pieces of that period. However, some of his pieces are extremely ornate, while some are extraordinarily contemporary in feeling, with simple curved lines. Much of the work he produced during this period is highly sought after by collectors, as are other Art Nouveau pieces. The ornamented surfaces are interesting contrasts to today's

Favrile glass vase was made by Louis Tiffany about 1900. (Collection, The Museum of Modern Art, New York. Phyllis B. Lambert Fund.)

Favrile glass vase also made by Louis Tiffany, about 1900. (Collection, The Museum of Modern Art, New York. Phyllis B. Lambert Fund.)

Crystal wine and champagne goblets designed by Josef Hoffmann in 1920. Although he was considered a foremost proponent of Art Nouveau, Hoffman worked in simplified and classic design. The precision and clarity hardly seem to belong to Art Nouveau. Hoffman was active in Vienna, Austria. The far-right goblet was designed by Oswald Haerdtl in 1924. (Collection, The Museum of Modern Art, New York. Gifts of A. J. van Dugteren & Sons, Inc.)

Michael Thonet designed this flamboyant bent beechwood chair in 1860. (Photo: courtesy of Elaine Sewell.)

machine-oriented interiors with simple rectangular lines.

Art Nouveau was not destined to remain a strong and vigorous movement. It only served as a steppingstone to brighter and more permanent design philosophies. It did, however, present a traditional world with a cue to the future of designing in the arts. It helped bring about an awareness of the necessity of re-evaluating our position with the machine and industry. While one group of designers rejected the machine for its bastardization of material, the other group attempted to show how artists could utilize the machine as a tool of expression in the arts. With the Art Nouveau movement, the door was opened a crack; with a slight push, the world would enter into a real marriage of industry and art.

BIBLIOGRAPHY AND SUGGESTED READINGS

Drexler, Arthur and Greta Daniel, *Twentieth Century Design*, Museum of Modern Art, New York, 1959.

Giedion, Sigfried, *Space, Time & Architecture*, Harvard University Press, Cambridge, 1943.

Hitchcock, Henry-Russel, *Gaudi*, Museum of Modern Art, New York, 1957.

Pevsner, Nikolaus, *Pioneers of Modern Design*, Museum of Modern Art, New York, 1949.

Richards, J. M., *Modern Architecture*, Penguin Books, Inc., Baltimore, Maryland, 1948.

Selz, Peter, *Art Nouveau*, Museum of Modern Art, New York, 1959.

Schmutzler, Robert, *Art Nouveau*, Abrams, New York, 1964.

Vallance, Aymer, *William Morris, His Art, Writings, & Public Life*, George Bell and Sons, London, 1897.

This Thonet chair, designed about 1870, is still considered a classic in the furniture field because of its simple, direct, and honest use of materials. (Collection, The Museum of Modern Art, New York. Gift of Thonet Industries, Inc.)

Composition *by Theo van Doesburg, 1924.*
(Gemeente Musea, *Amsterdam.*)

Schroder house at Utrecht, The Netherlands, 1924, designed by G. Rietveld and T. Schröder. (Photo: The Museum of Modern Art, New York.)

Chapter 4 DE STIJL

The artists and designers of Art Nouveau had opened the eyes of Western man. It was inevitable that additional avant-garde philosophies would follow, prophetic of more important contributions to the revolution in architecture and furniture design. The ideas following Art Nouveau may not have been readily acceptable to the layman, but the layman had witnessed revolution in the arts and could be prepared to understand a little more of the visual images he was yet to find encompassing his daily environment.

The *de Stijl* group followed Art Nouveau. Its main force was active in Holland from 1917 to 1928. However, this movement certainly was not limited to the Netherlands, for it slowly inched forward until all of Europe and the United States felt the impact of its ideas.

THE INCEPTION OF *DE STIJL*

In 1917 Theo van Doesburg began publication of the famous *de Stijl* magazine, and around this publication the *de Stijl* group formed. It was from this magazine that the group took its name, which means "The Style." This small publication spread the ideologies and philosophies of this important twentieth-century design group, acting as its spokesman in all forms of art—architecture, painting, graphics, typography, and sculpture. Besides the painters van Doesburg and Piet Mondrian, the architects C. van Eesteren, G. Rietveld, J. J. P. Oud, and the sculptor Vantogerloo, there were many other contributors to the success of this movement. Together they formed a strong and spontaneous vanguard heading toward a common and constructive purpose.

Theo van Doesburg

Theo van Doesburg was considered the leader of the *de Stijl* movement, although he was certainly not the most noted of the group. Besides being the originator of the *de Stijl* magazine, he was also a painter. In 1921 and 1922 he made a grand tour of Europe, spending much of his time in Berlin and Weimar, in Germany, influencing architects such as Walter Gropius, Mies van der Rohe, and Le Corbusier. During his lifetime he collaborated with Jean Arp, the artist, and with the dadaists; and he spread the philosophy of *de Stijl* throughout Europe—especially to Germany. Van Doesburg died in 1931.

Piet Mondrian

Mondrian was one of the important artists and painters in this movement. In 1912 he met Picasso and was highly motivated by his work. By the following year, Mondrian was a completely changed painter. He had rejected nature and representational objects and moved into full acceptance of nonrepresentational form as his method of expressing his philosophic ideologies. He had this to say about the way of seeing:

"The emotion of beauty is ever restricted by the appearance of the 'thing'; that is why the thing had to be eliminated in the representation. So long as there is no entirely new art of building, it is up to the art of painting to perform that in which the art of building—such as is generally apparent—has failed; i.e. to represent purely

Color Construction (*project for a private house, 1922), by van Doesburg and Cornelis van Eesteren. In this arrangement of squares, rectangles, and flat planes, one can easily see how the architectural characteristics of a home are being developed. (Collection, The Museum of Modern Art, New York. Edgar J. Kaufmann, Jr., Fund.)*

Rhythms with Black Lines *by Piet Mondrian, dated 1935 to 1942. (Collection of Mr. and Mrs. Henry Clifford, Radnor, Pa.)*

well-balanced proportions or, in other words, to be abstractly realistic representation. The abstract realistic art of painting is therefore meanwhile the life-saving substitute'' (*de Stijl*, cat. 81, p. 63).

In the *de Stijl* group Mondrian came into close contact with the architects who were working toward a new expression in building materials. He was very much aware of the relationship of his advances in painting to those in architecture. The new understanding that he was finding in space, light, and line was being discovered by the architects in new materials of industry, such as glass, steel, and concrete. Mondrian continued to paint and when he moved to New York in the early 1940s, he brought his *de Stijl* influence to the United States. He died in New York in 1944.

City in Space *by Frederick Kiesler for the International Exposition, Paris, 1925. (Photo: The Museum of Modern Art, New York.)*

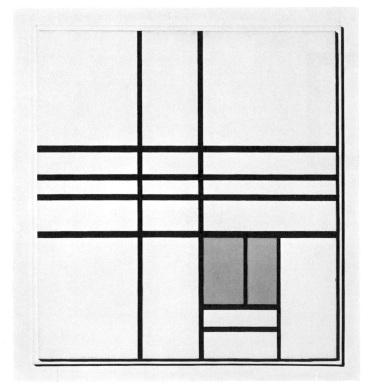

Composition *by Piet Mondrian, 1936. (Louise and Walter Arensberg Collection, Philadelphia Museum of Art.)*

Frederick Kiesler

Kiesler, who was very active as an architect, joined the *de Stijl* in 1923 but contributed his work from Vienna. In 1925 Kiesler designed an intricate City In Space for the International Exposition in Paris, using all the required spatially oriented squares and rectangles which were the mark of the *de Stijl*. The work was an imposing sculptural and architectural solution in space. What is so very interesting about Kiesler's work is his rejection of natural shapes in 1925 and his eventual absolute acceptance of forms from nature, as shown in his contribution to the 1961 Visionary Architecture Exhibition, held at the Museum of Modern Art in New York. While most of the *de Stijl* members continued to work only in abstract forms, Kiesler reverted completely to nature for his inspiration in "endless" space designs as the years went on.

Gerritt Rietveld

The major furniture designer of this group was Gerritt Rietveld, who was also an architect. Usually when one thinks of furniture of this movement, one immediately visualizes a Rietveld piece. As we can see in his chair designed between 1917 and 1919, Rietveld applied the *de Stijl* philosophy to seating as well as to other household items and architecture. Although one cannot say that the pieces he designed are the most comfortable in appearance, they do express the ideological goals sought after by the group and offer to the world new materials in conjunction with new ideals. But, while squares and rectangles are very easily incorporated into tables and case goods, one must conform to the contours of the human body when designing chairs. Without this appearance of comfort and functional usefulness, his furniture was not acceptable. For the same reason, other *de Stijl* furniture designers met with failure. Rietveld's house at Utrecht, Holland, is probably one of the best examples of the architecture constructed by the group members. It was constructed in 1924.

Chrome-plated and painted metal table lamp designed by Gerrit Rietveld in 1924. (Collection, The Museum of Modern Art, New York. Gift of G. Rietveld.)

Armchair of painted wood designed by G. Rietveld in 1917. The same line and flat-plane characteristics that are found in the paintings and architecture of de Stijl *are seen in this chair. (Collection, The Museum of Modern Art, New York. Gift of Philip Johnson.)*

Design for a café by J. J. P. Oud, 1925. Café de Unie, Rotterdam. (Photo: Gemeente Musea, Amsterdam.)

CHARACTERISTICS AND INFLUENCES OF *DE STIJL*

Out of this small but active group of artists and architects came a style of architecture that was to make a considerable mark on future generations. The hallmark of *de Stijl* was the use of flat planes, rectangles, and squares, and a composition that replaced formal balance with active and informal balance. Symmetry gave way to asymmetrical design. This was a balance of contrast in which "the right angle as the point of intersection of two lines provides the simplest form of contrast" (*A History of Modern Architecture*, Jürgen Joedicke, p. 100). Often this contrast was aided by the use of the primary colors, which

Model for a de Stijl *building for Rosenburg by Theo van Doesburg.* (Gemeente Musea, Amsterdam.)

the *de Stijl* members used exclusively. The cubes and squares and formal masses, which characterized this movement, were not limited only to architecture and painting but were used as well in sculptural forms and in typography. Experimentation was a part of this movement, and no form or object was sacred. While traditional layouts in graphic design utilized carefully formalized balanced design, the *de Stijl* members introduced asymmetrical balance here too.

The germination of *de Stijl* did not take place by itself but was helped along by several other sources. Cubism, which Picasso and Braque had established in Paris in the early 1900s, was a great light in the eyes of the Dutch designers. Here, in painting, were some of the same philosophies that could be translated into their work in architecture, city planning, and interior spaces. Frank

Lloyd Wright, the American architect, also helped influence the movement, after two less well-known members of its group visited the United States. In many of Wright's early buildings there can be seen a definite affinity to the *de Stijl* style. Many of his small domestic homes are constructed of the same rectangular and square forms but are ornamented with Art Nouveau-influenced designs for which Louis Sullivan had been so well known. Even in the furniture that Wright was designing until his death, the familiar shapes of *de Stijl* are evident. Probably this is one area in which Wright was, to some extent, a failure, as were the furniture designers of the *de Stijl* group.

The *de Stijl* began to influence Germany through the Bauhaus; as we look at that movement more carefully, we will see many characteristics that can be directly traced back to Holland and the *de Stijl* group.

Disintegration of *de Stijl*

The *de Stijl* group began to disintegrate when its various members left the country because the Dutch were not ready to accept them. Holland at that time was extremely conservative, and few people in that country could appreciate what the group had to offer to the world. Many members went to Germany and became active in the Bauhaus school; several members died; Mondrian went to Paris and finally to New York.

IMPACT OF *DE STIJL*

De Stijl had an enormous impact on designing concepts, not only in Europe but in America also. Architecture and painting felt the major effects of *de Stijl*, which had as its most important contribution the new asymmetrical approach to design. It is not difficult to see the mark of asymmetrical design in architecture in the United States. In many of our main streets and suburbs there is architecture that reflects the *de Stijl* philosophies; store fronts, ranch-type homes, and building balconies furnish examples of *de Stijl* impact.

Much of twentieth-century American design can be traced back to European roots—artistic efforts from graphic design to architecture. Although these European influences are not always easily seen, they do exist, often heavily disguised in bad reproductions. The reader will probably question the reasons for even considering *de Stijl* as a contributing force in interiors of today; but although furniture, fabric, and interiors as such were very weak and minor in this movement, the over-all impact of the Dutch aesthetic development has been a lasting influence on design in all areas of artistic endeavors. American designers can not turn their backs on the origin of today's design even though it is "seemingly" unimportant. The American home is a depository for pieces characteristic of *de Stijl* and the Bauhaus, from the packaging that enters after an afternoon shopping trip to the furniture purchased for the living room or kitchen. The *de Stijl's* major contribution to us is through architecture, and this plays an extremely vital role in the building of homes for our family units. We therefore are deeply in debt to *de Stijl*, but we are even more in debt to the Bauhaus movement that was taking place in Germany at approximately the same time and was even more directly involved in changing the image of the American interior.

BIBLIOGRAPHY AND SUGGESTED READINGS

Drexler, Arthur and Greta Daniel, *Twentieth Century Design*, Museum of Modern Art, New York, 1959.

Joedicke, Jürgen, *History of Modern Architecture*, Frederick A. Praeger, Inc., New York, 1959.

Lewis, David, *Mondrian*, Faber & Faber Limited, London, 1947.

Museum of Modern Art, *De Stijl 1917–1929*, New York, Bulletin Vol. 22, No. 2, Winter 1952–53.

Stedelijk Museum, *De Stijl*, Amsterdam, Cat. 81, 6.7.1951–25.9.1951.

Sommerfield House, Berlin, designed by Walter Gropius in 1921. Members of Bauhaus workshops collaborated in decorating and furnishing the rooms. (Photo: courtesy of The Museum of Modern Art, New York.)

The Bauhaus in Dessau designed by Walter Gropius in 1925 and 1926. (Photo: courtesy of The Museum of Modern Art, New York.)

Chapter 5 BAUHAUS

The Bauhaus was active during much of the time that the *de Stijl* movement was operating in Holland. However, the Bauhaus was a more organized unit that housed itself in a particular building and was a formally planned movement.

THE DEUTSCHE WERKBUND

The Bauhaus was extremely active, much more so than the *de Stijl* movement. It certainly had more influence on the world of design than did the Dutch group. Its relation to other movements was described thus:

"In Germany, Hermann Muthesius sought a synthesis between the 'machine style' and the Morris 'arts and crafts' movement. He founded the Deutsche Werkbund in 1907 in an effort to effect real cooperation between the best artists and craftsmen on one hand, and trade and industry on the other. At the first session of the *Werkbund* Theodor Fischer said, 'Mass production and division of labor must be made to produce quality.' Therewith the fallacy of Morris' 'craftsman's culture' seemed to have been overcome'' (*Bauhaus 1919–1928*, Herbert Bayer, Walter Gropius, and Ise Gropius, p. 13).

FOUNDING THE BAUHAUS

The Bauhaus had as its leader Walter Gropius who was one of the members of the *Deutsche Werkbund*. Gropius was an architect of fame who later came to the United States to practice his profession. He was especially interested in seeing a unification take place among all the arts, and this desire led him to the formulation of the German Bauhaus.

Walter Gropius wrote the following account of his founding of the Bauhaus:

"This idea of the fundamental unity underlying all branches of design was my guiding inspiration in founding the original Bauhaus. During the war I had been summoned to an audience with the Grand Duke of Sachsen-Weimar-Eisenach to discuss my taking over the Weimar School of Arts and Crafts (*Grossherzogliche Kunstgewerbeschule*) from the distinguished Belgian architect, Henri Van de Velde, who had himself suggested that I should be his successor. Having asked for, and been accorded, full powers in regard to reorganization I assumed control of the Weimar School of Arts and Crafts, and also of the Weimar Academy of Fine Art (*Grossherzogliche Hochschule für Bildende Kunst*), in the spring of 1919. As a first step towards the realization of a much wider plan—in which my primary aim was that the principle of training the individual's natural capacities to grasp life as a whole, a single cosmic entity, should form the basis of instruction throughout the school instead of in only one or two arbitrarily 'specialized' classes—I amalgamated these institutions into a *Hochschule für Gestaltung*, or High School for Design, under the name of *Das Staatliche Bauhaus Weimar*" (*The New Architecture and The Bauhaus*, Walter Gropius, p. 35).

Bauhaus at Dessau. Corner of the workshop wing showing bridge and, beyond it, the technical school. (Photo: courtesy of The Museum of Modern Art, New York.)

Masters' houses of the Bauhaus in Dessau. The architect was Walter Gropius, who designed them in 1925 and 1926. (Photo: courtesy of The Museum of Modern Art, New York.)

Weimar, Germany, was the site picked by Gropius in 1919 for the establishment of his school. However, his school was not an accepted unit of culture in Weimar; it was highly criticized and was constantly put on the defensive concerning its goals and aspirations. The press, as well as the community, was very confused and completely misunderstood the aims toward which Gropius, the faculty, and the students were reaching. It was for this reason that the Bauhaus left Weimar in 1925 and went to Dessau, where the local government and community were willing to let the group experiment and even erect a building of their choice. There they were able to practice their ideologies without the interruptions that they had found stifling them in Weimar. The building was designed by Gropius and has been a landmark in every architectural survey since it was constructed. Few art historians leave out this important contribution to the field of architecture. In this building, the walls of which were reduced to a curtain of glass, the creative arts were practiced throughout most areas of individual expression.

Not only were the visual arts practiced with great intensity, but theater, drama, and other performing arts were participated in by the students during their evening hours. The Bauhaus was a closely knit community that offered a whole world of excitement to the student.

Artists, industrial designers, craftsmen, photographers, and architects were on the faculty. The teachers in the Bauhaus were little known when the school opened, but their names have echoed through the art world since they established the school in 1919. Men like Paul Klee and Lyonnell Feininger, Wassily Kandinsky and Oskar Schlemmer, and Moholy-Nagy and Joseph Albers all contributed varied points of view to the totally new educational program in the field of art.

BAUHAUS PRINCIPLES

The Bauhaus, it has been noted:

". . . established principles that even now, the contemporary designer and artist might well heed, recommending that:

"1. mass production and industrialization should be the primary concerns of the student and not that of individual craftsmanship.

"2. schools of design should bring together the arts of paintings, architecture, crafts and industrial design and eliminate the differences between 'applied arts' and 'fine arts.'

"3. schools of design should have faculties some of whom are progressive in thought and creative in practice to balance those who are primarily interested in the preservation of traditional techniques and theories.

"4. students should be a part of and participate in current twentieth century activities and should not seek refuge in the security of the past"

(*Design At Work: Its Forms and Functions*, Edward Adams, George Pappas, and David B. Van Dommelen, p. 4).

As can be recognized in the principles stated above, the Bauhaus presented a well-formulated slate of ideas for the pursuit of a close understanding of handicrafts, architecture, and mass-production. Walter Gropius wrote:

"The *Bauhaus* workshops were really laboratories for working out practical new designs for present-day articles and improving models for mass-production. To create type-forms that would meet all technical, aesthetic and commercial demands required a picked staff. It needed a body of men of wide general culture as thoroughly versed in the practical and mechanical sides of design as in its theoretical and formal laws. Although most parts of these prototype models had naturally to be made by hand, their constructors were bound to be intimately acquainted with factory methods of production and assembly, which differ radically from the practices of handicraft. It is to its intrinsic particularity that each different type of machine owes the 'genuine stamp' and 'individual beauty' of its products. Senseless imitation of hand-made goods by machinery infallibly bears the marks of a makeshift substitute. The *Bauhaus* represented a school of thought which believes that the difference between industry and handicraft is due, far less to the different nature of the tools employed in each, than to subdivision of labour in the one and undivided control by a single workman in the other. Handicrafts and industry may be regarded as opposite poles that are gradually approaching each other. The former have already begun to change their traditional nature. In the future the field of handicrafts will be found to lie mainly in the preparatory stages of evolving experimental new type-forms for mass-production" (*The New Architecture and The Bauhaus*, p. 37).

The faculty and students were extremely sure of their destiny in bringing about a true amalgamation of the various concepts of existing design. Their school was a playground of thought and experimentation, where each student was required to build a vocabulary in many fields of individual expression. The contributions from the mixed faculty of artists, architects, and craftsmen made a program that was powerful; the environment of the school generated concrete suggestions, all of which had the definite purpose of improving industrial design standards and techniques and of promoting the use of handicrafts in architectural designs.

Disruption of the Bauhaus

Most of the active members of the Bauhaus are known throughout the world. They have continued to influence design even though the Bauhaus was disintegrated in the early 1930s. Nello Ponente wrote:

"The Bauhaus was now in disruption, its ideals and its very existence violently threatened by the reactionary forces irresistibly on the rise in Germany, which stigmatized it as an instrument of internationalism. Gropius was withdrawn in 1928; in 1933 the Nazis, having come to

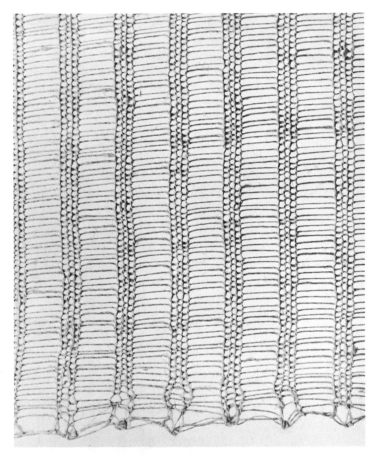

Knitted casement cloth designed in 1959 by Anni Albers, as an experiment for industry. (Photo: courtesy of American Craftsmen's Council.)

power, closed down the Bauhaus. Klee had already left it in 1931 for a professorship at the Düsseldorf Academy. Storm clouds were gathering over Europe, ... Peace, freedom, and the rediscovery through the work of art of man's social vocation—these were the aims the Bauhaus had set itself and struggled for. In their stead came war, dictatorship and social anarchy'' (*Klee*, p. 95).

Because these people are so important as makers of twentieth-century design, we should stop here for a brief look at a few of them. It is startling to see how many of them actually made specific contributions to the long list of home furnishing designs, and are still making important additions today.

Anni Albers. Wife of the painter Josef Albers, Anni Albers was one of the outstanding weavers at the Bauhaus. Her work at that time was mainly geometric, but she still did a great deal of other experimental work in other types of weaving. Today she lives in the United States and has continued to maintain a high standard of weaving techniques. During her time at the Bauhaus in Germany, she often worked with industry. Here in the United States her work is also sought after by commercial firms. On her arrival in America in 1933, she taught at the Black Moun-

Tea glass and saucer two inches high, made of steel, ebony, porcelain, and heat-resistant glass. Designed by Josef Albers in 1925. (Collection, The Museum of Modern Art, New York. Gift of Josef Albers.)

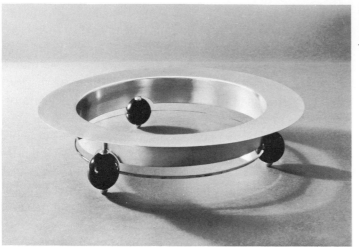

Fruit bowl of silver-plated metal, glass, and wood was designed in 1923 by Josef Albers and manufactured at Bauhaus metal workshop. (Collection, The Museum of Modern Art, New York. Gift of Walter Gropius.)

Armchair designed by Marcel Breuer in 1924 and manufactured at the Bauhaus carpentry workshop. (Collection, The Museum of Modern Art, New York. Phyllis B. Lambert Fund.)

tain College in North Carolina, where many Bauhaus members went after the Dessau school was closed.

Marcel Breuer. A Hungarian architect and sucessful designer, Marcel Breuer made unique contributions to the art of furniture design from the workshops of the Bauhaus. His introduction of tubular metal chairs opened up a complete new approach to furniture design, which, although revolutionary in conception, now is accepted in thousands of households around the world. George Nelson described his innovations:

"When Marcel Breuer developed his tubular steel chair 26 years ago, he dramatically demonstrated a fact that had been hinted at by Thonet's bentwood chair and the old-fashioned ice-cream parlor chair; namely, that the mainspring of progress in the *technique* of manufacturing furniture lies in bringing new materials into the field. Breuer's achievement was twofold: first he used a new material; and second he applied a new design principle to the chair by substituting a double S-shaped support for the conventional four legs. This move eliminated many joints; gave the chair comfortable resiliency at low cost. Soon the idea was applied to other metals beside steel . . ." (*Chairs*, p. 18). Few homes in the United States have been without some furniture that incorporated tubular steel, furniture such as dinette chairs and lawn chairs. Several of the chairs Breuer designed in the 1920s are now being produced by Knoll Associates for the contemporary home. Breuer is still actively working in architecture in the United States where he came after the Bauhaus was closed.

Wassily Kandinsky. Born in Moscow, Russia, in 1866, Wassily Kandinsky went to Munich, Germany, to study painting, in 1896. Eventually he found a place for himself at the Bauhaus, where he not only taught painting, but also became vice-president. Klee's influence on Kandinsky's work is evidenced by the fantasy and mystical content of his painting. His work, like that of most of the Bauhaus faculty, was chosen by the Nazi Government for inclusion in the "Degenerate Art" exhibition the Nazis circulated in Germany. He died in 1944.

Paul Klee. An artist from Switzerland, Paul Klee taught at the Bauhaus from 1920 to 1929. He was fully aware of the freedom he had at the Bauhaus to experiment

Side-chair design made by Marcel Breuer in 1928 using chrome-plated steel tube, wood, and cane. It was produced by Thonet. (Collection, The Museum of Modern Art, New York.)

Armchair designed by Marcel Breuer in 1925 of chrome-plated steel tube and canvas, and produced by Thonet. (Collection, The Museum of Modern Art, New York. Gift of Herbert Bayer.)

Armchair designed by Ludwig Mies van der Rohe in 1926 of chrome-plated steel tube and leather. (Collection, The Museum of Modern Art, New York. Gift of Edgar Kaufmann, Jr.)

Side chair designed in 1926 by Ludwig Mies van der Rohe, using chrome-plated steel tube and cane. It was produced by Gebrüder Thonet A. G., Germany. (Collection, The Museum of Modern Art, New York.)

with teaching. Ponente wrote that "he was aware of the semantic power of points, lines and space, and their movement on the picture plane; now he set out to test, experimentally, their effectiveness as vehicles of representation and interpretation" (*Klee*, Nello Ponente, p. 70). His work is full of inventiveness, improvisations, excitement, and whimsy. He drew from all life's experiences for his work with the students at the Bauhaus. He died in 1940 just after World War II struck Europe.

Lazslo Moholy-Nagy. Another extremely important figure at the Bauhaus was Lazslo Moholy-Nagy. He began teaching for Gropius in 1922 and remained at the Bauhaus until 1928. His work was extremely experimental in nature, for he investigated new materials and methods of expression. He produced much of the printed material and publications that originated in the Bauhaus. After he left the Bauhaus, he, like so many Bauhaus members, came to

Chess set designed by Josef Hartwig in 1924 at the Bauhaus. (Collection, The Museum of Modern Art, New York. Gift of Alfred H. Barr, Jr.)

Josef Albers tapestry, designed in 1924. Handwoven by Gunda Stadler-Stölzl of black and white wool, silk, cotton, and metal thread, it is 71 by 44 inches in size. (Collection, The Museum of Modern Art, New York. Phyllis B. Lambert Fund.)

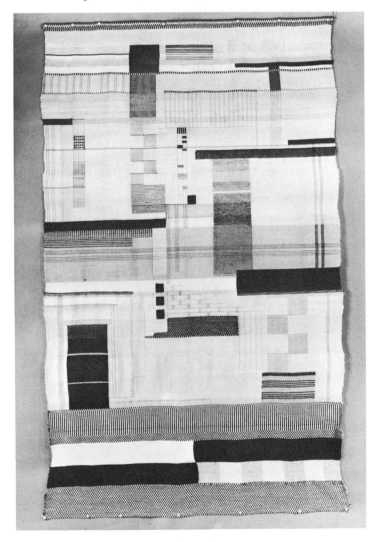

the United States. Here he became the Director of the New Bauhaus in Chicago. Later, he opened the School of Design in that city. His most famous contribution to the field of art was his book *The New Vision*, published in 1946, the year he died.

Ludwig Mies van der Rohe. An architect, Mies van der Rohe replaced Walter Gropius as director of the Bauhaus in 1930. Because of the active early Nazi organization in Dessau, he moved the Bauhaus to Berlin. There it remained until 1933, when Mies van der Rohe found it necessary to close the school altogether. He left Germany in 1937 and came to the United States, where he has participated in architecture very actively ever since. He is especially well known for his methods of breaking the four-walled box structure of a building into spans of glass that permit nature freely to enter his structures. His most famous contribution to furniture design is his "Barcelona" chair, which he designed in 1929. It is still considered one of the few chairs of the century that have offered major design solutions to furniture evolution.

SPREADING BAUHAUS IDEAS

When the Bauhaus was dissolved, its members went their different ways and carried its ideologies and principles across more of the world as they resettled. Most of its more prominent members arrived in the United States to continue teaching their philosophies. They made a great impression on the American scene. In Chicago, Mies van der Rohe, along with several other members, joined the department of architecture at the Armour Institute, while Moholy-Nagy and Gyorgy Kepes went to the New Bauhaus. Black Mountain College, in North Carolina, had Josef and Anni Albers and Alexander Schawinsky as new staff members; Marcel Breuer and Walter Gropius went to the architecture department at Harvard. In these ways they were able to continue to teach:

". . . the guiding principle of the Bauhaus . . . the idea of creating a new unity through the welding together of many 'arts' and movements: a unity having its basis in Man himself and significant only as a living organism.

"Human achievement depends on the proper coordination of all the creative faculties. It is not enough to school one or another of them separately: they must all be thoroughly trained at the same time. The character and scope of the Bauhaus teachings derive from the realization of this" (*Bauhaus 1919–1928*, Herbert Bayer, Walter Gropius, and Ise Gropius, p. 25).

BIBLIOGRAPHY AND SUGGESTED READINGS

Adams, Edward, George Pappas, and David B. Van Dommelen, *Design At Work: Its Forms And Functions*, The Pennsylvania State University, Center For Continuing Liberal Education, 1961.

Bayer, Herbert, Walter Gropius, and Ise Gropius, *Bauhaus 1919–1929*, Museum of Modern Art, New York, 1938.

Giedion, Sigfried, *Space, Time & Architecture*, Harvard University Press, Cambridge, 1943.

Gropius, Walter, *New Architecture and The Bauhaus*, Museum of Modern Art, New York, 1936.

Joedicke, Jürgen, *History of Modern Architecture*, Frederick A. Praeger, Inc., New York, 1959.

Kepes, Gyorgy, *New Landscape*, Theobald and Co., Chicago, 1957.

Moholy-Nagy, Lazslo, *Vision in Motion*, Theobald and Co., Chicago, 1957.

Nelson, George, *Chairs*, Whitney Publications, Inc., New York, 1953.

Ponente, Nello, *Klee*, The World Publishing Co., Cleveland, 1960.

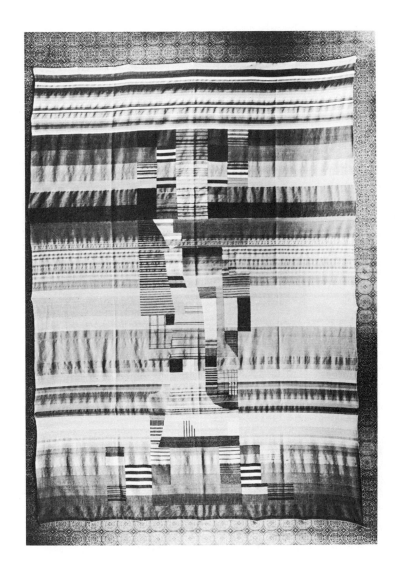

Wall hanging by Stadler-Stölzl at the Bauhaus, made about 1924. (Courtesy of Gunda Stadler-Stölzl.)

Carson Pirie & Scott Company store (formerly Schlesinger and Mayer Department Store) Chicago, designed by Louis Sullivan from 1899 to 1904. (Photo: courtesy of Carson Pirie & Scott Co.)

Frank Lloyd Wright's Robie house, Chicago, built in 1909. Its style was a forerunner of the contemporary style that has become popular throughout the country during the last 20 years. (Photo: Hedrich-Blessing.)

Chapter 6 AMERICAN DEVELOPMENTS

American developments in home design were rapidly taking place even before the various movements in Europe began to germinate. Of course, the European contributions to the fields of architecture and interior design were great and cannot be pushed aside. We have seen that many technological and structural innovations were introduced in Europe in movements that were both exploratory and experimental. However, American designers were not sitting back and assimilating these new achievements without doing some interesting work themselves. Too often we underestimate the contributions that Americans have made to our world, and we must therefore look at these in relation to those strong continental forces of Art Nouveau, *de Stijl*, and Bauhaus.

Certainly the American home has reached a pinnacle of success as compared with the homes of Europe. Our homes are better designed, better 71 equipped, and better planned. In the United States, we did not stop with architecture, outside appearances, or great ideologies, but we went directly on to the core of the complex practical problems of organizing efficient work space, storage areas, traffic lanes, and of developing the best household equipment in the world.

CATHERINE E. BEECHER

While William Morris was revitalizing the field of arts and crafts in England, the first home economist emerged to make improvements within the heart of the home in the United States. Catherine E. Beecher, sister of Harriet Beecher Stowe, examined the problems of the American housewife in 1842 in her book *Treatise on Domestic Economy*. Although the words "home economist" sometimes arouse some resistance, a writer of the stature of James Marston Fitch recognized the work and the contributions Miss Beecher made, in his book *Architecture and The Esthetics of Plenty*. It was because of her experimental ideas that the housewives of today are able to have houses that are more effectively designed. Miss Beecher played an important role in releasing the American woman from servitude to the ill-planned home. Even though Fitch did not discover Miss Beecher's work until 1961, home economists have long been interested in her ideas; she studied and made profound investigations of nearly every aspect of the home. Fitch commented:

"The one respect in which Miss Beecher's plans are distinctive is in their provision of clothes closets, pantries, and storerooms (which show that she already has well-developed concepts of specialized storage) and 'bed-presses,' i.e., beds that folded into closets (which forecast her interest in multiple use of space). She understands that her kind of housekeeping implies specialized rooms (her Gothic cottage has a combination study and guest room, a nursery, a sewing room) but she is not yet able to visualize their special architectural character" (*Architecture and The Esthetics of Plenty*, p. 71).

She overlooked, however, the aesthetic aspects of what she was planning, and this is still characteristic of many home economists. They become very involved with the mechanics and with technical problems and do not see the beauty that could also be achieved at the same time. Fitch's comments on Miss Beecher's relationship with Frank Lloyd Wright are interesting:

"In this long and encyclopedic book she has covered every aspect of woman's profession—the management of a middle-class American family. This family is essentially modern, and so is the house she evolves to shelter it. From a functional point of view, she is decades ahead of specifications for that free-standing, middle-class suburban house which Frank Lloyd Wright was to bring to esthetic perfection, thirty or forty years later" (*Architecture and The Esthetics of Plenty*, p. 81).

Miss Beecher's work in home planning inspired a long line of home economists to explore built-in devices in various parts of the home. Today the home management specialist is still deeply involved in many aspects of designing the interior and the furnishings of a house.

While Miss Beecher was investigating problems within the structure, others were beginning to experiment with architectural solutions by introducing new techniques in construction.

THE CHICAGO SCHOOL OF ARCHITECTURE

Henry Hobson Richardson was one of the architects who helped start the revolution in the United States that would eventually change the facade of American building—not only in the commercial structure, but also in family dwellings. Richardson, from 1885 to 1887, built the Marshall Field Wholesale Building, which introduced honest and straightforward use of materials in the construction of a building. His was an architecture that belonged to the famous Chicago School that developed the "using of steel skeleton in the construction of multi-storey buildings" (*A History of Modern Architecture*, Jürgen Joedicke, p. 24). In this school of architecture, the load-bearing wall adapted new form concepts when D. H. Burnham and J. W. Root created the Monadnock Building in Chicago in 1891. The pure understanding of clearly defined elements of the structure and its use reached a plateau at this point but would be carried on further by later architects. The architects were beginning to understand what materials could do and that materials could do much without help from unnecessary ornamentation.

Louis Sullivan

Another member of the Chicago School who worked a little later was the architect Louis Sullivan, whom we discussed in relation to the Art Nouveau movement. Sullivan did a great deal to promote the skyscraper, and from his research and considerations grew the concepts of a type of building that one day would become the symbol of American cities. Sullivan's greatness lay in his ability to see and to understand the social implications of his art and its place in society. This meant that Sullivan, along with other architects and designers of the Chicago School, in order to pursue architecture honestly had to cast aside the styles and influences of past cultures and proceed to answer current problems. From this conviction came Sullivan's famous phrase, "form follows function." In *The Autobiography of An Idea*, Sullivan wrote in relation to this phrase:

"He could now, undisturbed, start on the course of practical experimentation he long had in mind, which was to make an architecture that fitted its functions—a realistic architecture based on well defined utilitarian needs—that all practical demands of utility should be paramount as basis of planning and design; that no architectural dictum, or tradition, or superstition, or habit, should stand in the way. He would brush them all aside, regardless of commentators. For his view, his conviction was this: That the architecture art to be of contemporary immediate value must be *plastic*; all senseless conventional rigidity must be taken out of it; it must intelligently serve—it must not sup-

press. In this wise the forms under his hands would grow naturally out of the needs and express them frankly, and freshly. This meant in his courageous mind that he would put to the test a formula he had evolved, through long contemplation of living things, namely that *form follows function*, which would mean, in practice, that architecture might again become a living art, if this formula were but adhered to" (p. 257).

Sullivan left many important buildings as his mark in the progress of architecture. The Wainwright Building, built in 1891 in St. Louis, was the culmination of his ideas. It was like no approach to architecture that had been used before, and it reverted to no past dynasty of previous architectural dictum. Instead, it stood alone as an indicator of what would be done, in the years to come, by other architects. Its walls were not load-bearing walls but simply protected the steel skeleton and provided the delicate ornamentation Sullivan desired. The building stressed vertical shafts and height; he turned later to horizontal emphasis in the Carson, Pirie & Scott Building.

His Transportation Building at the 1893 Exposition in Chicago is often referred to as the beginning of modern architecture. At the time, it was completely out of place in a "midway" of white fake marble facades of eclecticism and Greek Revival.

FRANK LLOYD WRIGHT

Sullivan's work did not stop at his death, for one of his students was destined to become the architectural genius of the twentieth century. Frank Lloyd Wright's contributions to architecture have been so numerous that they outweigh those of any other architect in this century. His work was controversial throughout his life, and it continued to be so after his death, when the Guggenheim Museum in New York was opened for public inspection in 1961.

Organic Architecture

Wright followed Sullivan's philosophy of "form follows function,'' but he would have preferred to be known by his ''organic'' architectural approach. In 1953 Hugh Downs of NBC talked to Wright concerning his work. Mr. Downs asked Frank Lloyd Wright the meaning of ''organic architecture.'' Wright answered:

''. . . modern architecture is merely something—anything—which may be built today, but organic architecture is an architecture from within outward, in which entity is the ideal. We don't use the word organic as referring to something hanging in a butcher shop, you know.

''Organic means intrinsic—in the philosophic sense, entity—wherever the whole is to the part as the part is to the whole and where the nature of the materials, the nature of the purpose, the *nature* of the entire performance becomes clear as a necessity. Out of that *nature* comes what character in any particular situation you can give to the building as a creative artist'' (*The Future of Architecture*, Frank Lloyd Wright, p. 12).

Few artists, designers, or architects have had as colorful a personality as Wright's. His outspoken words stabbed and jabbed the mediocre and the fake around him. He set his standards high, and few (or none, in his view) were able to climb the heights to his level.

Although Wright has given heavily to the architecture of commercial buildings, his inventiveness has influenced the domestic structure to an even greater degree. We find many innovations related to his ideas.

Wright's Contributions

Probably one of Wright's most significant contributions to the American home, though one not yet fully assimilated by many architects, is the amalgamation of the structure with its surrounding environment or landscape. The rocks and trees of a hillside became part of the walls and floors of the houses he designed. This is part of his *''organic''* idea. In Chapter 13 we shall investigate more carefully the site and its relationship with the structure.

Wright was also the introducer of the open plan. Today in many of our homes one room slowly merges or

flows into the next, often without a wall section or separator. Although in many earlier homes, the kitchen, dining room, and living room were all one, Wright reintroduced this old concept into the contemporary house. In the ''typical'' ranch-style floor plan, we see the ''dining L'' as an offspring of the open plan.

The prairie house, which Wright designed when he built the Robie house in Chicago in 1909, was basically

The Willey house, built by Frank Lloyd Wright in 1934, has a hallway that is called a gallery and is utilized as a library. The bedrooms open on this open space. (Photo: Hedrich-Blessing.)

Malcolm Willey house, Minneapolis, Minn., built by Frank Lloyd Wright in 1934. The dining area has built-in table and storage space, typical of Wright's houses. Notice the use of brick flooring, considered an innovation in the 1930s. (Photo: Hedrich-Blessing.)

designed to echo the horizontal landscape of the midwest beyond Chicago. Although the modern ranch style is far from Wright's original idea of the prairie house, it is a part of the heritage he left, as are the ribbon-type windows, patios in northern climates, cantilevered roofs, and large areas of glass—better known as picture windows. It is hard to think of the monotony and ugliness of the picture windows and ribbon windows used in development houses as being branches of Wright's architecture; but the pilfering of ideas from great men and the subsequent bastardization of these ideas is not unknown in our society.

The Usonian House

A great and very important contribution to architecture and the American home was Wright's Usonian struc-ture. His Usonian house was designed with gravity heating or what we generally call radiant heating. This he developed in order to be able to construct a house that was inexpensive and available for the average man with an average income. Most of his good Usonian houses were built before World War II and ranged in price from $4,500 to $9,500. For his Usonian home he also conceived the idea of indirect lighting—lights hidden in panels reflecting their beams off the ceiling. Limited decorative elements and simplified construction techniques were also utilized to lower the costs.

An interesting Usonian house that Wright designed is the Goetsch-Winckler house near Okemos, Michigan, built for two women art professors teaching at Michigan State University. It was built in 1939 at a cost of $9,500.

The Goetsch-Winkler house in Okemos, Michigan, built in 1939, is one of the best of Wright's Usonian houses. Notice the ribbon windows and the floor-to-ceiling glass doors opening to the yard. (Photo: Hedrich-Blessing.)

Incorporated in this house are the many developments that Wright contributed to American architecture. It has an open floor plan that gives an unusual feeling of space, even though the house is actually small in dimensions. Along with the open plan, cantilevered roofs and carport and large amounts of brick used in extending walls deceive the spectator when viewing the house from the exterior; inside it is spacious, airy, and light. In the interior, his use of textures in wood, brick, and flooring creates a warm atmosphere which, instead of being cold and uninviting, is *gemütlich* and comfortable. A limited amount of built-in furniture is used, and through the years the occupants have added those items needed to make it even more personal than it was in Wright's conception. The house was designed around two exceptional women, and Wright was extremely successful in keeping the character of the house in tune with the dwellers. Nature surrounds the building, enters through the ribbon windows and gallery doors, and the outside environment is part of the total structure.

By designing a house like this, Wright was able to bring to Americans a new understanding of people in relation to their own surroundings. Although Wright alone did not feed the fire in the revolution of home designing, it can be fairly well asserted that he was the major force in the changing architectural scene in the United States for the first half of the century.

During his career, Wright completed commissions in several parts of the world. Japan played an important part in influencing his work, and Americans became more familiar with Oriental trends in architecture and home furnishings. By 1938 many young architects were being swayed by Oriental forms, and various publications illustrating this art ideology began to appear. In 1938 Antonin Raymond published *Architectural Details* in Japan, and in this publication suggested many important thoughts necessary to our successful continuation in a new phase of architecture. He wrote:

"It must be constantly restated to laymen as well as to professionals, that contemporary architecture is not the desire for expressing individuality, not the desire for new and bizarre form, nor is it merely another fancy of designers. The work of those modern designers whose efforts are chiefly in this direction, will soon be added to the heap of discarded fashions."

This was a lesson that could easily have been heeded

The Lloyd Lewis house, Liberty, Illinois, was designed by Frank Lloyd Wright in 1940. Observe the interesting textures employed in furnishings and building. The furniture was designed to fit the home. (Photo: Hedrich-Blessing.)

Lloyd Lewis house, Liberty, Illinois, was designed by Frank Lloyd Wright in 1940. (Photo: Hedrich-Blessing.)

by the designers of Art Nouveau. Wright undoubtedly understood Raymond, and Raymond's following paragraphs seem completely fitted to Wright's philosophies:

"The first principle which all great architecture teaches us is to regard local conditions as the one known factor from which to start, and to allow the structure to take the most logical shape dictated by these conditions. Thus flowers and animals do in differing climates.

"From the Japanese we have learned the value of the natural substance and surfaces of materials, and we avoid artificial finishes and condemn imitations. When selecting materials we consider not only their practical values but also their natural colors and textures, creating in that way true harmonies which outlast any fashion. This requires excellent workmanship which is an essential in a truly good

The Sol Friedman house designed by Frank Lloyd Wright in 1949. A feeling of space and nature is found in this interior with its fieldstone walls and Indian objects. (Photo: Ezra Stoller.)

modern building as is its pure and perfect structural engineering.''

It was not until after World War II that foreign influences really began to hit the United States with a strong impact. Because the world was generally getting smaller in light of more rapid transportation, and because veterans from the war brought back new cultural ideas, we discarded our provincial attitudes and adopted more cosmopolitan ways of looking at architecture, crafts, and furniture design. Today the women's magazines, the department stores, and most shops feature goods that were not available in this country a few years ago. Along with this influx of ideas from lay sources, the arrival of European architects and designers just before the war greatly changed the American design world.

Mr. and Mrs. Sam Sabean's house was designed by a student of Frank Lloyd Wright about 1938. It emphasizes the role of the outdoors, as do all of Wright's own building designs. (Photo: courtesy of Sam Sabean.)

BIBLIOGRAPHY AND SUGGESTED READINGS

Beecher, Catherine E., *Treatise On Domestic Economy*, Thomas Webb and Co., Boston, 1842.

Fitch, James Marston, *Architecture And The Esthetics Of Plenty*, Columbia University Press, New York, 1961.

Joedicke, Jürgen, *History of Modern Architecture*, Frederick A. Praeger, Inc., New York, 1959.

Peter, John, *Masters of Modern Architecture*, George Braziller, Inc., New York, 1958.

Raymond, Antonin, *Architectural Details*, Seisho-Kwan, Kyobashi-Ku, Tokyo, 1938.

Scully, Jr., Vincent, *Frank Lloyd Wright*, George Braziller, Inc., New York, 1960.

Scully, Jr., Vincent, *Modern Architecture*, George Braziller, Inc., New York, 1961.

Sullivan, Louis H., *Autobiography of An Idea*, Dover Publications, Inc., New York, 1956.

Wright, Frank Lloyd, *Ausgeführte Bauten*, Verlegt Bei Ernst Wasmuth A.–G., Berlin, 1911.

Wright, Frank Lloyd, *Future of Architecture*, Horizon Press, New York, 1953.

Wright, Frank Lloyd, *Natural House*, Horizon Press, New York, 1954.

PART TWO COMMENTS

By understanding past events, the layman and student can better recognize the developments that led to contemporary design. At his first glimpse of modern paintings, a viewer may be confused—and rightly so. Without adequate perspective on chronological and historical background, he has no measure for the assumed chaos he sees. For the same reason, persons interested in the fields of interior design and home furnishings must investigate the steps that led to the contemporary scene. With background he may look with pleasure and knowingly evaluate what he sees as being a rightful part of his society and his time.

We are now able to look in retrospect at the chaos that industrialization brought to our world and to see how the artist and craftsman approached new designing problems. The designer tried with difficulty in the Art Nouveau movement to bring about an honest revision of ideas. Although he failed in his own time, he opened up the door for other designers to begin further investigations. These were the designers who took the machine and integrated its usefulness into their work in order to make more meaningful contributions to manufacturing practices. Both *de Stijl* and Bauhaus artists investigated design not by rejecting the machine but by using it as a tool to express their ideologies. As we study the designers who have made contributions to the field of architecture and interiors, we find that we cannot divorce the architect from the interior designer, or the craftsman from the home furnishing specialist. They are all of equal importance in the destiny of the home. Too often the home furnishing specialists underestimate the contributions made by the architect in planning the home, and vice versa. However, we have seen that eminently successful architects have married these two interests into one. The architect may be busy designing furniture while he draws his structure, and a textile designer may be very involved in the study of crafts and interiors.

With this in mind, we will assume that the architect is a home economist when he designs the kitchen, and that the interior designer is an architect when he works on a project to rebuild or redecorate the interior of a dwelling. It may well be, however, that each will reject this idea, for he may be reluctant to relinquish his specialty.

Part Three: CONTEMPORARY DESIGNERS

Dr. Edith Farnsworth's house, in Plano, Illinois, designed by Ludwig Mies van der Rohe in 1950, is an example of the purist type of house. (Photo: Hedrich-Blessing.)

The Sol Friedman house in Pleasantville, New York, designed by Frank Lloyd Wright in 1949, is illustrative of the romantic personal approach. (Photo: Ezra Stoller.)

Chapter 7 THE CONTEMPORARY HOUSE: FAÇADES, MATERIALS, AND PLANS

The façade or exterior of the contemporary home cannot be left out in a consideration of the house in our contemporary society. This, after all, is the first part of the home that the visitor sees when he arrives. The designer and architect have made great strides since World War II in changing the image and façade of the American home. We can no longer generalize about the appearance of the American home, if we ever were able to, for a great diversity of domestic structures has spanned the nation's landscape. Because of the designing and imagination of young architects and the changing needs and requirements of the family, the old homestead is slowly disappearing.

FAÇADES: PURIST, ROMANTIC, AND MODERN ECLECTIC

The following classification of American architecture has been made:

"If we look around us we can discover many interesting examples of architecture that fit into three categories, as well as others that stand by themselves because of some more individual characteristics. Mies van der Rohe's scheme for Dr. Edith Farnsworth's home is among the most convincing of recent designs created within the discipline of the purist: a highly rationalized and ultra-refined direct statement of technic and purpose. Frank Lloyd Wright's Sol Friedman house surely represents the opposite end of the scale: a highly personal romantic approach to organic architecture. And the skillfully designed house by Techbuilt Corporation represents a happy fusing of design approaches [which we will call modern eclectic]. It makes conscious and sympathetic allowance for the psychological need for texture, for color, and essentially livable qualities" (*Design At Work: Its Forms And Functions*, Adams, Pappas and Van Dommelen, p. 63).

To elaborate further on these three divisions of American architecture, we find that the purist approach to a structure is more clearly defined than the others; machine-like precision is its outstanding characteristic. The details are fine and acutely manifested, as in both the Farnsworth house and the Philip Johnson house. There is a sense of space that is sandwiched between two surfaces, held together with an invisible force, and framed with delicate, almost nonexistent steel molding. The purist's boxed room presents an antinature statement, similar in intent to the *de Stijl* ideal. The beauty of the purist house is the void—giving the beholder the ultimate in simplicity and an architectural essay that is logically clarified.

In the romantic house, one finds less clarification of form but more consideration of environmental forces. Individuality is paramount, as can be seen in Frank Lloyd Wright's houses. In this type of architecture, nature is given an important role in the transition from the building to the landscape, by the designer's incorporation of materials from the surrounding countryside into the structure. This type of house gives a feeling of warmth and hand craftsmanship and a lack of machine orientation.

The third division we might call modern eclectic, for it draws from both the other types and presents an amalgamation of approaches. Machine precision is combined with the softness of natural materials. Parts of such a house suggest the machine orientation, while other areas seem more closely allied with the countryside. Fieldstone fireplaces are in juxtaposition with clean planes of glass, while some parts of the house utilize textural glass and concrete brick, which form rich patterns seemingly from other cultural backgrounds. The fusion of two styles in this type of building is not unlike the eclectic architecture of past ages when many styles of architecture were put together for

Techbuilt house in Marblehead, Massachusetts, is a fusing of purist and romantic styles. (Photo: courtesy of Techbuilt Inc.)

desired effects. But in the modern eclectic, the architect is more concerned about the *happy* fusion of these varied parts of the building; when he blends these parts successfully, his structure is infinitely more pleasing than the eclectic architecture of the nineteenth century. His eclecticism also extends to the use of a great variety of new materials.

MATERIALS

With the advent of new design for houses, new materials and construction methods inevitably came into use to make this renewed effort in designing more successful. Before 1946, homes were generally made of wood and brick, and only at times were other materials such as stucco included for diversity. But as new processes have been developed by industry, materials of all types are now available for home construction. Some are completely new, while others are simply new approaches to old standard supplies.

Wood

Wood, of course, is one of the oldest of building supplies and has been used for the exterior of homes throughout the ages in many varied forms. From the Norwegian farmhouses to the log cabins of early America, roughly hewn logs were used as beams, lintels, and siding. Wood taken directly from the tree was and still is used in many primitive cultures. For the American Indian lodge structure, branches were bent in a span across a space, and smaller twigs were woven into the side walls.

Again today, the home is being sided with the beauty of unpainted wood as it was in the days of the early Western settler. For many years house exteriors were painted in various colors ranging from deep red to pastel pinks in the

Southwest, but we are now finding that wood left in its natural state, with only a sealer or filler applied occasionally, gives the outside of the home a warmer and richer feeling and integrates the structure more beautifully with the environment. Frank Lloyd Wright used wood exteriors extensively, and today's architects have continued his practice of utilizing wood for exterior building. For instance, not long ago the Haystack Mountain School of Crafts built a compound of buildings along the coast of Maine, and since the exterior was not prepared in any way, the wood has aged to a mellow grey, most appropriate in the surrounding fir and rocky landscape. A similar practice is used for the houses of Nantucket, Massachusetts.

The use of wood does mean that more maintenance and upkeep of the exterior will be necessary, but it is substantially less expensive initially than other materials. Of course, the builder can incorporate other materials with wood for interesting results, as long as the designer has used moderation in planning for these additional materials.

Wood used in the days of the Algonquin Indians is still a favorite material of housing today. (Photo: courtesy of Jamestown Foundation by T. J. Williams.)

Wood and glass are combined in a mixture of the purist and romantic moods. (Photo: courtesy of Pittsburgh Plate Glass Co.)

Besides its application in horizontal strips around the house as seen in conventional homes, wood can be applied vertically to the side of the house to enhance the structure, if the over-all design calls for vertical siding. Horizontal clapboard tends to make the building appear shorter and longer, while vertical siding will add height to the home. The choice of siding should be left to the designer, who is able to judge which kind a particular structure needs.

Fencing, as well as the actual house, can be made of wood; it can be used in the old manner of the plain picket fence and also in woven boards that introduce interesting patterns around the patio or play yard. Many homes today present only a wooden fence to the street side. Painted or unpainted, the fence lends great privacy to the family within and may also project a sense of mystery to the passerby.

Plywood has come into its own in the last few years. It was used only as wall boarding, in furniture, and in other smaller forms, for many years, but the contemporary architect has discovered that plywood can make great contributions to the façades of contemporary houses. It is not necessarily less expensive, but it can be quickly installed and can span space in very effective ways.

Brick, Concrete, Tile, and Stone

Brick, another widely used building material, has been part of homes for many thousands of years. Egyptians used various forms of brick, adobe, and tiles before the birth of Christ, and this material has continued to be extremely popular. In recent years, however, brick has become more expensive, and fewer houses are made of brick than of wood. In the last few years, enameling of brick has become popular, for it enables the homeowner to have colored exteriors. Brick, of course, has been used for small sections in homes throughout the history of man, even when it has not been the major part of the structure. Often only a portion of the exterior is bricked; of course, bricks have been utilized consistently in fireplace and chimney construction.

The Haystack Mountain School of Crafts illustrates the use of unfinished weathered wood in architecture.

Town houses faced with brick have traditional overtones and yet can be purely contemporary in design. (Photo: courtesy of Eichler Homes.)

Decorative forms of brick, tile, and cement block have been used a great deal since architects began to employ them as ornamentation of the façades of domestic homes and of large public buildings, such as Edward Stone's United States Pavilion at the World's Fair in Brussels. Other architects have used ornamental brick and concrete as pattern accents on the surface of buildings. Ornamental brick and concrete can often be seen in fences and garden entrances.

Brick, one form of ceramics, is made of clay that has been hardened in the sun or in a kiln. Ceramic tile is of the same nature as brick, basically, except that it generally has to be fired in a kiln at a higher temperature, it is thinner and finer in texture, and it often has some type of decorative glaze over the surface, so that a large range of colors can be introduced. Adobe is not fired in a kiln but is hardened by drying in the sun, and it contains other components mixed with clay, usually concrete, giving it more

enduring qualities in climates that are not always completely arid.

Many houses are now constructed wholly of concrete blocks, most of which are more refined than the old cinder block. However, for really inexpensive houses, cinder block can be used.

Although we still think in terms of standard sizes for bricks and block, in reality there is such a diverse selection that no one brick can be considered standard any more (unless it would be the ordinary red brick that is about 2 in. by 4 in. by 8 in.). There are now bricks in grey, white, pink, green, and other colors. They are used not only as part of the outside of the building but also in attractive patterns on the floor within the home. There are many houses being built today with entryways of varied types of brick, stone, and tile.

Using stone in the construction of a house is like using unpainted wood: both help bring the building closer

A room is shown to illustrate the contemporary use of concrete for interior spaces. Frank Lloyd Wright pioneered this practice. (Photo: courtesy of National Concrete Masonry Association.)

Philip Johnson's house in New Canaan, Connecticut, utilizes glass with steel beams. This is a classical and purist approach to individual housing space. (Photo: Ezra Stoller.)

to its surroundings and landscape, and both seem to add a feeling of warmth. Stone generally adds a casual feeling to the house, whether it is employed on the inside or on the exterior. This is especially noticeable if the stone is rough and raw from the earth. If the stone has been carefully trimmed, a spirit of comfort and coziness is less likely to result from its use. Houses that are built from the natural fieldstone of the immediate region at once seem to be part of the landscape, just as does a house of wood in a forest.

In the area of stone, besides the heavy fieldstones, there are black slates, which can be used for floors, hearths, and sills, and there are limestone and marble. Use of marble, of course, leads to a very expensive house, often impractical for the average house builder.

Glass

There has been a rapid development of the use of glass in architecture recently, and many new forms of glass are being introduced into the construction of modern buildings and homes. There was a time when one could find glass only as a transparent material, but now we are able to buy it in many textures, patterns, and colors. Beaded, striped, and frosted glass are important parts of a great many homes. Nontransparent types of glass panels can be used in areas where more privacy is required, or they can simply be incorporated as design elements on the exterior of the home. Unusual glass is often found in office interiors where dividers are needed to wall off areas that are closed to the public.

Stained glass has had a revival in architecture, especially in large public buildings, and it is also being used in homes for ornamental purposes. Stained-glass techniques were important factors during the Art Nouveau period when stained glass was used not only to decorate windows but also for lamps and accessories, which were often heavily embellished with mosaic designs in glass.

Glass introduces into the home the feeling of space as well as the sparkle of another material. Walls that are made of glass help bring the outdoors into the living room or kitchen or help make visual extensions of a room to a patio on the outside. Ceilings with studio effects are now designed with clerestory architectural details, derived from the architecture of medieval days. The clerestory aids the room by instilling a spacious and airy quality, much as do the large plate-glass or Thermopane picture windows of development houses.

For Alden B. Dow's architectural office and home, the designer planned a combination of copper roofing and concrete blocks. The structure, built in 1937 by a student of Frank Lloyd Wright, was intended to become an integral part of nature. This photograph, taken in May, 1937, by Wright, shows a building that now is completely surrounded by trees and shrubs and seems to melt into the earth and water. (Photo: courtesy of Alden Dow.)

Domes and skylights have been introduced into the domestic home by many architects. From the exterior, these make important contributions to the over-all effect of the building, especially at night. A dome skylight illuminated at night throws beautiful beams of light up into the surrounding trees, giving a mysterious effect to the house as well as adding a nighttime ornamental detail.

Glass, used as a part of the façade or the structure, adds to the ease of maintaining the house. Obviously, it does not need yearly painting. Heat loss is no longer a problem, for modern Thermopane windows keep the heat in and the cold out and at the same time eliminate the window moisture condensation that was for so many years a nuisance to the housewife.

Of course, glass is used in the home in ways other than for the actual building and construction. An aspect of glass that can be seen very readily from the outside and that plays a major role in some houses is the drapery made of glass. Fiberglas has become exceedingly popular in the last several years, and in many homes of glass the drapery is the messenger of color or pattern that meets the glance of the passerby. Fiberglas will be treated in more detail in Chapter *Eight*.

Metal

In the latter part of the nineteenth century when the use of metal was first introduced into architecture as a major component, it would have been hard to imagine that metal would become an extremely important part not only of large public buildings but of the small domestic house as well. Of course, metal is now used throughout the home and in ways that would be almost mundane and ridiculous to mention. One of the great achievements of the metal industries has been the persuasion of homeowners that their homes should have aluminum siding rather than wood. Of course, the advantages are great for the homeowner. Aluminum siding reduces maintenance a great deal and at the same time gives the appearance of wood after it has been painted.

Another use of aluminum can be seen in the dome structures designed by Buckminster Fuller. Fuller's mathematically conceived dome is designed with equilateral triangles of aluminum tubes covered with translucent plastic or filled with glass triangular panes. The house is then placed within the resulting sphere, and the effect is that of a space satellite.

The use of metal in building has really taken its place beside and in combination with the use of glass. The Philip Johnson house is an example of how these two materials can be utilized to change the façade of the American home. Although not everyone would be able to live in such a house, it has answered the architectural needs of some individuals. In the Johnson house, steel has been used exclusively as the framing device to hold the glass in place and gives the structure a clean, sheer line that is of the classic, or purist, type of architecture. Here is a description of it:

"The house is a single room 32′ x 56′, with walls entirely of glass. There are no columns inside the house: all structural elements are part of the exterior wall, and the carefully articulated transitions from glass panel to steel column, as well as the subtle punctuation of space inside the house, constitute all its architecture. There is a single door in the center of each façade, establishing symmetrical axes for the whole house. Inside are low cabinets—one for kitchen equipment and another for storage—and a brick cylinder containing a bathroom and, on its outer wall, a fireplace. The exact placement of cabinets, brick cylinder, and a large piece of sculpture creates 'rooms'" (*Built in USA: Post-War Architecture*, Henry-Russel Hitchcock and Arthur Drexler, p. 35).

The Charles Eames house, another building incorporating the use of metal, is quite different in presentation. The steel structural elements are not only part of the architecture but are aids in dividing the exterior walls into *de Stijl*-like divisions. It was described thus:

"For the exterior he chose a combination of glass walls and cement, painted in great squares of colour, red, grey, and bright blue, tremendously effective against the green trees, ... Inside the house there is a superb feeling of space because of the eighteen-foot-high ceiling of open steel decking and open-webbed joists. In building these two cubes [which comprise the total house, living area and studio], Eames used only factory materials, existing in ready-made sizes; nothing was made to order" (*Vogue*, August 15, 1959, "Eames," by Allene Talmey). While the Johnson house reflects the images of nature surrounding it, the Eames house presents a contrast to its environment in the brilliant colors of a Mondrian painting.

Of course, other metals have been used in houses in many ways; some for hundreds of years. Copper, a metal used since nearly the beginning of historic time, oxidizes and adds patina of soft greens to a building. Alden Dow, a Michigan architect, often uses copper as a decorative element on the exterior of his houses.

Plastic

The material most likely to make continued major impacts on designing for American homes, and most likely

The Charles Eames house in Santa Monica, California, was designed by Eames in 1949. He used factory-produced steel window and door units along with other manufactured parts. Metal is the major material. (Photo: courtesy of Herman Miller Inc.)

An experimental plastic house in Disneyland was built by the Monsanto Chemical Company. (Photo: courtesy of the Monsanto Co.)

A General Electric experimental prefabricated plastic house was designed by Eliot Noyes. (Photo: courtesy of General Electric Company.)

to change radically the image of the home, is plastic in its various uses. Plastic has been developed to withstand low temperatures, as well as extremely high temperatures, without cracking or melting. Plastic permits a wide range of colors to be used for decorative elements. Sun porches and outside patios can now have adequate protection from climatic changes with this new material. Slowly plastic has been improved and developed until it can be used for the complete construction of entire homes.

Monsanto Chemical Company has contributed to the research in this field. It sponsored experimentation that produced the plastic house, introduced at Disneyland in California. The experimentation took four years of testing and research with the Massachusetts Institute of Technology. The exterior of the house is composed of 16 molded polyester-urethane-foam "sandwich" sections, while other forms of plastic are used within the structure. Testing of this house for several years at Disneyland has demonstrated the strength and durability of plastics. The house itself has settled only three-tenths of an inch after receiving six million visitors in three years. We shall see in a later chapter how furniture designers have used plastics as new materials for chairs and accessories.

These materials, then, all contribute to the over-all image of the façade of the home. New materials appear each year, and each year new approaches are advanced for use of old materials. Young new architects and forward-looking older architects continue to search for new forms that will answer the new needs of a fast-moving world. It is impossible to consider that the *status quo* will remain as we now see it, for in the space age progress and movement cannot be halted. American homes will be as different in the year 2000 as the homes of the 1960s are different from those of 1900. It will be as difficult for the coming older generation to accept the devices and façades of the new

The apartment building here employs a combination of materials—glass, brick, steel, and paneling. (Photo: courtesy of Eichler Homes.)

century as it is for the grandparents of the 1960s to understand glass-walled houses and plastic chairs. But the development of new shapes and images will not stop, and we need only look at a few homes designed by architects and shown by the Museum of Modern Art in its Visionary Architecture exhibition to catch a glimpse of what is in store for future generations.

The house designed by Frederick Kiesler and exhibited in the Visionary Architecture show is of special interest to us because Kiesler was also a designer of a structure called City In Space, which used the forms of the *de Stijl;* thus the newer work seems at first glance to be in

Frederick Kiesler's "Endless House" is prophetic of the future use of materials for family living spaces. Unusual and startling, this house offers an extreme contrast to most houses that are being built today. (Photo: courtesy of Frederick Kiesler.)

The Sam B. Short home in Baton Rouge, Louisiana, features a vaulted plywood roof in combination with areas of glass and concrete. (Photo: courtesy of Douglas Fir Plywood Association.)

direct contradiction to his earlier designs. Both concepts, however, are very much alike in that they are both studies of endless space. The house with which Mr. Kiesler presents us is a house that *is* part of the earth. It is like the rocks and mushrooms in the forest. Each room flows freely into the next, in a way that is even more free than Frank Lloyd Wright's work. The house is simple, lives within the natural world, and is the creation of an exceedingly brilliant architect. However, the majority of persons seeing a structure such as this would immediately reject it, for it is much too foreign to them. It is highly unlikely that we will see suburbs with homes like this in the next ten years, but we cannot project ourselves into the twenty-first century when, for all we know, all men *might* be living in homes like this one. Through architects like Kiesler, who constantly move ahead of the masses, home façades will evolve and change into shapes we do not at first understand, but later learn to accept without hesitation. These odd shapes and forms must and will be built

with new materials—some of which are not even developed today.

FLOOR PLANS

In order to obtain a more exact picture of the contemporary house, we must of course also examine its interior development and plans. While the outside façade integrates the building with its surroundings or contrasts the structure to its environment, the inside plan tells more of the story of the family who lives there. The shape of the floor plan, the freedom of the interior or its formality, all help to make up the important image that the house projects. While the façade must beckon the visitor into the house in one way or another, the floor plan and physical arrangement of the rooms must lead him throughout the interior with interest and purpose.

Whereas once the interior was likely to have a basic, stereotyped center-hall arrangement with rooms off a center core, we now find that this pattern has given way to more fluid arrangements. We have already seen that Frank Lloyd Wright was responsible for a great deal of this change, but credit must also be given to those designers and architects who have continued to discover new formulas for developing floor plans and for modifying old techniques of planning interior arrangements.

The Square Plan

The square floor plan is one of the most common types. The chief appeal of this floor plan is the cost; it is less expensive to build, because less land is required and because less foundation is needed for either the one-story or the two-story house. However, this plan tends to be uninteresting in design. The house is often dark, if eaves are projected too far beyond the outside walls, and, of course, is very limiting as to the placement of the rooms. It is a compact design, with all rooms easily reached from any part of the house. There are normally fewer hallways and connecting arteries throughout the house.

Frank Lloyd Wright was especially interested in

eliminating the square type of plan from architectural practice because of its box-like appearance. This approach led him to more flexible and versatile floor planning.

The Rectangular Floor Plan

The rectangular plan is more costly to build than the square plan, but there is more manipulation possible in the placing of rooms within the rectangle. Sleeping areas can be located further away from activity areas, so that the quiet part of the house is more isolated. Of course, longer halls are often the result and are apt to introduce more unusable space if the house is badly designed. Exterior walls, however, can be designed with more interest than is possible with the box or block type of construction necessitated by the square plan.

Atrium or Court Plan

The atrium plan has been reintroduced in the last few years, but it is in no way a new formula. Greek and Roman houses used this plan extensively to introduce the visitor to the main house. The atrium plan is expensive, because it requires more land and a larger foundation. This building plan provides a wall-surrounded outdoor

The square plan. (Courtesy of Techbuilt Inc.)

The rectangular plan. (Courtesy of Techbuilt Inc.)

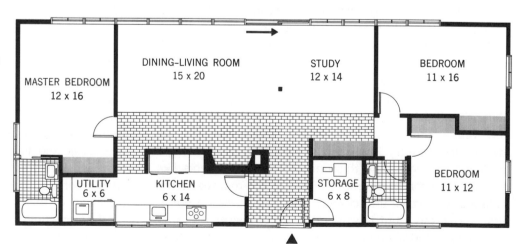

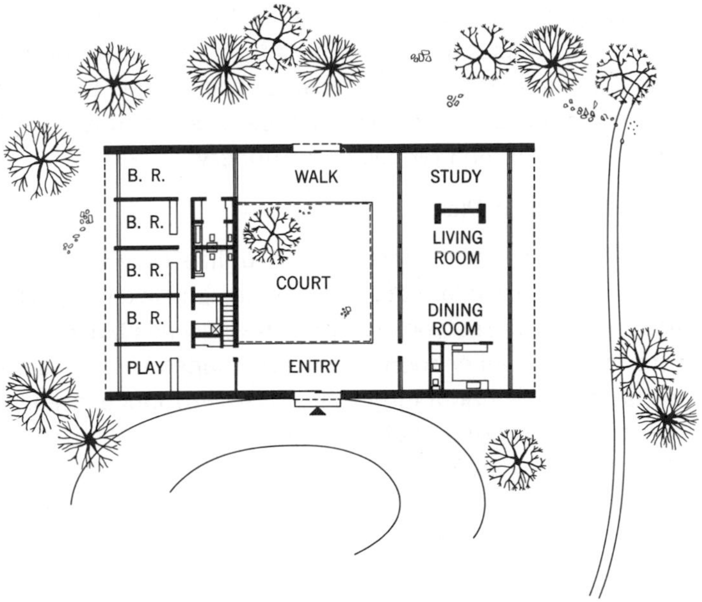
B. R.
WALK
STUDY
B. R.
LIVING ROOM
B. R.
COURT
B. R.
DINING ROOM
PLAY
ENTRY

The atrium or court plan. (Courtesy of Eliot Noyes.)

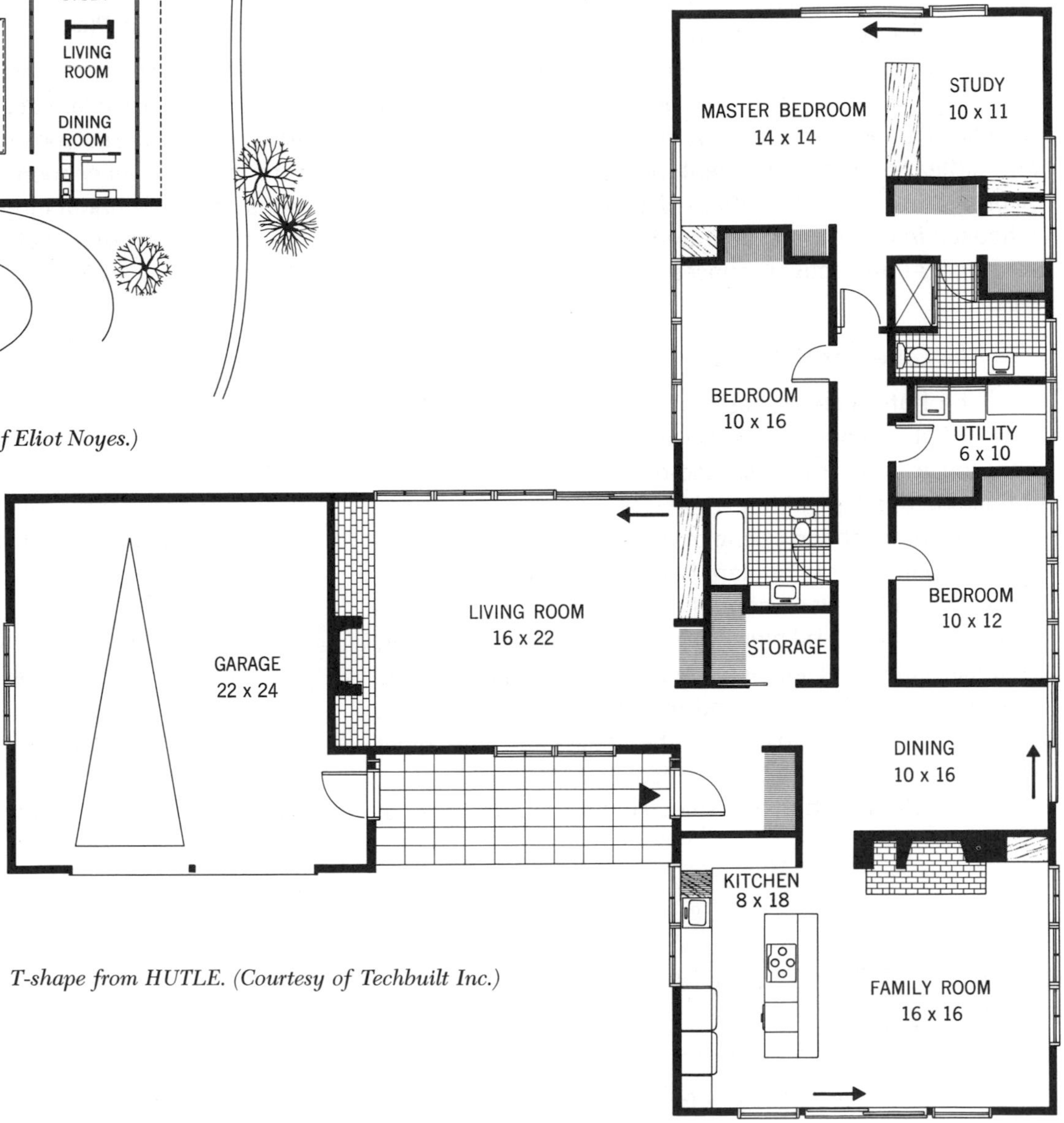
MASTER BEDROOM
14 x 14
STUDY
10 x 11
BEDROOM
10 x 16
UTILITY
6 x 10
GARAGE
22 x 24
LIVING ROOM
16 x 22
STORAGE
BEDROOM
10 x 12
DINING
10 x 16
KITCHEN
8 x 18
FAMILY ROOM
16 x 16

T-shape from HUTLE. (Courtesy of Techbuilt Inc.)

area for personal activities, such as eating and sunbathing. In contemporary usage the outer walls are often solid, while the walls facing the atrium may be of glass from floor to ceiling, permitting a good quantity of light to enter the house from the center court, although a blank wall is turned to the street. The court does not need to be placed exactly in the center of the plan but can be off to one side. The atrium plan often results in a house with two parts, connected by some type of covered walkway. Different activities can occur in the separated sections of the house with little or no infringement of noise on those areas incorporating quiet activities. Usually the sleeping area is housed in one of the separated divisions, and the living area and group activity spaces are housed in the other area.

The Letter, or Hutle Plan

The hutle plan is based on one of several letters—H, U, T, L, E, among others. Because this plan needs more land and a large, more spread-out foundation, the price of building this type of house is higher. Of course, a house designed in the shape of one of these letters is much more flexible than a square-plan house, and certainly more interesting in the placement of the rooms within the space available. Heating and plumbing costs are generally higher, because baths and kitchens are not always placed next to each other in this plan and require more pipe footage. Again, in this kind of plan, the noisy and the quiet activities can be separated and isolated from each other. Branches of the letter are selected for various types of rooms, permitting the unrelated activities to be farther apart. With this plan, it is easy to obtain private outside living areas in the spaces between wings and branches. There can be partial courts and secluded patios without the addition of high fences or shrubbery.

Curvilinear Plan

The curvilinear plans, which utilize curved lines as their main characteristic, are unique and exciting. They adhere to no stereotype and are extremely flexible. Besides offering the dweller rooms that are shaped in curves and walls that are undulating, they also introduce areas of courts and carports that blend slowly into the structure. Obviously they are expensive to construct, for they require adequate grounds, more foundations, and wall constructions that depart from the normal straight-line styles. Wright used the curvilinear plan in some of his designs, and he achieved his ultimate in the use of a curvilinear pattern with the Guggenheim Museum. A floor plan with curved lines naturally fits into many landscapes and is very suited to sloping hillsides where a box or rectangular structure might look out of character.

Multilevel Plan

The multilevel plan is by far one of the most popular with the public, because it offers inexpensive qualities. First, it is not necessary to have a great deal of land to design a successful house of this type; second, the foundation is not necessarily spread out too much. In the multilevel house the plumbing can be economically stacked,

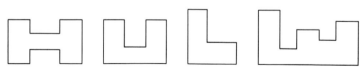

Outline of H, U, L, E from HUTLE.

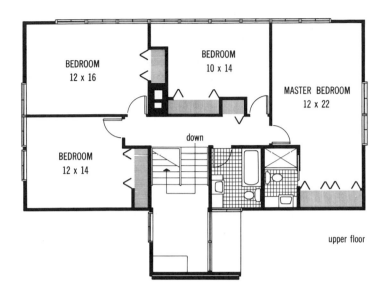

BEDROOM
12 x 16

BEDROOM
10 x 14

MASTER BEDROOM
12 x 22

down

BEDROOM
12 x 14

upper floor

Multilevel plan. (Courtesy of Techbuilt Inc.)

with the bath over the kitchen area or bath over bath. The stairways can be planned in a stacked relationship also, with less wasted space. The connecting arteries are generally placed in the center of the building or at its extreme side.

The multilevel house is either a two-story stacked or a split-level arrangement. The split-level house is good if well designed, for there are not as many stairs to the different levels as there are in the house where all the rooms on the second story must be reached by a full stairway. The major problem with the split-level house, as we so often see it, is the tendency of many builders and contractors to make this house look completely out of proportion and out of character with its landscape. A split-level house is and should be designed with a sloped lot in mind. When a split-level house is placed on level ground, it is generally pretty ridiculous in appearance. This type of plan is used in housing developments outside major cities, such as Detroit, with such abandon and lack

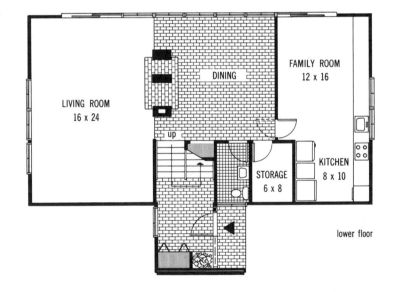

FAMILY ROOM
12 x 16

DINING

LIVING ROOM
16 x 24

up

KITCHEN
8 x 10

STORAGE
6 x 8

lower floor

of thought that it is hard to remember that a split-level house can actually be well designed and attractive.

In the last analysis, it is the family who must make the selection of the house in which to live. Each family, looking at available houses, will need to weigh the various aspects of each type of plan, each type of façade, and the general character of each structure. Some will find that a multilevel house answers their needs better than a court-centered house—perhaps because of economic factors or perhaps because of personal preference. In their investigation, some will find that wood appeals to them because of its feeling of warmth, and others will prefer glass because it opens up spaces and lets in the surrounding landscape.

BIBLIOGRAPHY AND SUGGESTED READINGS

Adams, Edward, George Pappas and David B. Van Dommelen, *Design At Work: Its Forms And Functions*, Center For Continuing Liberal Education, The Pennsylvania State University, 1961.

Architectural Record (edited by), *Treasuries of Contemporary Houses*, 2 Vols., F. W. Dodge Corp., New York, 1959.

Choay, Françoise, *Le Corbusier*, George Braziller, Inc., New York, 1960.

Drexler, Arthur, *Mies van der Rohe*, George Braziller, Inc., New York, 1960.

Fitch, James Marston, *Walter Gropius*, George Braziller, Inc., New York, 1960.

Hitchcock, Henry-Russel, Arthur Drexler, *Built in USA: Post-War Architecture*, Museum of Modern Art, New York, 1952.

McCoy, Esther, *Richard Neutra*, George Braziller, Inc., New York, 1960.

Scully, Vincent, Jr., *Frank L. Wright*, George Braziller, Inc., New York, 1960.

Talmey, Allene, "Eames," *Vogue*, August 15, 1959.

GENERAL PERIODICALS

Architectural Forum
Architectural Record
Arts & Architecture
Progressive Architecture

Wire shells without upholstery that were designed by Eames. (Photo: courtesy of Herman Miller Inc.)

Molded plywood chairs and table by Eames.
(Photo: courtesy of Herman Miller Inc.)

Chapter 8 CONTEMPORARY DESIGNERS: FURNITURE AND FABRICS

The designers of today have a rich heritage on which to call when they create furnishings for the contemporary home. We have seen how Art Nouveau broke from traditional patterns and how the European *de Stijl* and Bauhaus groups developed new design philosophies that our designers today feel strongly when they work with new materials and concepts. In addition, the contributions of American artists and architects introduced a whole new vocabulary of ideas and technology into the making of twentieth-century design. Architects are responsible for various facets of our contemporary design world, for it is through the many individuals from this discipline that furnishings have been reborn in new forms and exciting plastic concepts. Because architects possessed knowledge at 103 highly skilled technical levels, they were able to proceed into areas of design that many other artists could not tread.

Other art disciplines, too, have contributed greatly to contemporary design, for many artists and craftsmen, in addition to architects, have given much to our culture today. The artist has discovered that he can translate his materials into forms that the layman can more readily recognize and appreciate in the home. As both the *de Stijl* and Bauhaus exhibited, the plastic arts need not be limited to the "unfunctional" object of art.

The list of contemporary designers for furnishings within the home is long and varied, but there are some designers who have contributed more than others, just as there are furniture companies that have taken the necessary steps to keep up with the development of design in this century. There were industrial concerns involved with producing well-designed objects before World War II, but it was not until after the war that the really stimulating sources began to manufacture in amounts significant enough to make a strong, long-lasting impact on furniture design. Obviously it is impossible to list all the companies that have made these steps forward, but it is necessary to examine one or two in order to gain an insight into the organization of these firms. Two companies seem to stand out as being most responsible for promoting acceptable twentieth-century design in this country as well as in Europe. Some of the most avant-garde ideas in furnishing that this country has ever seen were introduced by Herman Miller Inc. and Knoll Associates, Inc. These two companies have also brought from other countries products that have helped in some way to change the face of American design. These companies have managed to do this with the help of many inspired and accomplished designers, both American and foreign.

Furniture companies like Knoll and Miller, which have kept their standards high, have been able to set and create rather than follow trends. Today we need only glance through advertisements in national magazines to see the designs which have been based on one or more of the designs sold by Miller and Knoll.

Herman Miller Inc.

The Herman Miller company is located in the small town of Zeeland, Michigan, the center of the Dutch tulip farms. There in western Michigan the company can enjoy the services of the skilled woodcraftsmen who come from many generations of specialists in the execution of fine furniture. Zeeland is only a few miles from Grand Rapids, Michigan, which was at one time the furniture capital of the world and to some extent might still be considered so. Herman Miller Incorporated was at one time a producer of period reproductions, but its chief designer, Gilbert Rohde, convinced the company that reproductions were insincere and aesthetically dishonest. With a new philosophy of design, the company began hiring highly capable designers to produce new images in modern furniture. The firm's goals were cited in 1950 when the company published a book titled *The Herman Miller Collection:*

". . . its goal is a *permanent* collection designed to meet fully the requirements of modern living. The collection is to be permanent in the sense that it will not be scrapped for each market, or for each new 'trend' as announced by the style experts. It is designed to grow, not necessarily in size, but in the perfection of its component parts. No piece will be kept if a better design can be developed to take its place, nor will a given way of making things be followed simply because that's the way they were always made."

And this philosophy still seems to apply; it is still possible to purchase through Herman Miller pieces of furniture designed when these ideas were first formulated in the 1940s.

Herman Miller Inc., like some of the other companies producing fine furniture, does not necessarily employ designers to work at drawing boards in a company drafting room. Instead, Herman Miller Inc. retains three designers whose accomplishments are internationally

Teacart designed by George Nelson. (Photo: courtesy of Herman Miller Inc.)

Stereo cabinet designed by George Nelson. (Photo: courtesy of Herman Miller Inc.)

known. Herman Miller once used the designs of Isamu Noguchi, a Japanese-American sculptor; and Knoll Associates is today selling chairs designed by Harry Bertoia, a Pennsylvania sculptor. At Herman Miller and Knoll some of the top architects and designers of our time have been employed as designers of contemporary furniture. Charles Eames and George Nelson are two who have been designing for Herman Miller during the last decade.

George Nelson. Born in 1908 in Connecticut, George Nelson was trained as an architect at Yale and later traveled in Europe where he studied the architecture of past ages. He spent several years doing editorial work for *Architectural Forum* but turned to developing a large collection of furniture for Herman Miller during 1945 and 1946. Mr. Nelson now has his own company in New York, from which he works in the areas of graphic design, office interiors, architecture, furniture design, and industrial design. An accomplishment of the George Nelson Company was the American National Exhibition in Moscow in 1959, where a Buckminster Fuller dome was used to house the exhibitions that Nelson designed. Nelson's furniture

Stereo cabinet (open) by George Nelson. (Photo: courtesy of Herman Miller Inc.)

Chest by Nelson. (Photo: courtesy of Herman Miller Inc.)

Sofa by George Nelson. (Photo: courtesy of Herman Miller Inc.)

designs for Herman Miller are conservative in relation to those of some designers whose work we shall also study, but this comment does not imply any lack of imagination on his part. Nelson is a genius in the designing of furniture that answers the problems of storage not only in the home but also in the office. The small detailed devices that he incorporates into drawers and headboards are good examples of utilization of space and of inventiveness without sacrifice of the aesthetic qualities that make beautiful furniture. His pieces have a masculine architectural sense that is appealing to both men and women.

Charles Eames. Another of Herman Miller's free-lance designers, Charles Eames, extends his activities beyond furniture designing to a variety of fields. He has been called not a twentieth-century man but a man entering the twenty-first century. His imagination flows into film producing, architecture, lecturing, writing, and experimentation with toys. Along with his wife, Ray Eames, and a small staff, Eames has developed household products that have changed the face of furniture in the last two decades. Although Eames has attended various architectural schools, he has not received a degree from any of them. He studied with Eliel Saarinen at Cranbrook and worked on combined projects with Eero Saarinen. Charles Eames first recognized the diversified possibilities of plywood when he was commissioned by the Navy to develop splints for the wounded of World War II. This experimental work led him to create the eventually famous Eames chairs that were exhibited at the Museum of Modern Art in New York in 1946. Through continued research with the Herman Miller company, he has since introduced some of the most unique seating systems of our times. His latest seating units can be seen at the O'Hara Airport in Illinois where a unique system of suspended upholstery is employed: heat-sealed vinyl cushions are held in tension between frames of polished cast aluminum.

Eames has won the Alcoa Industrial Design Award for his imaginative uses of aluminum. His "Do Nothing Machine" is probably one of the most brilliant concepts of

Charles Eames. (Photo: courtesy of Herman Miller Inc.)

adult toys ever developed. Operated by solar energy, it dances and sparkles in the sun as various parts of its structure whirl for fun and aesthetic enjoyment.

Because of their interest in toys, he and his wife have produced several films utilizing the charms of the child's world. Their films "Parade" and "Toccata For Toy Trains" exemplify the excitement that both Ray and Charles Eames project into their work, be it for nonsense or for the development of a new piece of furniture. Eames's inventiveness can be seen throughout his activities; when he puts a room design together, color and excitement keynote his work.

Herman Miller Inc. is not only a furniture company but also a highly skilled educational organization that presents well-organized lectures, slide shows, and films to universities throughout the country. This is a service that is not necessarily gauged to sell chairs but rather to advance ideas, high standards, and improved understanding of the design world. The lectures presented at conferences and universities are packed with marketing thoughts, philosophical ideas, and aesthetic appreciation of the world in which we live.

Plastic-shell upholstered chair and table that were designed by Charles Eames. (Photo: courtesy of Herman Miller Inc.)

Eames Aluminum Group furniture, designed by Eames. (Photo: courtesy of Herman Miller Inc.)

Storage unit designed by George Nelson and rosewood lounge chair by Eames. (Photo: courtesy of Herman Miller Inc.)

Lounge chair of polished aluminum by Charles Eames. (Photo: courtesy of Herman Miller Inc.)

Bedroom setting designed by George Nelson. Furniture is kept to a minimum and yet provides ample storage and work space. Notice the trend toward combining and harmonizing traditional and modern elements in accessories and furniture. (Photo: courtesy of Herman Miller Inc.)

The furniture sold by Herman Miller is seldom found in department stores or small retail furniture shops but instead is handled through showrooms throughout the United States and other countries of the world. Many of these showrooms are parts of other organizations offering regional areas several lines of furniture together with interior design and architectural services.

Knoll Associates, Inc.

Knoll Associates, Inc. was founded by Hans G. Knoll and his wife, Florence, in 1946. The major offices and showroom are in New York, but the constantly expanding company now has showrooms in all major cities in the United States, subsidiary companies in Germany, France, Italy, Canada, and Mexico, and licensees in 18 other countries. The Knoll factory is located in Pennsylvania where the furniture is manufactured by highly skilled Pennsylvania-Dutch craftsmen.

Florence Knoll Bassett, design director, now lives in Miami, and some design projects originate from her research studio there. However, her most important activities are as head of the Design Development Group in East Greenville, Pennsylvania, and the Planning Unit in New York.

The Design Development Group is composed of several young designers, including Richard Schultz, Donald Petitt, and Vincent Cafiero. This group works closely with the Planning Unit in the research and development of furniture designs. In addition to the impressive staff of designers in the Planning Unit and Design Development Group, free-lance designers are called upon for various programs.

All new designs in furniture and textiles are developed under Florence Knoll's direction. As design director she is also responsible for the graphic presentation of designs in brochures and advertisements, showroom in-

Florence Knoll. (Photo: courtesy of Knoll Associates, Inc.)

Storage cabinets by Florence Knoll. (Photo: courtesy of Knoll Associates, Inc.)

stallations and exhibitions.

The Knoll Planning Unit has designed offices and public areas for many of the major buildings in the United States. Each project is planned in a miniature scale model before the actual work begins in the structure itself. Emily Post used this technique in the early 1900s to present various architects' work to clients. Mrs. Post worked closely with the architect John Russell Pope. Introduced again by Florence Knoll in the late 1940s, the technique is now widely used by other design firms.

Despite her influence on design of individual pieces of furniture, Florence Knoll strongly believes that these pieces should be designed not as independent units but related to something. In a Knoll Planning Unit job, the building, its environment, and function are considered as related components to form a harmonious entity with the interior. Florence Knoll's ideas are presented to the public

Sofa, lounge, and table designed by Florence Knoll. (Photo: courtesy of Knoll Associates, Inc.)

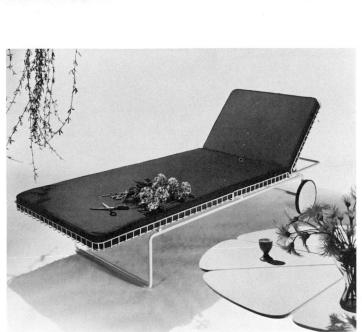

Upholstered plastic shell by Eero Saarinen. (Photo: courtesy of Knoll Associates, Inc.)

Outdoor chaise lounge designed by Richard Schultz of the Knoll Design Development Unit. (Photo: courtesy of Knoll Associates, Inc.)

"Womb" chair with molded shell designed by Saarinen. (Photo: courtesy of Knoll Associates, Inc.)

Brno chair designed by Mies van der Rohe in 1930 for a house in Brno, Czechoslovakia. (Photo: courtesy of Knoll Associates, Inc.)

Molded plastic chairs and marble-top table designed by Eero Saarinen (Photo: courtesy of Knoll Associates, Inc.)

The classic Barcelona chair, stool, and table designed by Mies van der Rohe in 1929 for the German Pavilion at the 1929 International Exposition, Barcelona, Spain. (Photo: courtesy of Knoll Associates, Inc.)

in lectures and slide programs all over the country; Planning Unit projects are shown as pilots and pioneers of new design concepts.

Since its origin Knoll Associates has used the abilities of many architects who understand engineering concepts and structural problems to assist in development of furniture designs. The list of designers who have contributed to Knoll is long and impressive.

Eero Saarinen and Mies van der Rohe: Architects. Eero Saarinen, the Finnish-born architect who lived in Michigan from 1931 until his death in 1961, developed the famous "Womb" chair for Knoll in 1945, and in 1956 introduced the pedestal chair of molded plastic. Both of these chair designs have particular effects and reflect Mr. Saarinen's philosophy: "A chair should look well as a piece of sculpture in a room. It should also look well when someone is sitting in it."

Another designer, whose main furniture designs are part of the Knoll collection, is the architect Mies van der Rohe. You will remember him as an important member of the Bauhaus. In the late 1920s he designed the famous Barcelona chair and also the Brno chair. These, with table and chaise comprising the Barcelona group, and two Tugendhat chairs are now manufactured by Knoll and are important pieces of twentieth-century design.

The list of architects who have contributed to Knoll designs includes Florence Knoll Bassett herself, Franco Albini from Italy, and Pierre Jeanneret, Corbusier's associate, who came to Knoll for one year to design especially for Knoll.

Harry Bertoia: Sculptor. The sculptor Harry Bertoia was encouraged by Florence and Hans Knoll to make investigations in the furniture field. In 1947 Bertoia had his first showing of furniture at Knoll Associates' showroom in

Plastic chair designed by Harry Bertoia. (Photo: courtesy of Knoll Associates, Inc.)

Furniture and sculpture designed by Harry Bertoia. (Photo: courtesy of Knoll Associates, Inc.)

Wire chair designed by Harry Bertoia. (Photo: courtesy of Knoll Associates, Inc.)

Invisible plastic chairs designed by Laverne. (Photo: courtesy of Laverne Inc.)

New York. There is a close relationship between his furniture and the sculptural forms he creates; in both, metal is used in freely expressed lattice patterns that are delicate and that manipulate space in a particularly strong way. His sculptural works can be seen incorporated in important architectural statements throughout the country. Both the General Motors Technical Center in Warren, Michigan, and the Manufacturers Trust Company in New York have room dividers composed of rectangles and squares of many sizes and shapes, which seem to dance across the façade of the room walls.

Knoll and Herman Miller are major influences in the contemporary world of furniture manufacturing; more than that, they are establishers of trends, movements, and the new twentieth-century image. They have built heavily on the experimentation that preceded them in the Bauhaus and *de Stijl* movements, neither copying nor blindly moving along but using these former ideologies as

a basis for more continued expression in interiors and furniture. Theirs is a fresh new approach that embodies new materials, new techniques, and—most important—the spirit of adventure and exploration.

Laverne Inc.

There are other smaller concerns producing many innovations in furniture design, and they rightfully should not be left out of this book, but it is impossible to list them all. A small but important organization, also exploring the use of new materials and forms, is Laverne Inc., which has developed a clear transparent plastic chair. The Laverne company has been honored by many national and international awards, as have Knoll Associates and Herman Miller. Although most of the awards granted to Laverne Inc. have been for contributions in wallpapers and fabric design, the "Invisible Chair" series is probably the most renowned of their designs. The Lavernes are purists and present to the public only the best results of their wide experimentation. Their work in furniture, textiles, wall coverings, and accessories expresses a quality of beauty, clarity, and integrity of design that has had a powerful impact upon the international design scene. Only Estelle and Erwine Laverne create the designs produced by this small but effective company.

George Nakashima

While the companies thus far discussed use mass-production methods of manufacturing furniture, George Nakashima still uses handcraft techniques for his furniture designs. In speaking of the triumvirate, we could probably have given him as an example of one craftsman who has managed to retain the closeness of the designer, the producer, and the consumer—at least in furniture designing. His work is very contemporary, but with a feeling reminiscent of the early American craftsman and his understanding of woods. Nakashima still designs and builds his own pieces with a minimum of studio help in his New Hope, Pennsylvania, workshop.

Other Designers

While all the contemporary furniture designers cannot be mentioned here, several have contributed much to the field, and their additions have helped bring high standards to the consumer. Paul McCobb introduced his low-cost Planner Group in the 1940s after World War II; this line

Storage units by Heywood-Wakefield. (Photo: courtesy of National Association of Furniture Manufacturers.)

High-backed chair by Metropolitan Furniture Manufacturing Company. (Photo: courtesy of National Association of Furniture Manufacturers.)

greatly influenced the use of stacked furniture in this country. Although his Planner Group is no longer on the market, McCobb is still designing high-quality furniture for the manufacturer. Edward Wormley has designed exclusively for Dunbar Inc., and the versatility of his work is astounding. Most of his furniture is high in cost, but at the same time it is equally high in quality. Robsjohn-Gibbings produced some of the first contemporary furniture after World War II, while Milo Baughman, Lawrence Peabody, and Sam Maloof are making new and exciting contributions as independent designers today.

Desk by Edward Wormley. (Photo: courtesy of Dunbar Furniture Corp. and Wesley Pusey.)

Wardrobe armoire designed by Merton Gershun for Dillingham Manufacturing Company. (Photo: courtesy of National Association of Furniture Manufacturers.)

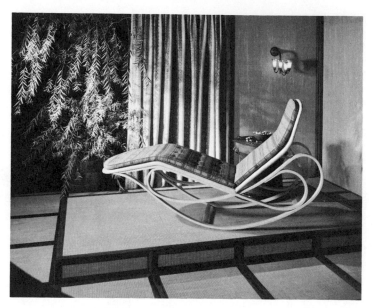

Reclining rocker-chaise designed by Edward Wormley recalls the nineteenth-century chair designed by Thonet. (Photo: courtesy of Dunbar Furniture Corp.)

Walnut end table by Paul McCobb. (Photo: courtesy of The Lane Co.)

Cocktail-table design by Paul McCobb. (Photo: courtesy of The Lane Co.)

Children's furniture of the "Erector" type. (Photo: courtesy of Kombi Kindermöbel GMBH, *Aachen, Germany.)*

Foreign Influences

American companies and designers have not been working alone in developing contemporary furniture of good design. Since 1949 the United States has seen a progressively stronger movement of Scandinavian influences in furniture and household accessories. This movement of Scandinavianism did not begin to mature until Finn Juhl, the Danish designer, turned over his designs to the Baker Furniture Company in Grand Rapids for production. It was through this initial step that Finn Juhl and Baker became the most important trend-setters in Scandinavian furniture. The words "Danish Modern" became synonymous with all furniture coming from the countries of Denmark, Norway, Sweden, and Finland.

Other designers and companies started to retail their products here in a major trend that is still potent. One of the biggest companies selling Scandinavian furniture in this country is Dux, Inc. Its principal designer is Folke Ohlsson. This company was founded in Sweden,

Three-seat sofa designed by Folke Ohlsson. (Photo: courtesy of Dux Inc.)

Swedish furniture designed by Folke Ohlsson.
(Photo: courtesy of Dux Inc.)

although most Americans still refer to its products as "Danish Modern," probably because some of the furniture was assembled in Denmark and carried the stamp of Danish craftsmanship. Dux now has a factory in the United States.

Another Danish designer of international reputation is Hans Wegner. His pieces of furniture have the handmade appearance that we find in Nakashima's. Although in recent years Scandinavian designers have been one of our biggest sources of influence, Italy, Germany, England, and other countries have also contributed designs to furniture.

It is not easy to draw distinct lines as to foreign influences in furniture production because, since World

Nest of tables. (Photo: courtesy of Dux Inc.)

War II, this country has received a tremendous influx of ideas from other countries. Some of these ideas are directly related to furniture, and others are more closely associated with accessories. Americans traveling throughout the world bring their impressions back with them and demand more internationalism in their homes. The veterans of World War II also helped to activate this interest in foreign furniture and objects. Having been stationed throughout the world, they were not satisfied with a provincial country but wanted to see a more cosmopolitan United States. The Far East has been a great contributor to our homes, but in architecture and accessories more than in furniture.

Today the furniture designer accepts his position in a highly technical world and is ready to improve his designs

Chair and footrest in teak designed by Fritz Hansen. (Photo: courtesy of Fritz Hansen Inc.)

Lounge chair designed by Folke Ohlsson. (Photo: courtesy of Dux Inc.)

Easy chair and footrest-table designed by Arne Jacobsen. (Photo: courtesy of Fritz Hansen Inc.)

Table designed by Arne Jacobsen and chairs by Hansen. (Photo: courtesy of Fritz Hansen Inc.)

for more useful incorporation into the home. He is constantly aware of the needs of the family, although the family might not be aware of his interest. Even when he is not an American, his contributions are essential to this country's growth. He is concerned with society and its lack of interest in the development of new ideas. Most of all he looks forward to new materials that will enter the field as chemists, scientists, and designers introduce them. He already has a tremendous accumulation of materials with which to work, and we shall look briefly at these.

Materials for Furniture

The materials utilized in the making of furniture are of utmost importance, for a piece of furniture is only as good as are its materials and the way the materials are employed. To make a piece of furniture in our mechanized world and not to relate it to today's living would be false and unreasonable. It is unlikely that consumers want refrigerators designed as they were 50 years ago, and so it seems illogical to expect furniture designers to maintain the *status quo* of past generations.

To use contemporary materials such as plastic, aluminum, and other newly developed fabrications in the forms of yesteryear is equally unfitting. Although many of the materials that are being utilized in furniture production are not new, techniques of manufacturing are new, and we should expect industry to move steadily toward new ideas.

Wood. The material that has been used throughout the history of man for furniture—wood—still has not lost its usefulness. In modern furniture, the tendency is to use fewer surfaces that cover up the grain and more finishes that bring out the warmth and color of the wood. French finishes with oil, rubbed surfaces bringing out the softness, and simple sealer finishes are recommended by experts who wish to see a natural product that gives a glow to the room setting. Furniture with heavy and thick varnish finishes applied to surfaces is more work to maintain, for the smallest scratches show up and the slightest dust dulls the slick shiny tops. Teaks, walnuts, and other woods that have been prepared simply and honestly are less apt to show wear over long periods of time. The more ornamentation that a piece of wood has, the more effort it takes to maintain the piece adequately.

Plywoods and laminated woods, although at one time not the most durable for furniture, have been so improved that most major companies are using them in some aspect of their products. In view of the new technical advancements, it is not necessary to insist on solid wood for good furniture. There is little, if any, warping in plywoods now, and after the layers have been laminated together, they will stay together for a long period of time. Eames's first laminated wood chair, manufactured in 1946, is still holding up under many situations and circumstances.

Of course, the joints utilized in the making of wood

furniture are especially important. A badly designed piece of case goods will soon begin to deteriorate as the joints pull and loosen. Some joints are better than others; construction that gives better wear includes dovetailed, mortise-and-tenon, and doweled joints. Of these, dovetailed construction is the best for drawers and case goods. All joints need some type of glue, and for even more strength in a piece of furniture, screws should be incorporated. Butterfly insets are often used in the construction of table tops. They not only hold together several pieces of wood very well but add simple ornamentation to the piece. Nakashima uses the butterfly inset.

When drawers are being designed, it is important that they fit properly and that the drawer has channels on which to run. In many good pieces of furniture today, metal runners with wheels are used which give more stability to the drawers and will last indefinitely. Other points to watch for are furniture protectors, such as leg guards, base strips, and hardware pieces. All of these can enhance the piece of furniture or make it too ornamented. All of these parts can be useful, but there are times when even a piece of case goods is of better design without obvious hardware.

Metal. An important part of our furniture today is metal. Since the introduction of new metals, many companies are incorporating more and more into furniture. Welding is a strong and very successful method of putting metal furniture together. It can be seen in Charles Eames's and Harry Bertoia's chairs. The use of nuts and bolts helps in furniture construction and can add the ornamentation that has been removed by utilizing simple materials. A beautifully polished chrome or stainless steel bolt is a very attractive part of a chair and certainly reflects the machine-oriented times in which we live.

Metal can be highly polished, as are the stainless steel legs of the Barcelona chair designed by Mies van der Rohe; or metal can be given a satin finish lacking high shine. Metal can also be painted with black or other colors; the problem with a black surface is its tendency to look like wrought iron.

Metal furniture requires less maintenance than does wood. There is little polishing needed to keep up its good appearance. A slight dusting occasionally will keep the legs, bases, and supports in very fine condition.

Metal is seldom used alone in a piece of furniture but plays instead only a small role in a total piece. Unless the furniture is for outdoor use, fabric, plastic, or some other type of material is combined with the metal.

Aluminum has been introduced by Charles Eames for indoor furniture, though once we thought of it only as a material for pots and pans or patio furniture. Eames's experimentation has brought this light material into the home for use in the living room.

Plastics. As we saw earlier, plastics have made a great contribution in the area of architecture, and their acceptance as a material for furniture construction is well-established. Both Knoll Associates and Herman Miller have produced elegant chairs using this new twentieth-century material. Lovely, soft sculptural shapes can be obtained with plastics, and the final product is extremely easy to maintain. Although plastics once cracked and pitted easily, they no longer deteriorate so quickly. Instead, they retain their brilliancy and strength for many years. Herman Miller's plastic is made of polyester resin reinforced with glass filament. A plastic shell chair, without upholstery, can be washed with soap and water indoors, or cleaned quickly with a hose outdoors. The plastic furniture now available comes in a large selection of colors and can be combined with coverings of vinyl material and fabric. Chairs composed of plastic are lightweight and can be moved readily from one room to another for dual uses. Eero Saarinen's "Womb" chair utilizes a plastic shell form under the fabric and foam-rubber upholstery, as do several chairs by Herman Miller.

The basic shells that are used by Knoll and Miller can be interchanged with various types of bases, so that each basic shape can have a more versatile use. Besides being used in offices and schools, shell chairs can be used in studies, dining rooms, living rooms, and bedrooms.

There is hardly a room into which they will not fit; if desired, they are available in a design for stacking.

Designer furniture, or what some people call "high-styled furniture," is generally more expensive. There are many reasons for this; in the end, good furniture is always more expensive. Good furniture designers, like Eames, Nelson, Saarinen, and Mies van der Rohe, do not give service cheaply. They are professional people, and their ideas and creative work demand recognition as do those of any well-known painter. Companies like Knoll, Herman Miller, and Dunbar pay royalty fees to the designer, much as a publisher does to an author. Therefore, the prices charged by such companies, reflecting royalties, must be higher than those charged by a company that hires a designer and pays him a yearly salary. In addition, a good company spends a great deal of money on research in engineering problems. Herman Miller has an engineering department that does nothing but test the designs of the furniture it plans to put on the market. Each piece is tested for strength and durability of construction; the upholstered pieces are tested for the wearability of fabrics. Herman Miller has also developed an elaborate and highly effective way of checking each piece of furniture that is going out to the public. Seldom does a badly constructed piece get beyond the shipper.

These companies, then, are attempting to produce goods that can satisfy a design-hungry public and to manufacture furniture of the highest quality, both as to design and as to material. Both Knoll and Herman Miller, along with many good furniture companies, offer a wide range of pieces from very low to rather high prices.

Fabrics

Before synthetic fabrics came into being, a consumer was able to recognize fiber content easily and without consulting many resource materials. With the many new synthetics available today, however, it is almost useless to go into detail concerning fabrics and their composition. Of course when a covering for a sofa or a material for drap-eries is wanted, the usefulness of a particular material should be understood before it is bought. The importance of investigating carefully the content of fabrics for special purposes cannot be overemphasized. Fortunately, it is now legally necessary for manufacturers to attach proper labels to define fiber content, so that the layman may have a better knowledge of what he is purchasing.

Four Basic Weaves. It will be helpful for the consumer to know about some basic weaves, when he is selecting fabrics. Although there are many ramifications of each weave, we will look at four basic weaves to obtain a better understanding of textiles to be used in the home. The four basic weaves are plain, floating, pile, and figure.

Plain. The most fundamental is the plain weave. It is composed of equal numbers of warp and weft per square inch, interlaced alternately. There are many variations of the plain weave, of which the basket weave is one. The plain is the weave we find most often. It is not expensive because of its uncomplicated nature.

Floating. The difference in the floating weave is the presence of free-floating *fibers* on the surface of the finished fabric. Consequently, the coarser the fabric, the more easily it can be snagged and pulled apart. Satin weaves and twills are made with a floating weave. In these weaves the weft skips over a set number of warp yarns at intervals. The satin weave has longer floating yarns than the twill, and the floating yarns are generally the warp instead of the weft. The satin is irregular and the twill is regular. Because of the regular characteristics of the twill, a diagonal pattern is achieved in the finished fabric.

Pile. Loops thrown onto the surface of the fabric make up the pile weave. These can be left uncut or they can be cut. Velvet is an example of cut pile; corduroy is uncut pile. Pile is the weave that is used for making rugs and carpets.

Figure. The figure weave is very complicated and results in a design such as a brocade or damask. It is a mechanized weave and was first introduced in France by Joseph Jacquard.

Plain weave.

Basket weave.

Twill weave.

Satin weave.

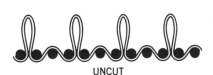

Pile weave.

UNCUT

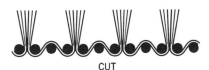

CUT

Unwoven Textiles. Felt is one material used in unwoven textiles; it is made by a process of matting fibers with steam and heat. Knitting is done by the manipulation of long needles or by machine. Twisting is the process by which lace is made; although it was out of fashion for many years, several fabric designers are reintroducing it for contemporary homes.

Printed Fabrics. Most of the woven fabrics can be decorated by various printing methods. There has been a great deal of excitement about printed fabrics in the last few years. There are basically three ways to print on a fabric.

Roller. The most common method of printing fabric is by roller. Cylinders of copper are etched with the design desired; the roller is put into the machine; the fabric is run through as in a newspaper press. A separate roller is used for each color.

Silk Screen. The other two methods of printing call for hand techniques. In the silk-screen process, a stencil is applied to the underside of a silk screen; with a squeegee, ink is pressed through the screen onto the fabric. This technique is sometimes partially mechanical, but only if a large quantity of a particular fabric is being produced.

Block Printing. Block printing is a printing technique done entirely by hand. This is the old linoleum-block method. If the design is not carefully planned, it can often look blocky and awkward. (See Chapter 10.)

Man-Made Fibers. A great number of man-made fibers are used today in textile manufacturing. These include Fortisan, Saran, Arnel, and Acrilan. There are pros and cons concerning each fiber invented by the major chemical companies such as DuPont. Probably the best man-made fiber on the market today is Fiberglas. Maintenance of Fiberglas is extremely easy and the price falls within the budgets of most average families. Fiberglas does not mildew, fade, or burn. Fiberglas draperies can be cleaned simply by being dipped in warm soapy water and rinsed. There is absolutely no pressing needed to bring them back

FIBER NAME	HOUSEHOLD USES	CHARACTERISTICS	CARE
Natural Fibers			
Cotton	Rugs, carpeting and upholstery, slip covers, bedspreads, curtains, and draperies	Great versatility, soft, durable, strong, and absorbent. Not expensive, easily manipulated. Can be treated to increase its performance.	Is easy to care for and generally can be machine-washed. Usually irons well.
Linen	Curtains, draperies, slip covers, some upholstery, table linens, and towels	More expensive than cotton. Extremely strong and durable except under direct sunlight. Soils and wrinkles easily unless treated.	Can be washed and ironed but is limited to certain dyes and finishes.
Silk	Curtains, drapery fabrics, and some expensive luxurious upholstery	Warm and pleasant to the touch. Dyes well. Is a luxury fabric. Usually expensive. May water spot, readily absorbs body oils and grease stains. Strong and naturally resistant to wrinkles.	Should be dry cleaned. Should be protected from prolonged exposure to light. Can be attacked by moths and carpet beetles.
Wool	Carpets, draperies, upholstery, rugs, blankets	Very durable, versatile, springs back into shape, has great insulating capacity.	Dry cleaning is best. Shrinks and felts in presence of heat and moisture. Must be protected from moths and beetles.
*Man-Made Fibers**			
Acetate (Triacetate and Diacetate)	Curtains, draperies, upholstery, bedspreads, blankets, and scatter rugs	Drapes well, inexpensive, dries quickly but generates static electricity. Loses strength when wet.	Dry clean unless labeled washable. Hand wash in warm water and mild suds. Drip dry to avoid wrinkles. Press at low heat.
Acrylic (Acrilan, Creslan, Orlon, and Zefran)	Pile fabrics, rugs, blankets, carpets, upholstery, curtains, and drapery fabric	Resistance to wrinkling, high bulking power, resistance to sunlight. Rubbing and wear may cause pilling. Silky texture if desired.	Dry clean or wash. Dries quickly with little ironing.

* Even as this book goes to press, new developments are taking place in textile manufacturing. It is virtually impossible to keep a printed record up to date, for the changes appear practically overnight. It seems, therefore, that more accurate material could be obtained from current magazines that report the newest improvements and inventions in man-made fibers. However, the consumer can usually depend on those natural old standbys such as cotton, wool, silk, and linen if he is apprehensive about the content of a new fiber, just introduced on the market.

FIBER NAME	HOUSEHOLD USES	CHARACTERISTICS	CARE
Fiberglas	Draperies and curtains	Low abrasive quality, fireproof, non-absorbent. New types constantly being developed. Resistant to rot, moths, mildew.	Hand washable and drip dry. Easy care, do not iron or rub.
Metallics	Draperies, upholstery, trims, and decorative yarn	Glittering and gleaming plastic-coated metal or a core covered by metal. Sensitive to flexing and abrasion.	Should follow manufacturer's care guides.
Modacrylic	Curtains, rugs, draperies, and blankets	Soft and resilient, resistant to wrinkling and chemicals.	Sensitive to heat. Generally washable but dry cleaning is often best.
Nylon	Carpets, rugs, upholstery, curtains, draperies, and bedspreads	Exceptional strength but builds up static electricity. Very light and retains shape.	Washes easily and dries quickly. Can be pressed at low temperature.
Olefin	Carpets, rugs, and outdoor furniture	Light weight, no water absorption, medium strength, and waxlike texture.	Very little care necessary except possible wiping with damp cloth.
Polyester (Dacron, Fortel, Kodel, and Vycron)	Curtains, draperies, upholstery, bedspreads, pillows, and comforters	Strong, resists abrasions, retains crease, and keeps sharp pleat.	Easily washable, little ironing needed.
Saran	Curtains, draperies, awnings, rugs, upholstery, webbing for outdoor furniture	Stiff, waxlike, does not absorb moisture. Heat-sensitive, resists soiling and staining. New improvements continue to be developed.	Easily washable and little ironing needed.
Rayon	Curtains, draperies, upholstery, table linens, carpetings, and blankets	Inexpensive, easily manipulated, but lacks resilience. Poor resistance to soil and abrasion.	Dry clean, can be laundered, but is not as strong as cotton and linen. Can stretch or shrink in washing unless treated.

127

to their former crispness, and the homemaker can rehang them a few minutes after washing them. There seems to be one handicap with Fiberglas—its tendency to pull apart when sharp objects are snagged in the warp. Because of the slippery nature of the materials used, the warp threads separate easily. This handicap is being overcome as new weaves are developed. Also, the old stereotyped appearance of Fiberglas is disappearing. The consumer can now purchase Fiberglas which looks like linen or cotton. The novelty weaves now being used make Fiberglas more interesting than it was a few years ago.

Nylon is another man-made fiber that is prominent among fibers being produced today. Nylon can be mixed easily with other fibers for variation in textures. It has great strength, dries rapidly, does not fade easily, and will not attract moths as does wool.

There are still the old stand-by textiles that have been around for many years, and they should not be overlooked. Cotton, for instance, is still a favorite fabric despite its many drawbacks. Of course, the great advantage with cotton is its low price. Inexpensive cottons can make numerous contributions to the home. Some of the more inexpensive fabrics and their uses will be discussed in Chapter 12, "Creative Interiors."

When purchasing a fabric it is important that we select a good protective finish, especially for upholstery fabrics, to minimize spotting and soiling. Many companies now include some type of protective finish on their fabrics, but the purchaser should check this for safety. There is little reason why a textile should not have this finish on its surface. It is impossible to detect these finishes, for they are carefully applied to retain color, softness, and brilliancy.

The Design. In a textile for the home, the design is of utmost importance. To many homemakers, the design may be more important than the fiber content. Each person selects a design or pattern for an individual reason. Considerable thought should always go into the final purchase. Designs usually repeat themselves over and over, sometimes in 12-inch repeats, sometimes in 18-inch repeats, sometimes in larger or smaller repeats. The repeat may be easily noticed in some designs, and hard to discover in others. A well-designed textile repeats very quietly and is not jumpy and harsh.

For a good background fabric, a material should be quiet in design, soft and neutral in color. A small over-all pattern, repeated in small sizes, gives the appearance from a distance of being a textured fabric. Seen more closely, the fabric reveals its small patterns. This type of design is excellent as a background for displaying objects and blends well with the rest of the room. Small designs can be lived with for longer periods of time. The larger the pattern, the more difficult it is to live with for any great length of time, especially if a complete wall is draped with the fabric.

Large-patterned designs make interesting focal points in a room, especially if they are used with care. If

Alexander Girard. (Photo: courtesy of Herman Miller Inc.)

Upholstery fabrics designed by Girard. (Photo: courtesy of Herman Miller Inc.)

these large-patterned fabrics are also brilliant in color, there is a greater difficulty in introducing harmony in the room. This is not to infer that bright colors cannot be used but only that they should be carefully planned to achieve the intended effect.

The designers contributing new textiles to the home-furnishing field are many. There is a constant flow of new experimentations and discoveries, which are introducing many new interpretations of fabrics and fabric design to the buying public.

Alexander Girard. A designer who has helped revolutionize the textile industry is Alexander Girard. Girard designs fabrics for Herman Miller Inc. and is probably one of the most inspired designers of our time in the field

of textiles. He was born in New York City in 1907 and was trained as an architect at the Royal Institute of British Architects. He practiced architecture and design not only in the United States but also in Italy, England, and France. His travels have taken him through many countries, and the fruits of his experiences abroad have been enjoyed by many in this country. One of his major accomplishments was the gathering of material for the exhibition, "Textile and Ornamental Arts of India," held at the Museum of Modern Art in New York in 1955. His wanderings throughout South America resulted in his decorations for the restaurant, "La Fonda Del Sol," which he completely designed, in the Time and Life Building in New York. In this design, he incorporated his fine textiles with primitive

objects gathered from the countries south of the border.

Like Charles Eames, he is fascinated by toys, and this interest is apparent in many of the stores he has designed. Although the toys he favors are primitive and almost crude, they become gems against the clear crisp designs of his fabrics and interiors. His colors are vibrant and strong, clearly illustrating his interest in many cultures of the world. The collections he has designed for Herman Miller sing with every imaginative hue for every possible type of room or structure.

A large part of the fabrication of Girard's textile designs is executed in countries around the world, where native craftsmen carry out their age-old techniques. Consequently, Herman Miller can not always depend on exact

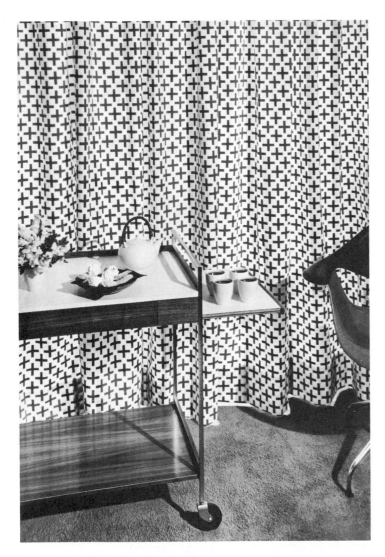

Plusses *by Alexander Girard. (Photo: courtesy of Herman Miller Inc.)*

nall Triangles *by Girard. (Photo: by Rooks, cour-sy of Herman Miller Inc.)*

Textiles and Objects Shop designed by Alexander Girard for Herman Miller Inc. (Photo: courtesy of Herman Miller Inc.)

Herman Miller Inc. San Francisco showroom designed by Alexander Girard. (Photo: courtesy of Herman Miller Inc.)

Jack Lenor Larsen. (Photo: courtesy of Jack L. Larsen Inc.)

delivery dates; the native craftsman works slowly and carefully, unregimented by a culture like ours. But the products brought into this country by Miller under the guidance of Girard are of the best quality. Girard uses many different weaves, but probably his printed fabrics are the most exciting. Clear, defined, and small in pattern, his textiles have a very wide range of usefulness.

Jack Lenor Larsen. Another fabric designer who has contributed greatly to the changing images of American textiles is Jack Lenor Larsen. Larsen received training in interior design and architecture at the University of Washington, and later he was awarded a degree in textile design at Cranbrook Academy.

"In the Fall of 1951 he came to New York to open a studio . . . and in 1952 Jack Larsen, Inc. was formed. Since its inception in 1952, Jack Lenor Larsen, Inc. has pursued both hand and machine weaving, with the technical knowledge and appreciation of each medium permitting the broad design exploration for which the organization is noted" (courtesy of Jack Lenor Larsen).

In 1963, Larsen introduced his new African line, which was inspired by a trip through that continent. Larsen uses native weaving and imported fabrics as does Girard for Herman Miller. Not all of the fabrics that are imported are designed by natives. Instead, the fabrics are often designed by Larsen or members of his staff, using the techniques of the natives, and frequently they are woven in the country that inspired the design.

Print Nouveau *by Larsen. (Photo: courtesy of*
Jack L. Larsen Inc.)

Swazilace *designed by Coral Stephens for Larsen's*
African Collection. (Photo: courtesy of Jack L.
Larsen Inc.)

Primavera *designed by Don Wright for Larsen.*
(Photo: courtesy of Jack L. Larsen Inc.)

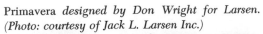

Kano Cloth *by Larsen. Inspired by the strip weav-*
ing of Nigeria and Ghana. (Photo: courtesy of
Jack L. Larsen Inc.)

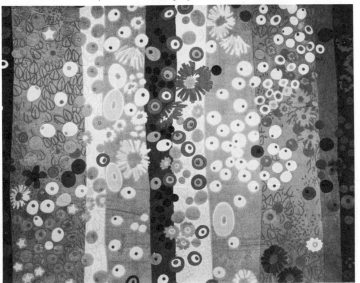

A Larsen forte is interest in and ability to investigate rare techniques for weaving cloth. While Girard seems to generate most of his excitement in the area of printed fabrics, Larsen makes a great contribution in the area of weaving techniques. Larsen has "made a sharp break from the accepted palette of primaries so closely identified with contemporary fabric design, searching instead to translate expressionistic and Oriental color theories, with their vivid, shimmering qualities" (courtesy of Jack Larsen).

Jack Larsen and Girard both work closely with architects and interior designers. Both have been trained in these fields and therefore have a good rapport with and understanding of the needs of these disciplines. Larsen and Girard have both been recognized nationally and internationally with awards for their work.

Laverne Inc. and Knoll Associates are also producers of interesting fabrics. Knoll has employed many well-known designers to contribute to the Knoll collection; Marianne Strengell, Stig Lindberg, Noemi Raymond, and

Moonstream *by Laverne. (Photo: courtesy of Laverne Inc.)*

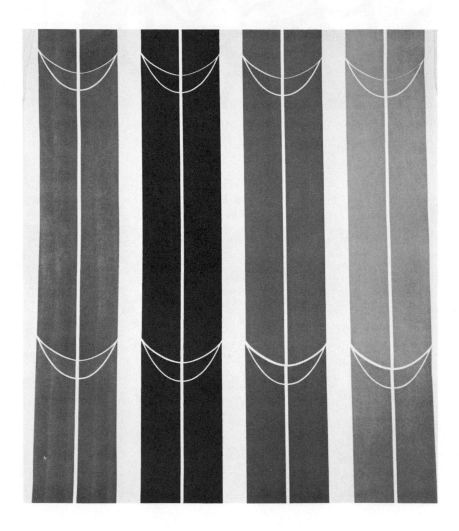

Angelo Testa are only a few of the designers who have at one time added to this collection. All of them are established names in textile designing.

Dorothy Liebes, Ruth Adler Schnee, and Ben Rose have been producing important textile design since the 1940s. Ben Rose especially has produced printed fabrics of high quality, and Dorothy Liebes has designed woven textiles utilizing metallic threads that have helped lead the way for contemporary textile design.

An exhibition, "Fabrics International," held in New York at the Museum of Contemporary Crafts in 1961, helped bring about a closer relationship between hand-weavers and industry. Some of the new developments experimented with by craftsmen were extraordinary, and the possibility that these techniques may be used by industry seems to be growing tremendously. Weaving is one craft that is easily understood by industry, and can be readily adapted to commercial enterprises.

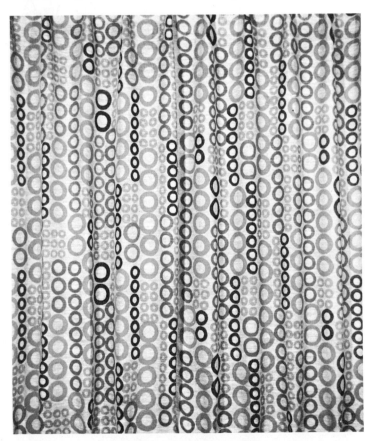

Haikkado *by Ben Rose. (Photo: courtesy of Ben Rose.)*

Trapeze *by Laverne. (Photo: courtesy of Laverne Inc.)*

Key Basque *by Ben Rose. (Photo: courtesy of Ben Rose.)*

Ebb and Flow *by Ben Rose (Photo: courtesy of Ben Rose.)*

Parenthesis *by Ben Rose. (Photo: courtesy of Ben Rose.)*

Two fabrics using "Antron" nylon designed by Dorothy Liebes. (Photo: courtesy of Stroheim & Romann.)

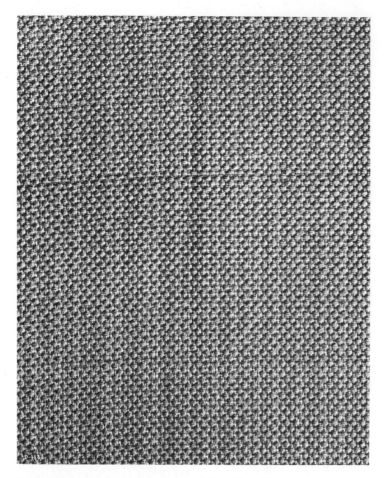

Bulky handwoven tweed designed by Dorothy Liebes for Stroheim & Romann. (Photo: courtesy of Stroheim & Romann.)

Textured stripe by Dorothy Liebes. (Photo: courtesy of Stroheim & Romann.)

Nocturne *by Boris Kroll. (Photo: courtesy of Boris Kroll Fabrics Inc.)*

Hoko *by Boris Kroll. (Photo: courtesy of Boris Kroll Fabrics Inc.)*

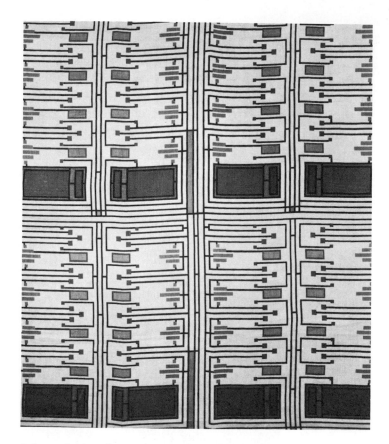

Schumacher's Taliesin Line of fabrics designed by Frank Lloyd Wright. This design is reminiscent of de Stijl. (Photo: courtesy of F. Schumacher & Co.)

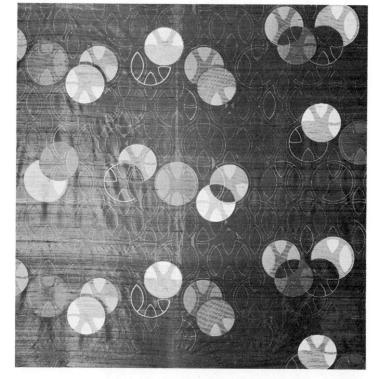

Taliesin Line fabric by Frank Lloyd Wright. (Photo: courtesy of Schumacher & Co.)

140

BIBLIOGRAPHY AND SUGGESTED READINGS

FURNITURE

Dal Fabbro, Mario, *How to Build Modern Furniture*, F. W. Dodge Corp., New York, 1951.

Hiort, Esbjørn, *Modern Danish Furniture*, Architectural Book Publishing Co., New York, 1956.

Nelson, George, *Chairs*, Whitney Publications Inc., New York, 1953.

Zahle, Erik, *A Treasury of Scandinavian Design*, Golden Press, New York, 1961.

FABRICS

Bendure, Zelma and Gladys Pfeiffer, *America's Fabrics*, The Macmillan Co., New York, 1947.

Birrell, Verla, *The Textile Arts*, Harper and Row, New York, 1958.

Conran, Terence, *Printed Textile Design*, Studio Publications, New York, 1957.

Hollen, Norma and Jane Saddler, *Textiles*, second edition, The Macmillan Co., New York, 1964.

Spearin, Jean, *Fibers, Fabrics & Finishes: Reference Manual*, Circular 378, Cooperative Extension Service, University of Maine, 1963.

Whiton, Sherrill, *Elements of Interior Design & Decoration*, J. B. Lippincott Co., Philadelphia, 1963.

PERIODICALS

American Fabrics
Design Quarterly
Furniture Forum

Furniture manufacturers have printed catalogs, sometimes available for distribution either free or at small cost. These are excellent reference and source materials. Fabric producers have textile files, usually available for a set fee that ranges from $15.00 to $25.00. Often this fee is returned after one purchases a certain amount of goods.

Copper enamel panel Lepidoptera *by Ella Marie Wooley can be used as a decorative element in the home. (Photo: courtesy of American Craftsmen's Council.)*

A mosaic table can be used in the living room, kitchen or dining room. Table by Krevolin and Constantine. (Photo: courtesy of American Craftsmen's Council.)

Chapter 9 THE CONTEMPORARY ARTIST-CRAFTSMAN

Important in designing a home and preparing its interior spaces for living are the many small accessories that express the individual.

These objects can be very expensive or very inexpensive, depending on the craftsmen who created them and, to some extent, the materials from which they were made. Contemporary craftsmen are offering the public a huge mass of products. Through careful buying, the consumer can collect objects of beauty and interest for inclusion in his home.

INDUSTRIALIZATION AND CRAFTS

Hand-crafted objects exemplified the democratic concept of beauty in preindustrial America, and their production was fostered by professional 143 and folk artists. But with the development of industrialization, the material as well as the aesthetic endeavors for sustaining such craft work were misused, and the artist-craftsman was unable to match the efficiency of manufacturing; he became an extinct type of the past, as we saw in the discussion of the "triumvirate."

If machine methods were responsible in part for killing the expression of the American craftsman and deeply wounding that of the European craftsman, then it has been said:

"The blame for the state of affairs can also be placed on the triumph of democracy—a triumph which exalted the taste of the ordinary man, however execrable it might be, to a parity with the taste of the elite . . . Not only in the United States, but throughout the civilized world, they [art and crafts] were at a low ebb during the middle decades of the nineteenth century. Everywhere those who looked only to the past for guidance failed to catch the spirit of the new age, while those who broke with the past and began to experiment made false starts" (John D. Hicks, *A Short History of American Democracy*, Houghton Mifflin Company, Boston, 1946, pp. 272–273).

Hand-crafted articles did not disappear completely, but they had reached a low level in quality, quantity, and status by the early part of the twentieth century. Today, the artist-craftsman once more is emerging, and he is insisting on his own distinct, necessary, and rightful place in this age of mechanization. He is earning a place for himself, not by returning to the old methods but by stating new values and satisfying new needs of our society in juxtaposition to those of our powerful industrial world. It is amazing in this renaissance that the present artist-craftsman has no real center of activity; he lives and works in many places throughout the country, wherever he can find compatible conditions for himself. He makes or discovers his own avenues for the distribution of his products and establishes his own markets when necessary.

The craftsman often avoids industry because he does not want to become involved in the creative vacuum of industry. Although industry has the technical knowledge, the facilities, and the money for experimentation, it seldom takes the bold step that is necessary to accomplish what the artist-craftsman can do in his personal studio. The industrial designer is lost in the role of stylist, attempting to satisfy the mediocre tastes of the man in the street who has had badly designed products crammed down his throat for so many years that he no longer has a good sense of values. We cannot expect the imaginative craftsman to get caught in this uncreative trap when he knows that it will retard his capabilities to think as an individual. Industry itself admits defeat in the area of creative endeavors not only in the United States but in many European countries as well. Stig Lindberg, of the Gustavsberg ceramic factory in Sweden, illustrates this point of view when he wonders why the Scandinavian designer should even try to be more creative when the American public will buy anything the Scandinavians market in America. The claim of industry that it is in sympathy with the artist-craftsman is insufficiently demonstrated when everything it produces for the public market has a "spit-and-polish" appearance with sterile surfaces and a plainly impersonal machine-made quality. In textile manufacturing some of these characteristics have been avoided, as we have already seen, for the facilities of the textile industry are better suited to reproducing the designs of the handweaver. The machinery is more flexible and versatile and more easily fits the needs of weavers. On the other hand, industry cannot, and perhaps should not, try to duplicate the aims of some artist-craftsmen.

CRAFTS AND FINE ARTS

The craftsman stands apart from industrial production; he is closely associated with the "fine" arts. We frequently find the strong influence of painting and sculpture in his work as well as similarity to these arts. Throughout the world of crafts, the craftsman seeks to escape from the limitations of traditional forms and conventional functions of the objects he creates. He does not neglect utilitarian values but rather explores new concepts of contemporary design just as does the architect.

For many years the crafts played a minor role in the arts, but recently a strong movement toward more important participation has become evident. In the field of copper enameling, for example, we can observe an increasingly close relationship with the field of painting. Many painters have been attracted by the sparkling colors of enameling to practice this craft but have kept a painter's discipline in their treatment rather than succumbing to the garish ornamentalism often found in enamels.

Enameling

Enameled products created by the artist-craftsman range from beautifully executed painting to bowls and trays of silver. Usually the craftsman uses copper as his background metal, but silver and other metals are also being used successfully as the base material on which fine enamels of ground colored glass are delicately fused at a temperature of 1500°. This is accomplished in a small kiln similar in construction to a ceramic kiln. The powdered glass can be applied through a sieve, or painted on the surface by brush. The resulting product can be used in any part of the home either as a utilitarian piece or a decorative object. An enameled bowl can be used as a vegetable dish, as an ash tray, or as a colorful object to sparkle a room. It is the individual owner's privilege to decide whether his piece will function in the home as a useful or as a purely ornamental accessory.

Copper-enameled paintings have made an especially interesting contribution in the craft world during the last few years, and they can be purchased at a wide range of prices. A medium-priced enameled painting may sell for around $50.00, while others may bring several thousands of dollars. Bowls and ash trays can be purchased from

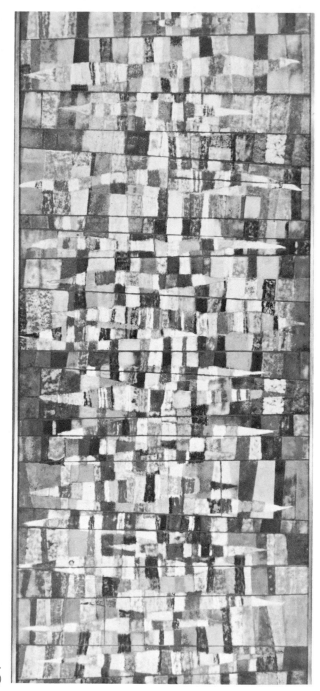

Enamel-on-copper wall panel by Peter Ostuni. (Photo: courtesy of American Craftsmen's Council.)

Stoneware pot with wax-resist glaze by Harvey Littleton. (Photo: courtesy of American Craftsmen's Council.)

$2.00 to $50.00, depending on the size of the object and the quality of the artist.

Other forms of enameling are returning to the contemporary craft world as artists rediscover interesting techniques dating back to the time before Christ. Cloisonné and Champlevé are two such techniques. In both of these techniques, small pieces of wire are put on the surface of the background metal, and enamel, placed between wires, is fused within the wire frames. The contrast of enamel and metal lines is very effective. Both methods are utilized for household objects, but they are seen more often in jewelry and ecclesiastic work.

Ceramics

Although the potter is often regarded as a creator of utilitarian pieces, many contemporary ceramists have achieved definite nonobjective sculptural effects in their

Creative ceramic and fabric dolls by Hal Riegger. (Photo: courtesy of artist.)

pots. We may question this deviation from traditional use of clay, but we can see that exciting new effects have resulted from such experimentation. These new potters seem to be completely unafraid of turning away from the conventional container that the machine can produce, and of giving new meaning to forms in clay. We must look objectively at this work, examine it, and decide upon its usefulness in the home. Some pieces, although seemingly useless, can make the same addition to the household that a sculpture makes. They can be purely aesthetic in manipulating space, light, and three-dimensional form.

Despite the advent of the sculptural potter, we cannot ignore the potters who are producing pieces of entirely utilitarian value. These potters are continuing the ceramic function that has existed since the Neolithic period. Their work rings with joy and manifests a certain familiarity, which we readily understand. There are many potters who approve of the utilitarian purpose and who adhere to this tradition. They are found much more easily then the more avant-garde potter, and their pieces are beautiful, useful additions to any home.

Stoneware, Earthenware, and Porcelain. Most potters today make *stoneware*. Stoneware is kiln-fired at temperatures ranging from 2000° to 2600°F., and therefore is considered high-fire ceramics. Because of its high fire, stoneware has very little absorbency, has a nice ring, and

Selection of ceramic pots from the collection of Mr. and Mrs. A. D'Amico of Bangor, Maine. Both utilitarian and nonutilitarian pottery has a place as enrichment in the contemporary home. (Photo: University of Maine.)

does not chip as easily as does earthenware. Stoneware is used by the potter in many types of ceramic pieces and is produced for dinnerware by commercial companies. Often the stoneware pottery made by an artist-craftsman has a mat (dull) finish and a nice earthy quality. The clay body is rich and natural, as if it were still part of the earth. However, the commercial pottery sold in retail stores is generally less earthy and more polished in feeling. Stoneware, although breakable, resists breakage much more than does earthenware. *Earthenware* is fired at a lower temperature, always under 2000°F. It is less vitrified and is certainly less desirable as dinnerware. Much pottery from native cultures is earthenware. The red clay bowls from Mexico and the Raku ware of Japan are earthenware, and their relatively soft bodies chip and break readily. Earthenware is at one end and *porcelain* at the other end of the firing scale. Porcelain is fired at very high temperatures (2300° to 2700°F.) and is therefore very hard, resistant to chipping, and unscratchable. Porcelain is translucent and very dense in composition. It is generally considered elegant for dinnerware. The making of porcelain is not recommended for beginning potters because working the clay is difficult. Porcelain clay is composed of a high percentage of kaolin, which helps to provide its white creamy color. *Chinaware* or bone china is porcelain, but a little whiter in color. Bone china is not necessarily better than porcelain.

Ceramics vary greatly in price. Small bowls and vases can be purchased for less than a dollar, and larger pieces are often priced as high as several hundreds of dollars. Much depends on the potter who has made the piece—his fame and the demand for his work.

Wall Hangings

A revival of interest has taken place in the production of wall hangings. Once seen only in palaces, wall hangings in various contemporary modes of expression are now seen frequently in homes of the middle classes. Uses of hangings have been described thus:

"The home has many wonderful places in which to display colorful and decorative wall hangings. In fact, there are so many places and uses for them that it is impossible to mention them all . . . wall hangings are meant to be seen. They are like paintings, and demand important situations within the home . . . they are unusual, and this is added reason for the individual with a sense of curiosity to have one in his home" (*Decorative Wall Hangings: Art With Fabric*, David B. Van Dommelen, p. 158).

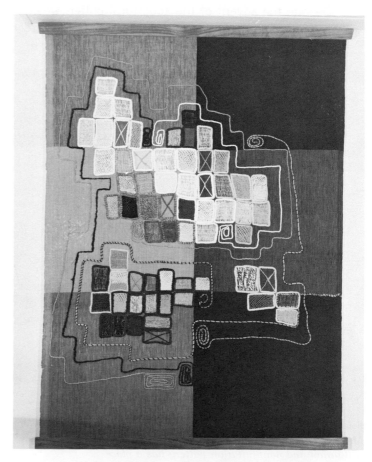

Wall hanging by Mariska Karasz done in stitchery on wool. (Collection of Montclair Art Museum.)

Hand weavers and "fine" artists have entered the field with enthusiasm, using every conceivable material and every imaginable device. Appliqué, stitchery, collage, and press-on tape are only a few of the ways in which the craftsman is expressing himself in this field. Even the sewing machine is being used as a creative tool to make unusual and aesthetically satisfying wall hangings for the family to enjoy.

Jean Ray Laury and Mariska Karasz are two among many who have contributed to this area of crafts. Both men and women are active in the production of wall hangings for the home.

If, at one time, there existed academic rules prescribing the techniques and methods by which a wall hanging or tapestry should be made, these have been largely discarded by the textile craftsman, just as the potter has overthrown the restriction of his traditional background.

Wall hanging entitled Stained Glass Window *by the author. It was made with stitchery and machine appliqué.*

Appliquéd pillow by Jean Ray Laury adds color and life to a sofa. (Photo: courtesy of Jean Ray Laury.)

A flossa rug by Anabel Schultz would add texture and warmth to any room. (Photo: courtesy of American Craftsmen's Council.)

A wall hanging by Jean Ray Laury is used as a headboard to add an individual touch to the bedroom. (Photo: courtesy of Jean Ray Laury.)

Rya rug by Alice Parrott. Rugs by craftsmen bring needed character and personality to rooms that are often unexciting. (Photo: courtesy of American Craftsmen's Council.)

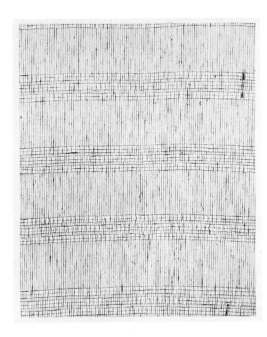

Handwoven casement fabrics such as this one by J. Anderson contribute interest to windows and walls. (Photo: courtesy of American Craftsmen's Council.)

Handcarved wooden bowl with inset ivory by George Federoff. (Photo: courtesy of American Craftsmen's Council.)

The Polish folk craftsman at his best retains the lovely grain and character of the wood in this container. (Photo: courtesy of Cepelia Corp.)

151

At the same time, many craftsmen are still working within the scope of particular traditional patterns but employing contemporary design as their vehicle of expression.

Wood

In addition to textiles, wood has been a favorite material of craftsmen through most of the history of man. The natives of every South Sea island, the Norsemen of Iceland, and the inhabitants of Africa have used wood for religious sculptures and ritual masks in most unusual and provocative ways. We find wood used in homes in every period of history, and in each period some unique way of exploiting its many possibilities was contributed. Today's craftsman, like his predecessors, continues to be attracted to wood as a material with which to express his ideas. To the sincere craftsman in wood, the grain is as beautiful as the lines and composition found in a painting. The natural color of wood as well as the natural pattern of the grain must be considered in the object to be created. We saw how wood was treated by designers of furniture, and it is as important to the makers of small objects that the item be honest and simple with every characteristic of the wood incorporated into it. The product of the craftsman who makes utilitarian pieces in wood is as valid as that of the artist-sculptor who works in the same material. The warmth of wood in the home adds to the over-all character of rooms and lends a richness that is often unattainable with other materials.

Mosaics

The art of mosaic is a very old one and in recent years has been used with great invention. The contemporary craftsman is not only using mosaic in architectural situations as it was employed in earlier times but is also incorporating it into tables, bowls, and other useful objects for the home. The technique of mosaic is simple compared with those of some other crafts. Small pieces of tile or stone are placed on a background surface and cemented by means of grout in the small surrounding crevices. The method is comparable with that used in making ceramic tile bathroom walls, but mosaic work is on a smaller scale. Today it is used as a form of expression by the ceramic artist and the sculptor. Mosaics can be purchased in a wide range of prices; size and artist will dictate the cost. However, the ambitious homemaker or designer can very easily make mosaic articles for the home with only a small amount of practice.

A mosaic wall panel like this one can be used inside or outside of the home as a decorative element. Designed by Ros Barron, this panel is composed of ceramic tile and concrete and is titled Blue Garden. (Photo: courtesy of American Craftsmen's Council.)

Glass

Glass making is an extremely old craft, which existed in cultures thousands of years before Christ. Glass is made by fusing silica (such as sand), alkali (such as potash), and another base (such as lime). Various characteristics can be added to plain glass by the inclusion of other chemicals. Color, for instance, is obtained by the use of cobalt for blue, copper for red, uranium for yellow, and any of a great variety of other chemicals and minerals for other colors. When lead is added, the glass is known as crystal. Crystal is considered the finest of glass; however, many companies produce glass that is extremely fine and

A collage mosaic of sea shells and driftwood made by Bill Dodge is a fascinating textural study for the walls of a hallway. (Photo: courtesy of the artist. Collection of Dr. and Mrs. David Gregory.)

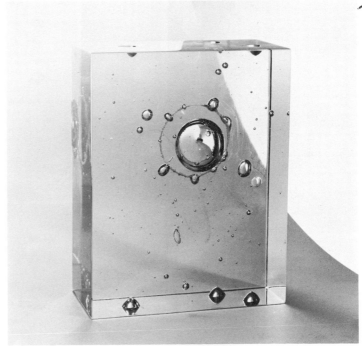

Detail of one block from the Palmqvist wall. Notice the clarity and precision with which the block is designed. (Photo: courtesy of AB Orrefors Glasbruk, Sweden.)

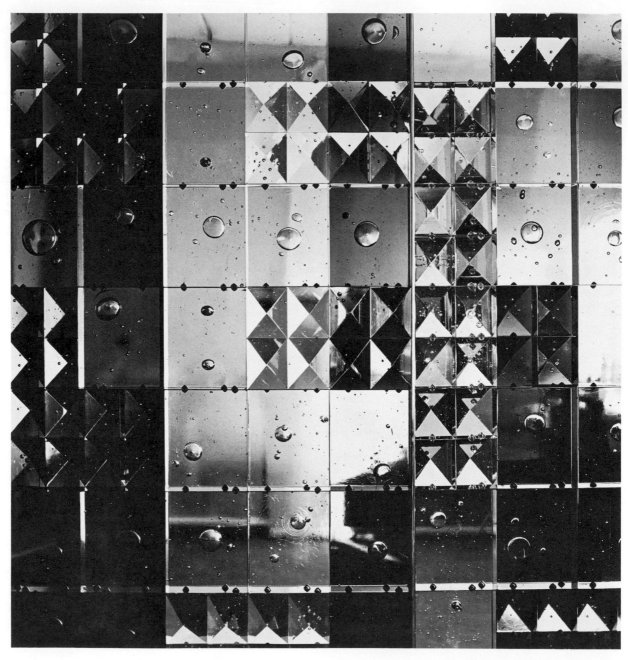

A glass wall designed by Sven Palmqvist utilizes both gray and white crystal and Ravenna glass blocks. (Photo: courtesy of AB Orrefors Glasbruk, Sweden.)

can be compared with some crystal. One of the finest glass and crystal producers in the United States is Steuben Glass; in the Scandinavian countries, names such as Boda and Orrefors are associated with fine glass. The United States has had very few glass craftsmen until recent years; now many craftsmen are exploring this area. Probably they were stimulated by the many distinguished craftsmen in the Scandinavian countries.

Glass objects serve many utilitarian purposes in the home. The hard, smooth surface of glass is good for all types of uses. Because it holds liquids well and has no taste, glass is most popular for drinking vessels. Its major handicap is fragility. It can be purchased in a wide range of prices. Flower containers, for example, may be bought for as little as $1.00 and for more than $1,500.00 (from Steuben Glass).

Ornamentation of Glass. The simplest way to decorate the surface of glass is *glass blowing,* done while the glass is still hot. The craftsman may add various small pieces of molten glass to the surface for ornamentation. *Glass cutting* is a technique for cutting a design through a surface layer of color to the clear glass below or cutting into the transparent clear glass to produce many-faceted surfaces that reflect light with a sparkling effect. *Engraving* on glass differs from cutting in that an abrasion wheel is used to incise shallow lines rather than faceted designs. *Glass etching* is a process of using hydrofluoric acid to eat away the surface, leaving a frosted effect. Generally the surface is not etched very deeply, but it can be etched to a depth of one inch, if the structure of the glass allows it.

Although all these techniques are interesting when used with moderation for the enrichment of glass, probably glass is most beautiful in its natural state. The polish and gleam of clear glass make a nice textural surface in any room. Even glass with only color added to it can be decorative enough. One of the faults of much glass designed by manufacturers is excessive ornamentation that hides the lovely surface qualities of glass and has a tendency to make the glass look cheap.

Metal

Objects made of metal, whether handcrafted or produced by a good manufacturer, can often introduce a needed texture into a room. Silver, brass, copper, and bronze are the most familiar metals seen in the home. Lovely lead bowls and stainless steel objects are also available. Each metal has a different characteristic.

Silver. Next to gold, silver is considered the best of the metals and is usually the most expensive. While tea sets and flatware are the most popular, silverware, small sculptures, bowls, and other objects can be used with great success in the home. The major problem with silver, in addition to the cost, is that maintenance requires a great deal of polishing. For a contemporary family without

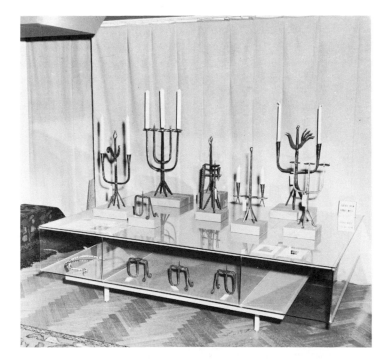

A selection of metal candle holders by Polish craftsmen on display at Cepelia Corp. (Photo: courtesy of Cepelia Corp.)

Paper cutouts made by Polish craftsman can be used as colorful accents in a child's room. This is only one example of hundreds of crafts being imported for sale in this country. (Photo: courtesy of Cepelia Corp.)

domestic help, other metals, just as elegant and beautiful, may be more practical.

Pewter. An alloy of lead and tin, pewter is especially beautiful because it has a quality of oldness about it. It is a dull gray-blue metal and as it ages adds a patina which gives it character. Newer pewters look more like silver than the older pieces and are less distinguished looking.

Copper. Because copper is a less expensive metal, many people can afford copper objects. When this metal oxidizes, it produces a lovely old patina that enhances, instead of marring, the beauty of an object. Copper serves many household purposes, and craftsmen use it as the background material for enameling. It conducts heat well and is therefore useful for holding food that is to be served warm; but because copper imparts an unpleasant taste, it is necessary to have another material between the food and the copper. Copper is used in many cooking utensils because it is a good heat conductor.

Aluminum, chromium, iron, and steel are used less often by the craftsman for small accessory pieces, but these metals have many uses in the home. You will remember some of these metals as important in furniture and architecture.

Influences from Abroad

The American artist-craftsman has been strongly influenced not only by the fine arts but also by the work of his fellow craftsmen abroad. The Japanese have affected the styles of our potters; the Scandinavians have had strong impact on our weavers; Danish woodcraftsmen have influenced our woodworkers. The artist-craftsman also has been influenced by the crafts of the American Indian and those of the Negro cultures of Africa. Many shops selling the work of foreign craftsmen have opened with great success in New York recently. One such shop is Cepelia, which sells the craftwork of Poland.

The men and women who have shaped the renaissance of craftsmanship are exploring new fields of design unimagined before our time, yet most of them have drawn inspiration from the vast amount of knowledge and technical research that preceded them for hundreds of years. The accumulation of the past cannot be forgotten or ignored but can be translated into a vocabulary that is in keeping with our age of space. Each day as contemporary craftsmen close the gap between the "fine" arts and the decorative arts, they are diminishing the misunderstanding that originally relegated craftsmen to a minor place among artists. The craftsmen are making people aware of their purpose, and, as they do this, they are gaining status in the field of art. Although society does not require craft objects as it requires food and other necessities for sustaining life, it is becoming more conscious of the value of such objects in the enrichment of life than it has been since the inception of the industrial age. The craftsman is making a place for himself in our society through his own experimentation and ingenuity. In his reappearance in this new role, he has created his own environment, discovered his own market, and given his consumers much pleasure that was previously unavailable to them. The American craftsman has made an enormous contribution by this achievement, which has yet to be completely recognized as an integral part of American life—the persistence of a handcraft culture existing stubbornly and ineradicably in the midst of our industrial society.

The role of crafts in the home is important, for it is through accessories such as wall hangings and pottery that the interior of a house expresses the individual. The objects that are utilized in the home tell us something about the occupants of the house and about the world they wish to construct for themselves.

There is no room in a home that can not have the work of the craftsman incorporated into it. The kitchen, where the housewife spends a great deal of time, can be made more enjoyable for her if she has utensils that are beautiful and easy to maintain. Earthenware and stoneware introduce a colorful and casual atmosphere into a room that we often overlook when we are decorating. The bathroom also can be given attractive objects to make it more interesting. There is no need for any room to be a dead area, lacking in character.

CRAFT DESIGN: STRUCTURAL AND DECORATIVE

The design of craft objects is important. It is not intelligent to place objects in the home unless they incor-

Rugs such as this one by M. Bujakowa of Zakopane, Poland, are becoming more popular as cultural contributions of the folk artists from around the world. (Photo: courtesy of Cepelia Corp.)

A tapestry rug designed by Lewinska of Poland. This is of the same type as the one designed by Bujakowa. (Photo: courtesy of Cepelia Corp.)

porate the basic considerations of good design. Any product of craftsmanship should have good structural and decorative design. The *structural design* concerns the size, form, texture, and color. These elements along with the *decorative* elements of the object, which are the surface ornamentation, must work together and function as one entity. The structural design must utilize materials honestly and simply. Raw materials for crafts should be used sincerely. Wood should not be made to look like some other material. Clay should not be made into "cow" creamers and sugar bowls, for example. The forms of objects should be suited to their uses and not designed to hide the purposes for which they were made. Proportion of an object is important if it is to function as a well-organized, useful piece. A badly proportioned pitcher, as everyone knows, is difficult to handle when full of liquid, while a piece that is successfully designed serves its purpose well.

The *decorative design* should fit the shape of the object as well as the material from which the object is made. The surface ornamentation should not overpower the piece with its excessive size, nor should it be too small in scale. The surface ornamentation should be an inherent part of the piece and not an addition applied as an afterthought. The more integrated the surface enrichment, the more successful the piece will appear. The surface design will usually (but not always) relate better to the piece if the design covers the surface quietly. The background is as important as the design placed thereon. Each should complement the other or harmonize with the other; neither should be considered alone.

Originality is a good asset in any work of craftsmanship, although there are some objects that should remain in traditional shapes and sizes for utilitarian purposes. If the craftsman makes the object different simply in order to be novel, there is a possibility that the object is no longer useful. When a cup and saucer are designed by a potter, they should be designed for the purpose of containing a liquid which is to be drunk. If the cup is too large or the texture too rough, the functional qualities will not meet traditional requirements for drinking. Simplicity is almost always desirable for pieces from which food will be eaten, and complex designs should be saved for objects of chiefly aesthetic interest to be used for display.

BIBLIOGRAPHY AND SUGGESTED READINGS

Hicks, John D., *A Short History of American Democracy*, Houghton Mifflin, Boston, 1946.

Karasz, Mariska, *Adventure In Stitches*, Funk and Wagnalls Co., New York, 1959.

Krum, Josephine, *Hand-Built Pottery*, International Textbook Co., Scranton, Pa., 1960.

Mattil, Edward, *Meaning In Crafts*, Prentice-Hall, Inc., New York, 1959.

Nelson, Glenn C., *Ceramics*, Holt, Rinehart, and Winston, New York, 1960.

Rhodes, Daniel, *Stoneware & Porcelain*, Chilton, Philadelphia, 1959.

Scharff, Robert, *Wood Finishing*, McGraw-Hill Book Co., New York, 1956.

Van Dommelen, David B., *Decorative Wall Hangings: Art With Fabric*, Funk and Wagnalls Co., New York, 1962.

Van Dommelen, David B., *Walls: Enrichment & Ornamentation*, Funk and Wagnalls Co., New York, 1965.

Waugh, Sidney, *The Making of Fine Glass*, Dodd, Mead, New York, 1947.

Composition *by Jean Arp, 1937. Torn paper, with*
India ink wash. (A. E. Gallatin Collection, Phila-
delphia Museum of Art.)

Long wide corridors can allow exhibit space throughout the house. Halls should be lighted well and have ample space for viewing. (Photo: courtesy of Eichler Homes.)

Chapter **10** FINE ARTS IN THE HOME

The fine arts are moving into the home as an expression of the interior designer and the home owner. Art has become an important element in the American society; young people throughout the country, as well as wealthy art collectors, are including various kinds of art objects in their buying lists in order to individualize their homes.

Some of these buyers are purchasing art primarily for investment purposes in hopes that they will be among the lucky owners when an artist becomes recognized. Others are buying mainly to solve decorative problems, which require them to seek paintings of a particular color, size, shape, or style. Still others are adding art to their homes simply because they enjoy lovely things around them. Each reason is supported by particular values and considerations.

Many people are impressed by the rapid growth of prices in the art world during the last few years and by the increasing number of new places where works of art are sold. Prices have become so high in recent years that monetary values may seem to be overpowering aesthetic values. All over the world people were stunned when a major New York art gallery auctioned a Rembrandt painting in the fall of 1961 for $2,500,000. This was an action that clearly pointed to the new materialistic importance that is being attached to art. Not only are the works of old masters urgently sought after, but the achievements and products of young artists are also eagerly purchased, often with the hope that their value will substantially increase. Each new painter appearing on the art scene today has a potential market for his products. It is probable that prices will continue to be elevated as the demand for art rises.

As we saw in the previous chapter, crafts also have an important role to play in the enrichment of the rooms of a home or office. However, while crafts usually play a functional part in the design of a house, the fine arts are regarded as solely aesthetic additions in interior decoration. This distinction is not always applicable, for some crafts lately have become nonutilitarian, but the generalization is rather safe. One can hardly expect a painting or a lithograph to be utilitarian—but they can and should add an element of beauty to even the most humble of rooms. It might be mentioned in passing that there are a few types of paintings and prints that could be considered utilitarian; these are the ones created for promotional reasons. Toulouse-Lautrec was essentially producing utilitarian lithographs when he made posters for various singers and dancers in Paris. Painters such as Norman Rockwell, who produces covers for magazines, are producing a utilitarian art, which could also be considered commercial art. It is doubtful, however, that both Rockwell and Lautrec should be mentioned in the same context.

Although we generally consider the area of "fine arts" to be expensive, it need not always be so. While not all of us can go to a gallery and purchase the successful artists' work, most of us can patronize some of the many painters, print makers, and sculptors who offer objects of art at very reasonable prices and whose work is of unquestionable quality.

To illustrate the position of "fine arts" in the home and the availability of works of art for lower-income families, we might look at the exciting opportunity offered by Sears, Roebuck and Company in a promotion of purchase of fine arts by the general public. With the expert advice of Vincent Price, the veteran actor and art collector, Sears, Roebuck offered the average-income consumer a fantastic opportunity to participate in the surge of art buying. The objects for sale were carefully selected by Mr. Price, who did not need to be persuaded to join in the enterprise, for he felt the urgent need for laymen to own and to enjoy art. He had this to say about the Sears project: "We're bringing art, fine art, to the people. To me the most exciting thing in the world is what man has made visually to prove he's a cultured human being" (*Parade*, Sept. 30, 1962, p. 4). The pieces were offered at reasonable prices ranging from only a few dollars up to about $3,000.00. The instantaneous success of this project attested the level of sophistication of the American people.

A home that is a receptacle for beautiful objects of art can be a very exciting and inviting place in which to live. It is not, however, necessary to overload the walls with paintings, sculptures, and wall hangings. Philip Johnson, in his glass house in New Canaan, Connecticut, hangs only one painting in a room. Its placement is important and becomes a major focal point in the house. Smaller objects or sculptures are placed discriminately on a table or in a corner where they do not interrupt the major emphasis of the painting and yet do contribute to a carefully planned interior. Because there are materials in the structure of this house that speak eloquently, enrichment with objects is necessarily limited. Very often, and certainly in this architectural essay, the understatement is most profound.

It is better not to make a gallery or small museum of a home. Each piece should serve its purpose well, and the end result of the room should be useful and economic in design. There are successful ways to incorporate many pieces of fine art into the home, but one must use care in approaching the use of great numbers of objects. If many pieces are to be exhibited in one room or throughout the house, they should be carefully arranged so that each piece will be easily seen and will show itself well. Each displayed object should be appropriate to its surrounding textures and immediately neighboring pieces.

Each piece that is exhibited should have something to say to the individual spectator. Communication is the primary role of a painting or sculpture. Without communication, the painting or sculpture will be a failure. This does not mean that every person will get the same message from an art object. In fact, a piece that creates a little discussion concerning its subject matter or treatment makes a more interesting addition to a room. It need not be controversial, but an unusual statement will contribute a great deal toward breaking a barrier that might be present when guests first arrive.

There are many subjects that can be treated in paintings and prints, and subjects are approached in an infinite variety of ways by different artists. Each individual should select objects that have meaning and beauty to himself. It will be up to the decorator or the household members to decide what subject matters can be used in the various rooms. There will be some subject matters that are completely inappropriate in certain rooms, but often the field is not as limited as most people think. Obviously an avant-garde painting could look out of place in a Chippendale salon, but a Russian icon might make an interesting departure from modern coldness.

The buyer should make a search of museums and galleries in order to become better informed about various styles of art. By reading the numerous art history books available on the market today, one can learn the different aims and philosophies of painters and the reasons why they painted as they did. Too often our likes and dislikes are not based on any logical or intelligent understanding of the arts. Instead of learning, we blindly continue to make rash statements about things concerning which we know nothing.

Besides coming to know something about the subject matter of a work of art and its origin, the individual interested in incorporating fine art into the home should have a knowledgeable understanding of the many media and materials used in constructing compositions. We might look at some of these art forms in order to understand them better and to recognize them more easily when we wish to purchase, rent, or incorporate them into the home. Unfortunately, it is really impossible to learn to identify all the art forms through a book such as this one, but the following definitions will give the layman a starting line from which to begin his investigation of fine arts. It is only after years of diligent studying that one can become truly familiar with painting, prints, and sculptures. Even art experts are sometimes fooled into buying fakes, although this seldom happens.

It is really impossible today to categorize works of art simply, because the contemporary artist tends to combine many media while he is working. Oil and watercolors can be mixed, as can fabric and paper, and ink and paint, and a hundred other combinations. But we might look briefly at some of the classical categories that have been used in past years.

Paintings

Paintings can be classified by pigment—oil and water color. Traditionally, an oil painting had much more importance attached to it than did a water color; however, nothing could be more misleading. A water color by a good artist is just as valid as an oil painting by an equally effective painter; at times the watercolor painting can be more expensive. The major differences are that the oil pigment is more likely to have textural effects than the water color, and the oil painting is produced on canvas or painting board, while water color is generally painted on a textured paper. Although textured effects can be seen on most contemporary paintings, they are not always seen in oil paintings of earlier periods. Many of the earlier painters carefully brushed out any signs of textures except those that they actually painted into the fabrics and materials of the depicted subject. However, contemporary painters use thick oil pigments and often mix other substances into the paint to make the texture rough and pebbly in feeling. Water color is generally used by itself and only seldom with another substance. Instead, the artist depends on his dexterity and manipulations to obtain the textural effect

The Old King *by Georges Rouault, painted between 1916 and 1936 in oil on canvas, 30 by 20 inches. (Collection of Carnegie Institute.)*

Painting (Autumn) *by Wassily Kandinsky, 1914. The medium is oil on canvas, and the size is 64 by 48 inches. Kandinsky was a member of the Bauhaus faculty in Dessau, Germany. (The Solomon R. Guggenheim Museum, New York.)*

desired. Rouault, in his painting *Head of a Clown*, mixed water color and oil together on paper to produce a very free interpretation of a clown.

An oil painting is usually not covered with glass, unless its value is so high that protection is needed from possible damage by vandals or climate. For instance, Da Vinci's *Mona Lisa* has been framed in glass for protection. However, a water color is and should always be framed and covered with glass, because the physical characteristics of water paint make damage more possible. Water colors are generally matted with a small margin of mounting board around the painting and within the outside frame.

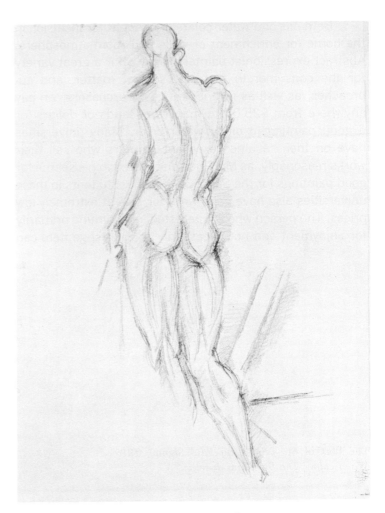

Study After Houdon's Écorché *by Paul Cezanne. Lead pencil on paper, 8 by 10 inches. (The Metropolitan Museum of Art, Maria DeWitt Jesup Fund, 1951, from The Museum of Modern Art, Lizzie P. Bliss Collection.)*

Head of a Clown *by Georges Rouault, painted about 1908 in water color and oil on paper, 23 by 18 inches. (The Dumbarton Oaks Collection.)*

Both oils and water colors are sought for inclusion in the home for enrichment of walls and room atmosphere. Abstract expressionist painters today offer a great variety for the consumer in textures, subject matter, and approaches, as well as in price ranges. Purchasers can pay anywhere from $25.00 to many thousands of dollars for a good painting in oil or water color. Many universities have on their faculties excellent painters who sell their works reasonably, as Mr. Price discovered in his search for good paintings for the Sears Collections. Students in these universities also have good work for sale at extremely low prices. The person who is interested in a painting primarily for enjoyment and not necessarily as a prestige item can certainly do well to shop in university or college art departments. People wishing to spend more on a painting should go to reliable art dealers and carefully examine various types of works, lest they purchase a picture that is below good standards and quality. If the purchaser is looking for a painting by a well-established artist, he should consult an expert before making any decision, lest he end up with a fraudulent painting.

Prints

Prints are different from paintings in that they are reproduced in large numbers by the artist. All prints are made by some form of printing process—and there are

The Port of St. Tropez by Paul Signac, 1916. Water color. (The Brooklyn Museum.)

many different ones. A print can be reproduced hundreds of times, or until the surface bearing the design is destroyed, and still remain an ''original'' piece of work. Usually prints are less expensive than oils or water colors, but that may depend on the artist who has created them and on how many prints he has produced at one printing. The artist numbers the prints as he pulls them from his press to indicate how many he has made. His first test copies are signed with the word ''proof'' or ''artist copies,'' and after that he begins to number them. The more he produces, the less value each has; when he signs some, those with his signature have more value, especially if he is a well-known, established artist.

Monoprints. The monoprint is produced by the artist's applying ink directly on a flat surface, which is often glass, and removing a certain amount of ink until he is satisfied with the design. The artist then places his paper on the surface of the glass and applies pressure to the reverse side. When he removes the paper, he has obtained his print. Because he has lifted the complete design from the face of his printing surface, he cannot reproduce exactly the same print that he obtained the first time. Therefore he produces only one print of a kind. This is the only type of print that cannot be reproduced many times. The monoprint is very exciting and experimental, for the artist gets new results from each printing. A monoprint can be mounted and framed just as any other type of print is prepared for exhibition.

Lithographs. Lithographs are printed from a drawing made on a large, heavy, flat stone. A special greasy crayon is used to draw the composition on the stone, and the design is then etched into the stone with acid. Ink is rolled on the surface, and an impression is made on the paper by applying a press. Toulouse-Lautrec did much to bring this technique to a high point of excellence during the late 1800s, when he produced posters for various performing artists in Paris. Although black and white is used most frequently, color can also be used in lithography very

successfully by the skilled artist.

Woodcuts. Woodcuts are the product of another form of printmaking that is full of possibilities. The design is cut into a block of wood with carving tools, and ink is rolled onto the surface of the wood before the impression is made. If the wood has an interesting and rather high grain, the grain can play an important part in the composition. The woodcut may be made in black and white or in rich, strong colors. Paul Gauguin produced many woodcuts during his artistic lifetime. Although earlier artists limited their work to small pieces of wood, contemporary artists have been using large pieces—some up to six feet high and three feet wide, producing forceful effects.

Silk Screen or Serigraphy. The process known as silk screen or serigraphy calls for applying a design on a piece of silk that is stretched over a frame. The design can be put on with glue, or a stencil can be adhered to the underside of the stretched silk. Either way, after the design is applied, ink is forced with a squeegee through the pores of the uncovered portion of the silk to the paper under the screen. A good silk screen will show the small fiber pores of the silk as tiny dots on the surface of the paper. The contemporary artist often runs his print under the screen several times, using a different ink color each time; the result can be a beautiful combination of colors and textures.

Etchings. There are several forms of etching; those seen most often are made by either dry point or acid techniques. In dry point, the design is drawn very lightly on the surface of a copper plate until the composition is composed of many small, delicate lines. In acid etchings, wax is put on the copper plate and removed according to the demands of the design—the acid eats the design into the plate wherever the wax has been removed. In both approaches, the ink is applied to the etched plate, the excess ink removed, and then the plate and paper are run through a very tight press. The resulting print has a slightly embossed edge surrounding the picture. Many artists have used one technique or the other in making prints, and some have combined the two etching techniques to create very interesting effects.

Reproductions. A reproduction, another kind of print, is a photographic likeness of an original painting or print. Sometimes it is very difficult to see the difference from the original, especially with lithographs and etchings. A reproduction is not necessarily bad, unless it is a poorly colored and photographed reproduction. It is not easy to tell how bad a reproduction is, unless you have the original

for a comparison study. It is then that even the layman can readily see how bad reproductions can be. There are some European companies that even emboss a reproduction to imitate the brush-stroke textures that are on the canvas of the original oil painting. If you are buying a reproduction, make sure you are getting one faithful to the original, with clear, good color and well-defined lines, shapes, and textures. It is better not to have a photographic reproduction, if it is a poor representation of the original.

Hanging. The way you exhibit your painting or print will make or break its effect on the viewer. Hanging a piece of fine art in the home is a challenge to your taste. It should be carefully placed in the right space on the right wall; each piece added to a home should have adequate attention given to its placement.

Water colors with glass coverings are exceedingly difficult to place because of the glare that is so often present. Do not use glareproof glass, for it ruins the effects of the painting. This is especially important for water colors, where delicate transparent effects have been incorporated by the artist. In determining a picture's placement, natural lighting as well as artificial lighting should be examined. If the glare has been eliminated, the piece may be hung; if glare is present, arrangements should be made to reduce it for more pleasurable viewing. Glare can be eliminated by placing artificial lighting at a new point; if the light is natural, soft draperies can be arranged so as to cut down its intensity.

Sculpture. The materials used in sculpture extend to almost every conceivable field of textures, fabrics, and surfaces. At one time sculpture was limited to marble, bronze, wood, and clay. The contemporary artist is using glass, plastic, old boxes, pipes, pails, mattress springs,

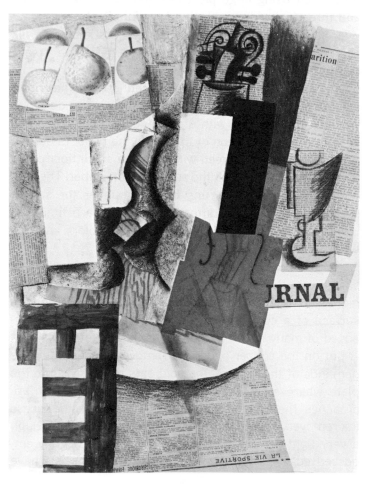

Violin and Fruit by Pablo Picasso, 1913. Collage. (A. E. Gallatin Collection, Philadelphia Museum of Art.)

Horizontal Spines *by Alexander Calder. Mobile.
(Addison Gallery of American Art, Phillips Academy, Andover.)*

Leda by *Aristide Maillol, Bronze. (Philadelphia Museum of Art Collection.)*

The Insect-Plant *by Theodore Roszak, 1960. Copper, 54 inches high. (Pierre Matisse Gallery.)*

Bird in Space *by Constantine Brancusi, 1921. Polished bronze with marble base. (Louise and Walter Arensberg Collection, Philadelphia Museum of Art.)*

Reclining Figure *by Henry Moore, 1935. Elmwood, 19 inches high, 35 inches long. (Albright-Knox Art Gallery, Buffalo, New York.)*

and even dishes that are painted white after they have been secured to some surface. It is not unusual to see an old piece of junk beautifully set on a pedestal and exhibited in the home or museum. The art of assemblage has opened unlimited avenues for the artist wishing to experiment in sculptural form. Art galleries offer such sculptures at very high prices; the individual, if imaginative enough, can create one suitable to his own taste.

A sculpture is a wonderful object to bring into the home. It can use up surplus or blank space very effectively, but again, as with hanging objects on the wall, the sculpture must be carefully placed and lighted to get the most benefit from its shapes and textures. Backgrounds for sculptures are equally important, for some must have clear, clean, contrasting backgrounds, while others are more effective against textured walls. Some should be placed in the center of the room to utilize the space surrounding the piece. No sculpture should merely be placed in an empty space in the room; instead, an attempt should be made to integrate it into the room. The sculpture should be related to its environment of colors, texture, and patterns, so that it may enhance the whole room. A sculptural piece that is set in front of a heavily patterned wall or drapery will lose its identity; neutral backgrounds will usually be more successful.

With all good work—painting, prints, or sculpture—the artistic expression is an important element of the piece. It expresses the artist's visual experience of the world around him or a particular experience that he has lived through. A successful work of art should speak to virtually any spectator and not be directed only toward a few elite people who surround the artist. Its content should be organized and orderly in presentation, and its color or lack of color should be integrated into the message it conveys. Furthermore, and very important, a work of art should be the result of a sincere artist's attempts to ex-

View of a European sculpture exhibition at the Bertha Schaefer Gallery in New York. There are many similar galleries in New York and other parts of the United States. (Photo by Budd: courtesy of Bertha Schaefer Gallery, New York.)

press himself. In the contemporary art world many fakes have managed to make themselves appear to be important as artists. These imitation artists will soon disappear from the scene, and it is highly unlikely that their work will be considered of lasting quality or value.

Good pieces of art are available at many places throughout the United States, and the location of the prospective purchaser will determine where he will buy his art objects. There are many excellent galleries in major cities and if the buyer is fortunate enough to be located near a city, he can visit these galleries. Although some galleries may seem to scare away the average viewer by an atmosphere of snobbishness, the gallery owner is really very pleased to have visitors at any time. Sometimes galleries are free, and sometimes a charge is made, especially to view benefit exhibitions. By looking in a local newspaper, one can determine which gallery will ask a small admission fee. To list all the recognized galleries would be impossible, but to give the reader an idea of several good galleries, the following list is presented:

Bertha Schaefer Gallery
32 East 57th Street
New York, New York

Martha Jackson Gallery
32 East 69th Street
New York, New York

Betty Parsons Gallery
24 West 57th Street
New York, New York

Pierre Matisse Gallery
41 East 57th Street
New York, New York

The Encounter Gallery, Inc.
2100 Classen Blvd.
Oklahoma City, Oklahoma

The Little Gallery
Birmingham, Michigan

Maxwell Galleries, Ltd.
551 Sutter Street
San Francisco, California

Ferdinand Roten Galleries
123 W. Mulberry Street
Baltimore, Maryland

Ankrum Gallery
910 North La Cienega Blvd.
Los Angeles, California

Esther Robles Gallery
665 North La Cienega Blvd.
Los Angeles, California

Many small new shops, as well as galleries, featuring the work of various fine artists from foreign nations, have been opening around the country. A shop of this type is Bonniers in New York City, which sells the work of Scandinavian artists. There are also Finnish, Italian, Mexican, Dutch, Polynesian, Danish, and many small Japanese stores that sell art objects to the consumer. And department stores in major cities and even in smaller towns often carry good art originals or reproductions. Some of these, such as Sears, Roebuck, continue to develop their fine arts departments so that eventually consumers in the most remote parts of the nation will be able to purchase art objects.

Whether the homeowner or decorator uses an original painting, a print, or a reproduction as a form of enrichment in the home is not important. What is important is that the painting play an integrated part in the design of the room and illustrate the individuality of the people who dwell there. It need not be expensive, but it does need to satisfy the feelings of the family and to be a meaningful addition to their aesthetic experience.

BIBLIOGRAPHY AND SUGGESTED READINGS

Boeck, Wilhelm and Jaime Sabartis, *Picasso*, Harry N. Abrams, New York, 1955.

Canaday, John, *Mainstreams of Modern Art*, Holt, Rinehart and Winston, New York, 1959.

Department of Art, *Looking At Modern Painting*, University of California, Los Angeles, 1957.

Erben, Walter, *Joan Miro*, George Braziller, New York, 1959.

Gombrich, E. H., *The Story of Art*, Phaidon Publishers, Inc., New York, 1951.

Myers, Bernard S., *German Expressionists*, Frederick A. Praeger, Inc., New York, 1956.

Parade, September 30, 1962.

Rewald, John, *Post Impressionism—From Van Gogh to Gauguin*, Museum of Modern Art, New York, 1956.

Robb, David M., and J. J. Garrison, *Art in the Western World*, Harper and Row, New York, 1942 (revised).

Sachs, Paul J., *Modern Prints and Drawings*, Alfred A. Knopf, New York, 1954.

Seuphor, Michel, *Dictionary of Abstract Painters*, Tudor Publishing Co., New York, 1957.

Soby, James Thrall, *Arp*, Museum of Modern Art, New York, 1958.

Watson, William, *Sculpture of Japan*, Viking Press, New York, 1959.

PART THREE: COMMENTS

The designing of a home, as we have seen, is more than a matter of combining colors and patterns; it requires an understanding of architectural structure, consideration of furniture, fabric, and enrichment, and knowledge of many other major elements. Once the designer can see what is available in the fields of crafts and fine arts, fabrics and furniture and architectural materials, he can start to pull together a statement of beauty in which the family can live. It is not enough, however, to know just what crafts are and what paintings are; the well-informed interior specialist will also have knowledge about the background of these things. He will have an understanding of the manufacturers' approach to the home, as well as of the needs and wants of his consumer or client.

But the specialist should not be the only person with a good understanding of these elements of the home—the home owner himself should be aware of the basic problems that face him. He should be aware of some of the fundamental characteristics of furniture and fabrics so that, when he is doing his purchasing, he will have criteria by which to buy. His understanding of crafts and fine arts will also help him throughout the establishing of a home. His ability to recall and recognize various companies will, in the end, be of great benefit to him in discussing problems with a designer (if he is using a professional person), and certainly will be needed if he is embarking on the venture of design without professional advice.

In this part of the book, the reader has been shown the structure of two important furniture companies, which have set the trends for contemporary interiors during the last 15 years; he has had the opportunity to examine characteristics and developments in crafts and fine arts, which are an important factor in any home; he has also seen some of the basic elements of architectural design, such as materials, floor plans, and exterior designs of houses. With this information well in mind, he is ready for the next step—the attempt to organize all the available data and to put it to work in the total picture.

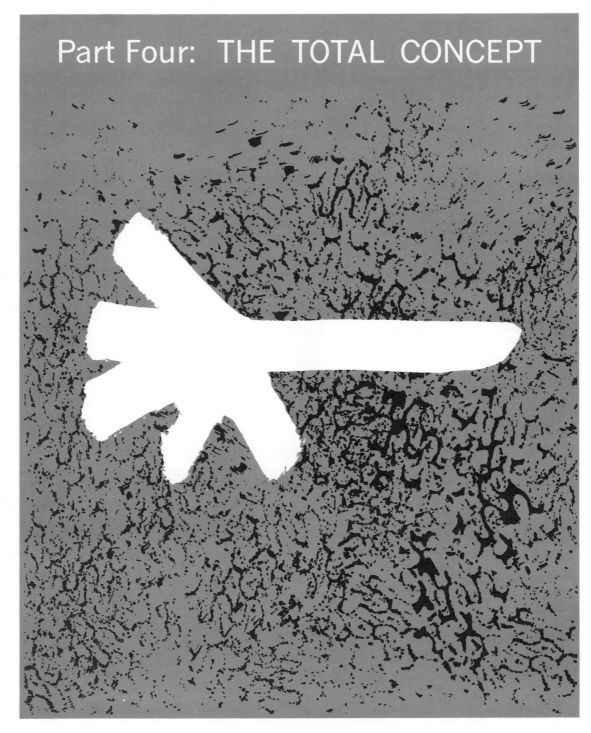

Part Four: THE TOTAL CONCEPT

An arrangement of conversational groups at the side of the room permits a good traffic lane to reach other parts of the house, by organization of space. Adequate surface areas are provided here for magazines, ash trays, and other objects. (Photo: courtesy of Knoll Associates, Inc.)

Storage facility designed by Charles Eames for dormitory room illustrates the compactness that is possible. Although this unit is designed for a dormitory, the homemaker can learn a great deal from Eames and his aesthetic approach to wall storage. (Photo: courtesy of Herman Miller Inc.)

Chapter **11** THEORY OF ORGANIZATION

The layman as well as the professional interior designer must carefully organize his thoughts and objectives before he attempts to redevelop an old interior or to start from the beginning in a new structure. Even such an expert group as the Knoll Associates' Planning Unit makes a thorough study of the complete project with which the association is involved before any furniture, accessory, or art work is placed in any room. For the new decorator or the layman, this practice is crucial. No good interior comes into being without thought. A careful plan must be evolved before an efficient and satisfactory living space or working area can be created. Every problem presents many different questions to be answered, and every individual reacts in his own special ways to the design of a space where he will live or work. Therefore, each family and each individual who will be involved must be carefully considered.

[One should remember that not all interiors are homes in which families will settle with their belongings. There are many institutions and public buildings that must be thoughtfully designed to make living for many persons more comfortable and aesthetically acceptable at all times. Sometimes we forget to consider as interiors those places away from home where many an individual spends a great deal of time. Although the mother and younger children in a family remain at home, the husband and older children live the larger part of their waking hours outside the home; wherever they are, their needs must be answered. The dentist's office, the schoolroom, or the busy secretary's corner can be improved and made workable with careful thought, organization, and the introduction of beauty. Studies have shown that the beautification of any area helps to produce more efficient work by employees and helps to establish a new image of their firm. Since business establishments and industries have become very concerned with their corporate images in the last few years, many have hired architects, designers, and artists to create new and better corporate images.]

There are many methods by which the designer or decorator can approach the problems facing him. Each person will have certain steps he will want to take to fulfill his plans; however, there are some basic steps and considerations that should always be followed. Although there may not be any required progression or chronological order for procedure, the following steps in the following order are suggested for the most satisfactory end result.

Evaluation

The first step to take toward the development of an interior is the complete evaluation of present pieces of furniture, other possessions, and available space. Activities of the family members should be included in this evaluation, for the individual interests of this complex unit will make the final differences in the planning of each interior.

What pieces of furniture are now available in the room or rooms that are being redesigned? Are there pieces that will be eliminated from the arrangement? Are there pieces that will be refinished? What architectural changes will be made, if any? After answering these questions with basic decisions, one will be able to determine what needs are manifest. The designer will have to know, for example, whether a library and music area are to be combined in one room or whether each activity—reading and music— will have a separate room. He will also need to know what other hobbies and activities are planned in the space under consideration. One must think about the needs and inclinations of each individual in the family in order to plan the kind and amount of space required and wanted by each one. If, for example, the people living in this house are extremely interested in the visual arts, it will be necessary to examine possible exhibition space, hanging areas, and lighting facilites for art objects.

The designer must make an inventory of personal and household objects, facilities, space needs, and comfort requirements. The completion of this close examination leads to the next step.

Needs

The logical step after the survey of current possessions is a listing of things to meet the needs and wishes of the residents who will occupy the space that is being designed or redesigned. As the evaluation took place, certain needs automatically became apparent. It is not always easy to separate the two steps; in fact, it is sometimes wise to conduct these two steps together. As the inventory is made, the needs can be listed as possible solutions to evident problems.

If seating is being eliminated by the removal of old furniture, it becomes obvious that new seating units will be needed. If daylight and a view would enhance the room, it becomes evident that an addition of more window area is desirable.

If there is only one room in which the family can congregate in the evening for various activities, it is indicated that storage space for hobby objects may be necessary, as well as library space for readers. Changing of traffic lanes and rearrangement of furniture are likely to be major needs.

Lighting, furniture, accessories, activities, traffic lanes, and architectural changes should all be listed. Each household has unique needs and puzzling problems to be solved.

EXAMPLE OF EVALUATION AND NEEDS STUDY:
Problem—change den to baby room

	EVALUATION	NEEDS	ESTIMATED COST
Walls	Blue flowered paper (soiled)	Painting (white)	$ 7.00
Woodwork	Grey	Painting (white)	1.00
Curtains	White Fiberglas	White cotton cafe (Sears, 2 pairs)	4.00
Window Canopy		Orange cotton (plain) (Grant's, 1 yard)	.69
Window Shade	Good condition	None	
Rug	None	Hand-hooked (orange and brown) Materials	6.00
Furniture	Remove all	Baby crib (from storage)	—
		White Eames rocker (from living room)	—
		George Nelson chest (tangerine and olive)	150.00
		Bathinette	20.00
Enrichment	Remove all	Japanese miniature kites (orange, red, pink etc.)	1.00
		Wall hanging (Materials)	.75
		Mobile (yarn pom poms) (orange)	.25
		Lion drawings (orange and brown)	gift
		Total estimated cost	$190.69

After these lists are completed, the designer is ready to embark on research.

Research

With a background of knowledge about current possessions and a list of things needed and desired, the designer is equipped to initiate a period of research and investigation. This is an important step; before any major changes involving large sums of money are made, specific means of attaining goals and aspirations must be clarified. Department stores and shops should be visited to study available furniture and current prices. One can never expect to find prices the same as they were a few years previously. Magazines and libraries should be consulted as to styles and types of furniture. Popular magazines are a good place to begin, but one must beware of trends that will be out of date within a few years or even months. Magazines and manufacturers seem to have a pact concerning the selling of furnishings, and the trends change rapidly. Therefore, the homeowner should look carefully and plan wisely, because furniture must last for some years, unless an unlimited budget is available.

Many popular magazines can contribute some ideas. *House and Garden* is an excellent magazine for young married couples wishing information on the new types of homes that are being built, the new furniture that is on the market, and the latest color trends that are being "pushed" for the current year. *Better Homes and Gardens* is a very good, down-to-earth magazine that gives plenty of ideas for converting old homes and old furniture into fresh new-looking items. One of the best magazines on the market for showing new furniture that is being manufactured is *Furniture Forum*. This magazine not only shows excellent photographs of furniture but offers detailed information as well. This may not be a magazine to which the average homeowner will want to subscribe, but it can be found in libraries. *Interiors*, a trade magazine, is not available on the newsstands, but it gives high-quality information on interior design. Other magazines that might be used in a thorough investigation include *Arts and Architecture, Craft Horizons, House Beautiful, Industrial Design, Interior Design, Progressive Architecture, Creative Crafts, American Home,* and *Design Quarterly.*

Each of these can answer different questions in one's research. From these sources, and from the many books that are available both in the textbook market and the trade market, many ideas should be gleaned.

During his investigation, the homeowner should decide on the character of his home and its rooms. Will there be a single style prevailing or different themes carried out in different rooms? One room might carry a theme of the sea, using the colors of the ocean and marine life, while another might employ accessories of a South American character. The pros and cons of the many different styles of furniture should be investigated as well as the materials to be incorporated into the furniture. The construction of pieces that may be added to the home should be carefully examined.

Articles of crafts and fine arts should also be investigated, for these will play an important role in the total appearance of the house. These are the small things that will echo the personality and individuality of the designer.

Financial Considerations

After the first three steps—inventory, requirements, and research—have been completed, the final process of financial considerations must be analyzed. Each family needs to develop an understanding of its housing budget and the most successful ways to carry out the desired project. Some people will be financially able to make their purchases and architectural changes immediately. Others will need to plan selectively, deciding which things they need first and for what pieces of furniture they can wait until their budget permits purchase. The prospective buyer should indicate on his list of needs the prices that he has ascertained during his period of research. Then the financial decisions, fitting plans into the family budget, can be made. (See Appendix for Costs and Budgets.)

General Considerations

In addition to the steps that have been discussed in organizing ideas for designing or redesigning an interior, there are other considerations of extreme importance. These will at times infringe on the steps already outlined, but fortunately they often will not require any financial consideration.

Traffic Lanes. The reorganization of traffic lanes throughout the house might not require the rebuilding of walls or doorways but only the moving of furniture to more suitable positions for family needs. In the final chapter this problem will be discussed more extensively in relation to each room, but at this point the focus is on the importance of traffic lanes and circulation paths in general. These roadways in the home should be planned so they will interfere with general activities as little as possible. They should be mapped carefully through the rooms used

Long wide corridors allow a good flow of traffic throughout the house. Halls should be lighted well and should be convenient to all rooms. (Photo: courtesy of Eichler Homes.)

for group activities and should end in logical places in individual rooms. They should be wide enough for adequate passage, especially if several people will be using the same lane at the same time. One should keep in mind that at various times of the day some circulation lanes are used more frequently than others. Halls are often too narrow; frequently they permit very little light to illuminate the stairs. When stairs are included in a traffic lane, as they are in two-story structures, adequate lighting should be carefully considered, as should proper floor surfaces. The floor surfaces are extremely important, and many people do not take into consideration the potential danger of the many small rugs they scatter around in the middle of traffic lanes. They are dangerous not only to elderly family members and to children but also to visitors who are unaware of their insecure nature.

Ventilation. The flow of air through the house is often a problem, and this should be given as much consideration

A corner furniture grouping helps to protect conversation from disruption. There should be plenty of space for legs, and there should be ample surface for objects. An arrangement of furniture like this is comfortable and relaxing. (Photo: Dux Inc.)

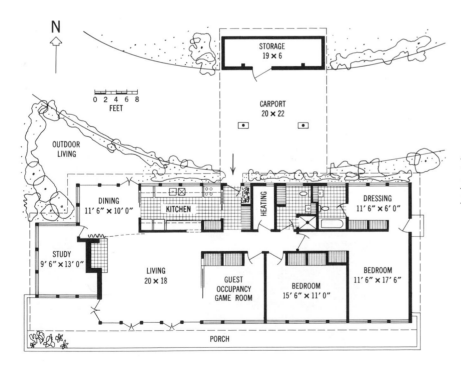

The traffic lanes in this house permit one to go from the entry into bedrooms, kitchen, and bath without going through the living room or other family rooms. The kitchen is situated near the front entrance, a convenience for the housewife.

Wall storage units can fit into many rooms in the home. Bedrooms, kitchens, living rooms, and hallways lend themselves to more efficient use with display and storage facilities. (Photo: courtesy of Eichler Homes.)

as the traffic lanes. Although two windows are not always necessary in each room, it does help to have windows that provide for cross-ventilation. In some areas, hallways and stairways permit adequate passage of air from one part of the house to another. In bedrooms where the door is usually closed at night, an adequate circulation of air is essential for healthy sleeping conditions. Of course, with the air conditioning of many contemporary homes, windows need not be opened, but in households where the budget does not allow for units of this nature, more concern should be given to the circulation of air from the doors and windows. Screens should be used where possible.

When a house is built, the architect and contractor should be sure to provide for adequate ventilation. There have been instances of well-known, highly esteemed architects who have failed to consider such basic points as screens and ventilation. If screens, windows, and doors are designed correctly in the initial planning, they become an integral part of the whole design and should not detract from the outside appearance of the building. Since proper ventilation is so important to good health, it should not be overlooked.

The kitchen is almost always lacking in sufficient storage space. Here is an all-electric kitchen that should please the housewife. (Photo: courtesy of Westinghouse.)

Storage. No house seems to have enough storage facilities. The complaint of housewives everywhere is the lack of storage space throughout their homes, whether these are newly built houses or older houses. Some houses built around the turn of the century have no closets whatsoever because wardrobe units were used for clothing storage. The lack of storage space in new houses is especially disheartening, for it would seem that people planning houses today would be sure to provide adequately for cupboards and closets. Linen closets are often badly placed in homes, necessitating extra walking for the housewife, and are also much too narrow to accommodate properly folded towels and sheets.

Kitchens are notoriously badly planned; there is seldom sufficient shelving and drawer space for kitchen equipment. In light of the knowledge available from home economists and architects, we should be able to design kitchens and storage units that serve all needs of the family well. Each room will be examined in greater detail in Chapter 14, and solutions will be proposed for storage problems. It should be remembered that no house need lack for storage space, because any house can be redesigned only slightly to accommodate more units.

The new types of wall storage units being manufactured by several furniture companies can solve many storage problems throughout the home. These storage units were first designed for commercial use, but their suitability for homes became so obvious that the furniture industry has since presented them in lovely teaks, burnished metals, and walnut wood. A few outstanding commercial names in this area are Herman Miller Comprehensive Storage System, Alma Furniture's teak units, Omni, Omnibus, and Kopenhaven. The use of wall units, although new in the United States, has long been standard in the Scandinavian countries.

The wall storage units are generally based on a modular system, so that various drawer units, shelf units, and desk units can be moved within groupings of poles or wall brackets. The great advantages of these systems are their versatility, the possibility of making additions as money is available, and their compact nature, which saves space in small rooms.

Lighting. In organizing plans for designing or redesigning a house, one must investigate the lighting. In new houses, bubble or dome ceiling units in kitchens, baths, and studies solve many of the problems in artificial lighting. But the natural light flowing into the house also needs to be considered. People very often close out the natural light with heavy draperies and window devices, only to add artificial lights that may be harsh and cold in character. The more natural light that is retained, the better will be the lighting effects throughout the house.

Of course, evening lighting is quite a different consideration and needs separate planning. There are those who want dramatic lighting and those who wish very plain lighting effects. In any event, each type of lighting should have careful planning.

Many lighting problems can be solved with indirect lighting, but people too often attempt to let indirect lighting also take care of the lighting problems that should be met by lamps and fixtures. Indirect lighting is good for general room illumination, but it is not good for close work, such as reading and sewing. A better, more direct light should be utilized for close work. While some individuals like direct light from hanging lamps, others prefer a soft light from a silk shade off to the side.

The color of lighting plays an important role in the general character of a room. The use of the incorrect color in a particular room can easily kill the décor that has been planned. White light keeps the colors as they really are, but at the same time does not add any character to the room. Cool light, such as blue, does what any cool color will do—gives more space to the room and at the same time adds a chilling effect. Warm light, such as yellow or pink, takes away from the cool effects of a room and dulls the cool colors.

Pure, raw colored lights should be avoided, unless they are being used for some special occasion. They take the individual characteristics from other colors and tend to be cheap in appearance.

Hallways and dark areas throughout the home should have special attention to lighting in order to eliminate unsafe areas. Movable table lamps and floor lamps are good to have because they can easily be transferred from place to place to solve different lighting problems at different times. Lamps with dual purposes are as important as furniture with several uses.

Location of light sources should also be considered. One should remember that a light source should never be at eye level, for it usually is distracting to have light pouring into one's eyes. When the light source is below the eye level, it helps to make the room more intimate and friendly. The higher the source of light, the more formal the room becomes. Small, direct lights introduce emphasis points, while large diffused light sources unify space.

The shape and size of a lamp base and fixture should be related to the lamp's function in illuminating the space where it is being used. One should keep lamp bases and especially shades simple and honest. A lamp shade in the form of an 18th-century ruffled gown is completely out of place in any room, and a lamp base designed to look like a telephone is also in bad taste. A lamp should look like a lamp or light fixture, not like some unrelated object.

Light switches and outlets should be planned carefully in the designing of a room. They should be convenient and easily reached. Mercury switches eliminate noise; one-button switches prevent floundering in the dark for the correct button to push and enable a person with loaded hands to put on the light with an elbow.

New developments are constantly being introduced in home lighting. Wall panel and ceiling lighting have now come into being, but in the next few years a whole new approach to room illumination will take place. Walls that will appear to be quiet white paneling will be able to be dimmed and brightened according to the function taking place in the room. These graduated light sources will make contributions of great importance to the home.

Furniture Arrangement. As one begins to look seriously at specific pieces of furniture, one should start thinking of how this furniture is going to be placed in the room where it will be used. One of the hardest problems faced by the layman is the question of what to do with a piece of furniture that is found to be too big for a room after it has been delivered to the house. One should not rely on one's feeling for size—this is generally fairly disastrous; few people can simply look at a space and know what size sofa will fit into it. One should use plenty of measurements to insure accuracy. One should write down wall and space measurements and take them along when one is shopping. Even if one is only buying a new chest for that small bedroom in the back of the house, one should be sure to refer to measurements lest the chest end up utilizing all the floor space.

When one looks at a new piece of furniture, one should take its measurements and then return home to ascertain how it would work out in the space planned for it. Possibly it will be necessary to rearrange the pieces already in the room or to remove a piece to another part of the house. This may be an occasion to wish for more dual-purpose furniture.

For really good planning, a floor plan indicating the placement of all the furniture should be drawn. Although this might seem tedious to the homeowner, it will save him from mistakes, headaches, and heartaches.

A floor plan can be drawn by marking off a large piece of paper in one-inch grids (see figure, p. 187). Each square inch will represent one square foot of the floor space. Measurements should be made carefully, for a slight mistake might mean that one entire piece of furniture would not fit. One should draw in the windows, doors, and other protuberances that would affect the placement of furniture. The location of electrical outlets should be indicated, for certain pieces of furniture will need to be placed near them. Using black paper, one should cut out furniture shapes (templates) using the correct dimensions for each piece of furniture. When enough templates have been pre-

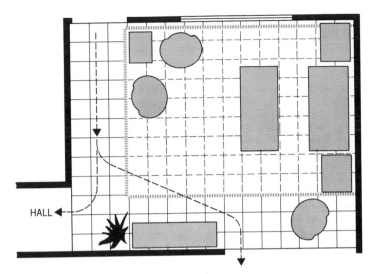

HALL ◄──

pared, they can be placed where the furniture is visualized. Arranging furniture in this way is easier and more enjoyable than carrying it around, and guaranteed not to cause backache or muscle strain.

It is important to watch for windows and doors, and to leave adequate space for ventilation, traffic lanes, and storage facilities in the room.

Sound. The home in which sounds easily penetrate from room to room is chaotic. This problem cannot be solved when the home is in an apartment building where the tenants cannot do their own soundproofing. Anyone who is thinking of renting an apartment should investigate this point. Draperies and thick carpeting can reduce noise a great deal within a room, but if partitions are badly constructed, as they are in many apartment buildings, sounds from other units will invade one's privacy and create unpleasant living conditions.

In the privately owned house, acoustical tile ceilings help to reduce noise, as do other soft materials, bookcases filled with books, and upholstered furniture.

Kitchens and baths are large producers of noise; these rooms especially should be adequately soundproofed, if possible. Walls utilizing air-void construction are the best barriers against sound. This type of construc-

tion was used in the barracks of the Thule, Greenland, Air Force Base as insulation against the cold and proved also to be excellent as a noise barrier.

Presenting the Plan

The presentation of an over-all plan for the room or rooms that are being designed might be a designer's important selling point to a client; and even if you are your own client, it is a good idea to organize the material that you have gathered into some visual order for your own benefit. The user or buyer of the room can more easily visualize what the end results will be if he can see a well-prepared plan. A professional layout is not always needed; even with a simple presentation, certain ideas can be formed as the result of seeing the various aspects of the design assembled in one spot. There are many kinds of presentations. Knoll Associates will render a very professional group of floor plans, elevations, and perspective drawings when presenting a client with a group of rooms, but the homeowner need not become involved in so complex a project. In any case, the plan that one puts together oneself will be helpful in many ways.

Color and Fabric Scheme. A simple color and fabric scheme can be put together very quickly after the investigation to discover what is available to meet certain basic needs of the family. To a simple piece of card board (or ordinary typing paper), one can paste or attach the pieces of fabric under consideration, and color chips can indicate colors that may be used. The colors and textures should be shown in proportion to the amounts to be used in the actual room. The wall color must be the largest color on the plan, while the smallest color swatches represent the tiny accessories to be in the room.

Fabric swatches can be collected on trips to stores and put next to others already gathered. Color chips are available wherever paints are sold. The small-size plan can be taken on a shopping trip and used in the stores in a study of fabrics under consideration. The fabrics as seen in stores, however, will take on different appear-

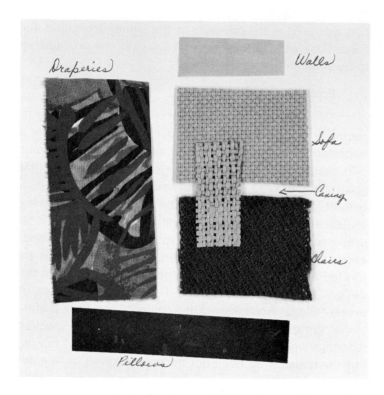

Draperies

Walls

Sofa

← Caning

Chairs

Pillows

A simple color and fabric scheme with paper chips and fabric swatches can begin to organize colors and ideas for a room.

ances under the light in one's own room. It is, therefore, necessary to study the fabric and color in its possible future setting before purchasing it in large quantities. Several small plans might be made up before any major purchases are made, to provide a range of choices for one's room. The small plan is not wholly reliable, especially as to the paint color for the walls: a small chip of paint tells only a small story about the large wall. Instead of depending on the color of a paint chip, one should buy a small can of the paint that is most favored and paint a portion of the wall behind the sofa, door, or draperies. After it dries, one will be able better to estimate its effect on and in the room.

Color, Fabric, and Furniture Scheme. In a plan that is basically the same as the first one, the color, fabric, and furniture scheme permits one to add pictures of furniture cut out from magazines and other sources. With the addition of furniture, the scheme becomes more complex but offers a more complete picture of the room and its different problems. If the scheme is for oneself, it need not be elegantly arranged and pasted, but if it is to be shown to a customer, the nicer and neater it looks, the more impressed the client will be. Also the client will see that one is well-organized and efficient in one's work. See the charts for examples of both types of scheme.

Floor Plan, Elevations and Perspective Schemes

A more complex presentation involves rendering rooms and drawings in either elevation or perspective—or both. Surprisingly enough, however, most people, with a little patience, can do both elevations and perspective drawings with at least some success. The advantage in this type of layout is that the client is able, at once, to visualize the total room and its future look.

Floor Plan. The presentation of all schemes should really include a floor plan. With a floor plan, the designer or homemaker is better able to show the projected arrangement of furniture. The plan should include doors, windows, fireplace, built-in furniture, and any other features affecting the arrangement of furniture. Simple heating units along the baseboards, for example, make a big difference in the placement of some pieces of furniture. Any object or part of the room structure that extends over the floor should be included in the drawings. The electrical outlets might very well be included also, for they determine the placement of lamps and other electrical devices.

Of course, the homeowner who is simply interested in having a floor plan to aid in the final arrangement of furniture need not make a complex one; lines designating the walls, doors, and windows may be enough. But the more advanced designer of floor plans will want to include the thickness of walls as well as all other parts of the structure

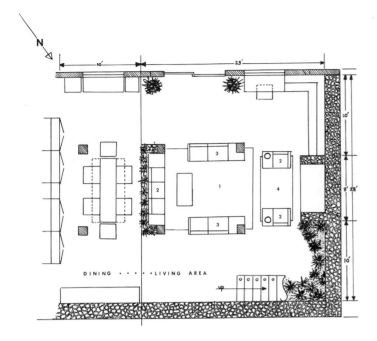

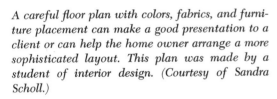

A careful floor plan with colors, fabrics, and furniture placement can make a good presentation to a client or can help the home owner arrange a more sophisticated layout. This plan was made by a student of interior design. (Courtesy of Sandra Scholl.)

that determine various placements of furniture, both built-in and free-standing. Chapter 7 shows an architect's floor plan and simplified drawings made from the architect's plans.

Elevations. To make an elevation drawing, one must first have finished the floor plan, with furniture placed as it will be when the room is completed in the actual situation. Now the elevation can be done in the following steps:

1. Above the floor plan and preferably on the same paper, draw (in scale) the wall to be elevated, first putting down the base line and then the ceiling height. Draw in their proper places such openings as windows and doors, that might show in this wall elevation.

2. The furniture to be projected on the wall elevation is measured for heights.

3. The heights are marked on the wall where the furniture will be seen.

4. The widths and lengths of the pieces are projected on the wall by lines from the floor plan to the wall elevation.

5. The heights and widths should be drawn in lightly until their accuracy is determined. Then they can be lined in with ink or darkened for later painting guides. The overall shapes of the furniture are now obvious.

6. Drawers, doors, knobs, and other parts of the furniture are drawn last, along with accessories such as plants and lamps.

7. After all parts of the drawing are on the layout, color can be added with pencil, water color, or by some other method.

Perspective. The perspective view of the room is more difficult to draw, but not insurmountably so for the be-

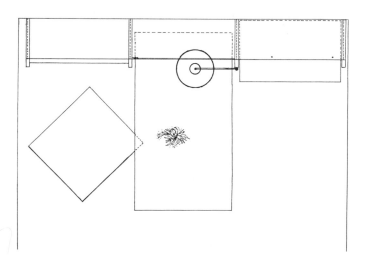

ginner. This differs from the elevation in its demonstration of depth in three dimensions. The wall elevation merely shows a head-on view of one wall without depth or three-dimensional characteristics, unless the drawing is cleverly rendered, probably by a professional, with shadows and optical-illusion tricks. Both perspective and elevation drawings have their purposes: the perspective drawing gives a realistic picture of a large portion of the room; the elevation drawing is presented for heights and wall positions of pieces of furniture. Here are directions for drawing a perspective view of a room.

1. The first step is completion of a floor plan, drawn to scale.

2. Mark the walls you wish to project into perspective view as Wall 1, Wall 2, and Wall 3, in order to avoid confusion.

3. Indicate on the floor plan the point from which you will be looking at the three walls. This point, measured from Wall 2 at a distance that should be about equal to the width of Wall 2, is called the *Station Point* (SP). It should not be placed exactly in the middle, but off-center to left or right for a more interesting view of the room.

4. Draw Wall 2 in scale (either one inch or a half inch to the foot is best). The size of the scale is determined to some extent by the size of the board or paper you are using. Generally a room is eight to nine feet high. Indicate a one-foot grid on the wall. This becomes the *True Height Wall* (THW).

5. Five feet above the base line of the THW mark a *Horizon Line* (HL). This is the level from which you will view all objects and furniture in the room. You can place the line lower, so that you can see the tops of things better, but do not place it higher, lest you obtain a strange view of the room.

A simple elevation of a Herman Miller storage wall. (Courtesy of James Watts.)

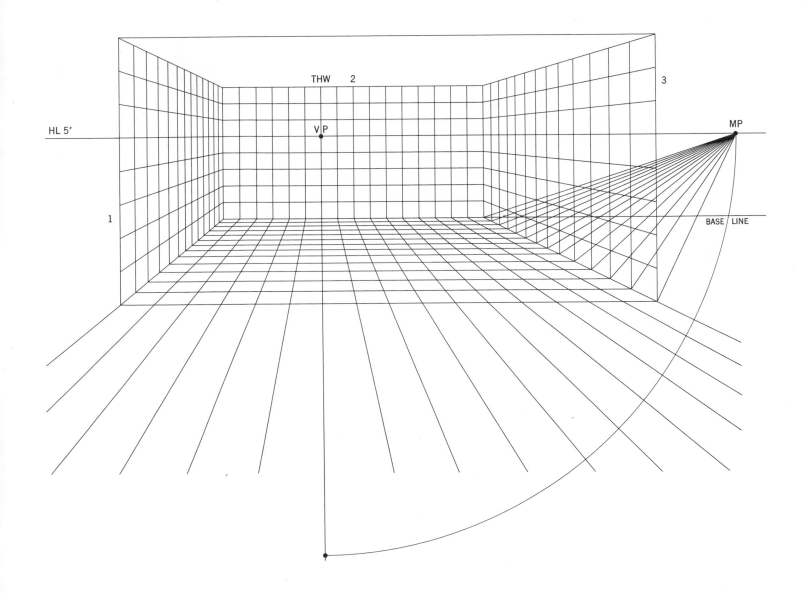

One-point perspective grid.

6. Place a mark or dot on the HL at the same distance from Wall 1 as the SP. This is your *Vanishing Point* (VP). All lines of Wall 1, Wall 3, and the furniture will meet here and vanish.

7. By placing one end of your ruler at one corner of the THW and the other end on the VP, and then doing the same with the other THW corners, you will have your lines for the ceiling and floor for Wall 1 and Wall 3.

8. Now extend the base line of THW out to the right and mark it in one-foot intervals.

9. The distance from the SP to Wall 2 is now marked on the Horizon Line. This becomes the *Measuring Point* (MP) from which you will draw all horizontal lines falling in the center of the room, making up the grids.

10. By placing the ruler on the base-line extension of the THW and the MP, you can place dots along the base line of Wall 3.

11. Draw horizontal lines across the space of the room over to the base line of Wall 1 and draw vertical lines on Wall 1 and Wall 3 from these same points. The walls now will be marked off in one-foot measurements.

12. By placing the ruler on the VP and at the bottom of each foot line on the THW and drawing a line, you will have a complete grid marked off in one-foot squares. Within the three walls, you should now have a grid system that appears larger in the foreground and diminishes in size as it goes back toward the THW. Within this space you can place the furnishings, according to the scale you have used for the THW.

Furnishing the Perspective Room Drawing. Now you must revert to the floor plan that you have been using as the guide for this room. Each piece of furniture drawn in the floor plan within the area of the SP and Wall 2 will be projected into the perspective drawing. You can draw directly on the grid system you have established, or you can place a piece of tracing paper over the grid. Use of tracing paper will allow you to keep the grid in good condition for use again. In fact, several rooms might be projected by use of modified versions of this grid.

ELEVATION 1

A FOLDING DIVIDER RE-VEALS THE BEDROOM, WHICH IS AN INTEGRAL PART OF THE LIVING AREA WHEN THE HIDE-AWAY BED BE-COMES A SEATING UNIT. THE DESK-STORAGE UNIT PROVIDES SPACE FOR BOOKS AND ALMOST ANY OTHER SMALL ITEMS.

ELEVATION 2

BURLAP-WEAVE PANELS ON THE DOOR ADD INTEREST TO THE ENTRANCE AREA.

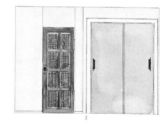

ELEVATION 3

THE DINING AREA MAKES USE OF A VERSATILE OVAL TABLE THAT TAKES LITTLE SPACE. WHEN NEEDED FOR GUEST DINING LEAVES EXPAND IT TO AMPLE SIZE. FLEXIBLE SEATING UNITS LIKE THOSE BELOW CAN BE REARRANGED LATER TO FIT CHANGED SPACE REQUIREMENTS.

A room design based on the one-point perspective grid, with elevations and color chip samples, makes a complete and professional presentation. (Courtesy of Sandra Scholl.)

APARTMENT LIVING

SPACE IS AT A PREMIUM IN MOST APARTMENTS. THEREFORE, FURNITURE GROUPINGS MUST BE PLANNED WISELY TO SAVE SPACE AND SEPARATE ACTIVITIES.

THE UPPER AND LOWER UNITS ABOVE PROVIDE STORAGE AND ALSO ACT AS A DIVIDER BETWEEN THE LIVING AND DINING AREAS.

HI-FI EQUIPMENT IS HOUSED IN WALNUT CABINETS, BUTTED TOGETHER FOR A BUILT-IN LOOK, AND THE SEATING GROUP IS COMFORTABLY ARRANGED FOR CONVERSATION.

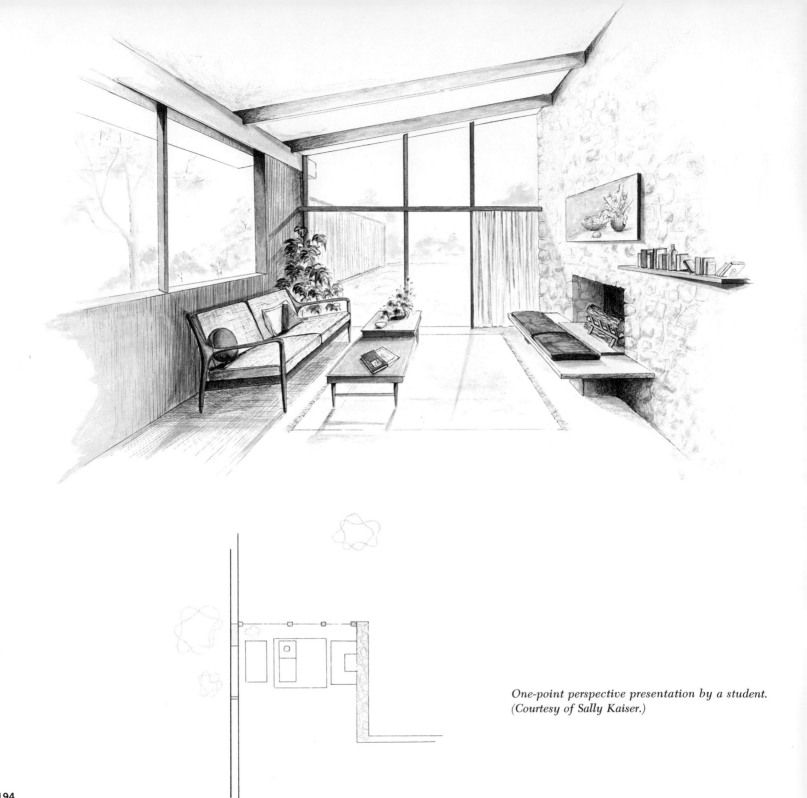

One-point perspective presentation by a student.
(Courtesy of Sally Kaiser.)

In projecting furniture into this room, you use the foot grid marks from all the walls and the floor. These are your measuring devices for obtaining the correct sizes of the furniture. The outline of each piece is drawn on the floor of the grid system according to its place and its floor-plan size. If you use tracing paper, you draw on it only the base and ceiling lines of the room. After you draw the base of each piece of furniture, you should project vertical lines up to represent the corners of the pieces of furniture; thus you indicate the corners *and* sides of the furniture. The height of furniture is shown by measuring the height on the side wall closest to the piece of furniture and projecting a horizontal line back to where the furniture is to be placed in the room perspective. At the place where this horizontal line falls between two vertical corner lines, the edge and top of the piece of furniture are delineated. The basic shape of the pieces should now be indicated. Legs, drawers, and other small hardware and accessories can be added. Most of your pieces of furniture will appear as boxes placed in the room, but as you break down the box shapes, the form of the furniture will be suggested. The legs should be included *in* the box—not added to the bottom. You should remember to include thicknesses of sofa backs and chair backs, or the furniture will have a very distorted appearance. One should always check the drawing before the lines are darkened with ink or heavy pencil. Probably the first attempt will be rather disappointing, but with each new try your drawing will become more accurate. Rounded edges are often difficult to put into the drawing, but with practice they can be made to look very nice. This is achieved by softening the corners in a freehand manner.

After the furniture is drawn, it can be painted. Always remember to work with the larger areas first.

BIBLIOGRAPHY AND SUGGESTED READINGS

Ball, Victoria, *The Art of Interior Design*, the Macmillan Co., New York, 1960.

Faulkner, Ray and Sarah, *Inside Today's Home*, Holt, Rinehart, and Winston, Inc., New York, 1960.

Kaufman, Edgar, *What Is Modern Interior Design?*, Museum of Modern Art, New York, 1953.

Obst, Frances, *Art and Design in Home Living*, the Macmillan Co., New York, 1963.

Pepis, Betty, *Guide to Interior Decoration*, Reinhold, New York, 1957.

Rogers, Kate, *The Modern House, U.S.A.*, Harper and Row, New York, 1962.

Schroeder, Francis de N., *Anatomy for Interior Designers*, 2nd ed., Whitney, New York, 1948.

Whiton, Sherrill, *Elements of Interior Design and Decoration*, J. B. Lippincott Co., Philadelphia, 1963 ed.

Wright, Russel and Mary, *Guide to Easier Living*, Simon and Schuster, New York, 1951.

Creatively placed furniture, objects, and plants fill Charles Eames's home with color and interest. Notice the ladder on the left hand side of the picture. (Photo: courtesy of Herman Miller Inc.)

An inexpensively furnished living area for a young couple shows the imaginative use of craftwork and objects found along the coast. (Photo: Thayer and Skinner.)

Chapter **12** CREATIVE INTERIORS

All the beautiful art objects, crafts, furniture, and architecture that we have discussed cannot make an interesting home by themselves. It takes more than money to create an integrated interior. And even if all the books on interior design and decorating were carefully studied, the application of the knowledge therein could still be chaotic and disorganized. The rules and guides can help the student and the homeowner, but the most important part of the interior is the part that is put into the project by the individual.

When we get right down to reality in evaluating interiors, we find that the room or house with the personal touch is the most inviting and exciting. The individual ideas developed by the homeowner bring color and life into an empty space. These need not be expensive, luxurious, or ostentatious but can be simple additions to a home that make the interior a fascinating place.

NATURAL ARRANGEMENTS

A short cut to bringing beauty into the home is the use of natural objects. Flowers, weeds, rocks, and shells can give texture, color, and pattern to a room and still be amazingly cheap; in fact, often these things make little call for any expenditure of family funds. Although there are many traditional styles of arranging natural materials, the casual and almost effortless placement of objects from nature can add needed enrichment and the creative touch to a room.

Plants and Weeds

Tall weeds and large green plants help fill space very easily, while extra furniture for the same area might be rather expensive and thus prohibitive for a young married couple or anyone else on a limited budget. A large stair landing or a corner in the living room can be excellent spots in which to place this type of arrangement. Little is needed except a pot with earth for a plant or a container for dried weeds; the latter can be inserted into the openings of cinder blocks and into other novel containers that cost practically nothing but inventiveness.

For subtle arrangements, dried weeds can be painted the color of the walls; this should be done with care, for painted weeds often look cheap. Painted or unpainted weeds can be very effective with lights that cast their shadows on a white or neutral-colored wall. Special lights, however, are not necessary, for if weeds are placed properly, the natural light will play soft and warm shadows on the wall. Lighted arrangements are very often hard and harsh.

Weeds do not have to be large and spectacular to be interesting in the home; small weeds can produce beautiful effects. Dried pods, fir cones, and other delicate weeds can be placed on coffee tables, tea wagons, and dinner tables in attractive natural arrangements.

Dried Plants. Here is a list of dried plants that can be used; these can be found without difficulty in different parts of the country. Of course, this is only a small list.

tall grass	cactus	seaweed
burrs	dried daisies	sea oats
wheat	smoke weed	milkweed
cattails	palm	tumbleweed
Japanese lanterns	love apples	pine cones
Indian corn	sunflower heads	

Rocks and Shells

Rocks and shells comprise another group of natural objects that can contribute interesting shape, color, and pattern to a room. A simple textured rock can have much more beauty than many an expensive object found in the home. Corners that seem dead are good places in which to pile rocks, perhaps with the addition of shells and other sea objects that have been collected on a summer trip. These could be placed in the bathroom or in an entrance hall; indeed, there are few spaces in the house where they could not be used.

Containers need not be used for rocks and shells. These objects can usually be placed directly on the surface of a piece of furniture or on the floor without damaging the grain or finish. Of course, it might be better to place some rocks on a small mat or piece of slate before setting them on the best piece of furniture in the room; discretion should be used. When some protection is desired, arrangement boards can be used; these are flat, sanded, and simply finished boards on which dried plants, shells, or rocks can be readily placed for display.

Creative Arrangement Material

It is not necessary to limit oneself to rocks and weeds in this type of arrangement; here the imagination can really take over. Rocks can be combined with a broken glass vase, or dried beans can be placed on a black tray for an arrangement. There are few things that cannot be included for enrichment with your prized possessions. Here is an interesting list of unusual materials that have been used for arrangements.

CONTAINER	MAJOR ITEM	ACCENT
Black lacquer tray	White navy beans	Orange glass ball
Black slate slab	White shells	Red glass chunk
Teak tray	Yellow jelly beans	Embroidered bird (yellow and red)
Round glass tray	Black polished stones	Orange shell
Delicate vase	Wispy weed and spider web	
Floor	Rocks and shells found in Maine	Lobster buoy
Floor	Fishing net and rocks	Pink puppet
Ceiling	Branches painted pink (hanging from ceiling)	Red and yellow paper balloon
Terra-cotta pot	Queen Anne's lace (dried)	
Crystal bowl	White eggs	Black coal
Table (white formica)	White shells	
Table (white formica)	Black rocks	Yellow salt shaker
Arranging board	Yellow broken glass	Dried lentils

Traditional Floral Arrangements

The kinds of arrangements just discussed are subject to no specific rules; they are completely free and unlimited as to manner of presentation in the home. Other arrangements are more formalized; these are the arrangements that we see in floral exhibitions and in restored eighteenth-century houses. Traditional arrangements are more restricting in character. They are categorized as triangular, oval, Hogarth S-curve, circular, and crescent.

General Problems of Arranging Dried and Fresh Flowers

Regardless of the type of arrangement that is to be used in a room, certain elements should be considered. One important factor is the background of the arrangement. This is an influence on the arrangement itself. The wall colors, textures, and patterns that will surround the arrangement should be considered as part of the design. One should study the various properties of the immediate environment before work on the actual arrangement is begun. A bold printed fabric behind a delicate arrangement of weeds or flowers will absolutely kill the arrangement. The furniture also will be part of the design.

The container is also of the utmost importance to the composition in objects of nature. The container should suit the kind of flowers or weeds that will be put into it. A delicate glass container would be completely out of character with cattails, while a heavy pottery container would probably be out of place used with delicate cymbidium orchids. One should carefully study the container in relation to the surrounding environment so that each will complement the other.

The same guides to design, found in the first chapter, apply to the designing of a floral arrangement. Color, texture, line, shape, and proportion should be watched as the arrangement is built. The leaves and their shapes, the blossoms and their size, color, and weight, dictate various solutions to the problems of arrangement.

The total effect should be one of color and warmth in any type of room, whether contemporary or traditional. Flowers and plants bring freshness and life into a room that might otherwise be deadly and dull. Any plant or flower will give some personality and character to a room. The more creatively the design is put together, the more fascinating its contribution will be to the room.

Space Arrangements

Most colorful and gay of room decorations are things that hang from the ceiling. Unfortunately, being earthbound people, we seem to be chiefly aware of space that is closely related to the ground below us. The ceiling, however, offers a whole field for new decorating ideas and creative experimentation. There is no need to keep attention at a low level in the house. Bringing the eye of the visitor up to the ceiling is rewarding and stimulating. With a single string, thread, or common pin, one can hang all kinds of objects from the ceiling to ornament a room. Small delicate branches, fabric hangings, or Japanese kites and mobiles, which can be purchased for a few dollars or cents, can add tremendous personality to a room. Charles Eames in his house in Santa Monica, California, hangs paintings parallel to the ceiling so that the spectator must look up in order to see them properly. This gives a unique character to an interior space that we usually neglect. The whole ceiling is free for experimentation.

Dime-Store Design

A successful, creative interior need not be full of expensive objects and furniture, although many people are under the impression that the more money one expends, the better the interior will be. This point of view seems especially prevalent among many of the house beautification magazines that appear monthly on the news stands. Actually, the creative household will have many places for inexpensive items, and one of the best places to purchase

A simple glass tumbler costing only nineteen cents has more good design qualities than have many expensive pieces of glassware. (Photo: courtesy of Owens-Illinois Glass Co.)

Ceilings of a room offer an opportunity to hang Japanese paper mobiles. Rocks can go in any room of the house and on all surfaces. Here rocks have been placed both on the chest and the floor. (Photo: Thayer and Skinner.)

such objects is the local dime store or variety store. Here, under apparent chaos, is a treasury of beautiful things to enrich the décor of any of today's homes without marring the aesthetic standards established by the best architect or interior designer.

Probably the greatest obstacle to variety-store shopping is the very abundance and confusion facing the consumer. However, a prospective purchaser must be able mentally to erase the surroundings from a piece that he is considering. Once an object is isolated from the array of color and pattern around it, one can examine it objectively,

Objects found in a "dime store" can make interesting contributions to the home. (Photo: Ed Leos.)

Colorful pillows found in a variety store add accents and emphasis to a dull room. (Photo: Ed Leos.)

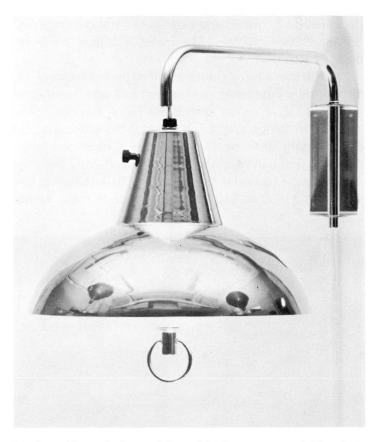

Simply and honestly designed, lamps like this one are available at little cost. Price of this lamp is approximately five dollars. (Photo: courtesy of Wolfe Creations.)

without distraction and prejudice.

Three basic criteria to use in reaching a decision to buy an article are the following:

1. The piece must be well constructed. Craftsmanship should be a primary consideration.

2. The piece must be simple and uncluttered. In general, the less profuse the ornamentation, the better the design. Forms and shapes should not be distorted. Textures added without meaning detract from the beauty of the piece.

3. The materials should be used honestly. This is probably the most important factor. Metals should not masquerade as wood, and clay should not be made into donkey-shaped planters. The material should be recognized as itself.

With these three guides in mind, the homeowner can select many interesting objects that will add beauty and creative touches to the design of a room. Besides selling such small things as glasses, vases, mixing spoons, and dishes, many dime stores sell furniture, rugs, and lamps at prices that can help any limited budget. Very beautiful lamps can be found for as little as $5.00. Jute rugs priced as low as $5.00 to $10.00 are available in many variety stores.

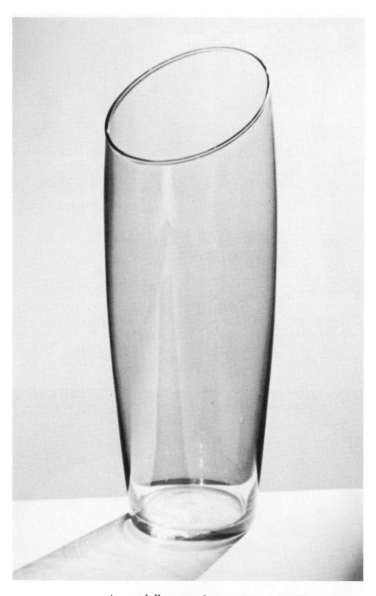

A one-dollar vase from a "dime store" can be just as beautiful as a piece of imported glass. The way one uses it and places it will determine its contribution to the interior. (Photo: Ed Leos.)

Standard candy jars add color to the kitchen or the living room if one places interesting things inside them. (Photo: Ed Leos.)

White plastic dishes, beautifully designed, can be used instead of expensive china and still bring elegance to the dining table.

In fact, with a little footwork and energy, the industrious shopper could probably furnish a whole room with objects from the dime store. A creative room can have in it objects of any price. The cost is not the final criterion, but rather the design together with the placement of the object.

Fabrics

Just as there are possibilities for enrichment with weeds and ornamentation with dime-store objects, so also low-cost fabrics offer a great many possibilities that few people employ. It is not necessary always to utilize fabrics and textiles in the same way or to pay high prices for them. There are available on the market many interesting fabrics that are inexpensive and can add the needed color and spark to the room. Decorative burlap is one of these fabrics. Although not a very durable textile, it is available in a huge range of colors. It fades easily, washes badly, and stretches out of shape quickly, but still there are many uses for such a material in even the most elegant home. Panels of burlap can be hung at the end of a dull hall, used to make draperies, or even used to back the rear of a metal bookcase that is being used as a room divider. Burlap with stitchery can add interest and pattern to a room, but the user of burlap must realize that it will probably deteriorate soon if it is exposed to the sun or if it is washed in the washing machine.

In addition to burlap, many inexpensive cottons from the dime store make beautiful decorative pillows, kitchen curtains, and even living room draperies. The great advantage of these cottons is that they are easily stored and easily replaced, without the loss of a large investment, if the family moves from one community to another. The cotton curtains that are put away after perhaps only one year

Either expensive or inexpensive fabrics can be used to conceal unwanted architectural elements. A back window hides behind this piece of Jack Larsen fabric. Notice the arrangement of shells on black slate on the table. (Photo: Thayer and Skinner.)

of use can very easily be adapted to another room in another house or apartment at a later date. This sort of arrangement is especially useful to the mobile family, which needs well-designed, inexpensive materials to satisfy the needs of many different situations. Families in the armed services have a particular need for inexpensive goods that can be used in many different situations in many different countries. Anyone can use low-cost fabrics for colorful, seasonal, decorative pillow cases, which can be changed often without big expense and add constantly changing room schemes to the household.

One should not limit oneself to strictly drapery or curtain materials for the hangings on the walls and at the windows; fabrics like fishnetting and dyed cheesecloth can be used for some problematic situations with success. Fishnetting can be used in room dividers, as casement draperies, or in seascape wall arrangements; cheesecloth can be used as a temporary solution to a large-window problem while one waits for the budget to accommodate more luxurious draperies.

Any kind of fabric panel can be hung in rooms to add color or to hide undesirable elements. The panels may range from very expensive Jack Larsen fabrics down to inexpensive denim, as long as they solve a problem and still add an aesthetic touch to the room. A plain unneeded window facing on a back porch might easily be hidden by a beautiful, patterned fabric. The same type of panel can hide unused doorways, radiators, open cupboards, and other unattractive elements.

Displaying Crafts and Fine Arts

Nothing brings more interest into a room than a fascinating display of craft work or an unusual arrangement of paintings. These decorations can be provided in ways that demand little financial means; or, if desired, very elaborate systems can be devised at high cost. An unused corner can become a complex network of cinder blocks or bricks topped with pottery and sculpture; a border of white marble chips around the carpet can become a

place on which to set such beautiful objects as paintings and ceramics; and the top of a radiator can be used for the displaying of various craft items. The character of the family dictates to some extent the way in which craft and art objects are displayed; however, even in a family with children, it should be possible to exhibit these items of beauty without much danger of their being damaged. However, it is undoubtedly easier to display objects of art more freely when small children are not a part of the household.

Like fabric panels, paintings can be used to hide undesirable things in a room or to bring more seeming wall space to a room. A window that is not needed can be covered by a painting, and the impression is given, inside,

Notice how Charles Eames hangs a painting from the ceiling—an imaginative way to display fine art. (Photo: courtesy of Herman Miller Inc.)

that the wall is larger than it really is. The importance of presenting a nice appearance on the outside of such a window, by pulling blinds or shade or by other means, should be remembered.

When exhibiting any type of art objects, one must consider whether the family wants a museum effect or not. When a family has a large collection of such things, the living room can become "museumy." Sometimes this is very effective, but at other times it is cluttered or destroys the homelike atmosphere. It is possible to show many beautiful objects and still not turn a home into a museum. This is done by placing the objects on table sur-

A large painting hides a strangely placed window, while a Pennsylvania Dutch pot holds interesting weeds. (Photo: Mike Lynch.)

Although this display is in the Textiles and Objects Shop in New York, it could just as easily be found in an interesting spot in the home. It was designed by Alexander Girard. (Photo: courtesy of Herman Miller Inc.)

faces, on the floor in corners, but seldom in lines on shelves. When objects are lined up carefully, they look too rigid. You should determine what kind of impression you wish to convey before you put too many objects into the space available.

Interesting arrangements of paintings, prints, and reproductions can be made above sofas, chests, and in other parts of the room by the use of many small and varied pictures and frames. This technique of showing paintings can become cluttered, overwhelming, and "busy," unless carefully planned. One should plan this type of arrangement on paper first or even tape life-sized pieces of paper on the wall in order to obtain a better idea of how the final design will look. Keeping similar types of work together contributes a consistency throughout groupings of pictures. Too much variety adds confusion to the wall; one should aim for organization. Frames with similar characteristics can be used to help unify a grouping, but

Here is an old stand-by method of displaying objects that is always good. Plain cinder blocks arranged under boards bring dead space into good use. (Photo: Mike Lynch.)

they should not be identical, or monotony will result. Small pictures are best in groups because small paintings by themselves tend to look spotty and lonely.

It is not necessary to have all paintings at eye level. In fact, nothing is more dull than a room with the pictures all in a row across the wall. Be daring; lower some to pick up the line of the top of the sofa; let one painting rest on the top of a chest and lean against the wall. It makes little difference where a painting is placed, as long as it can be viewed without difficulty. It can be placed very low, so that it can be viewed from a sitting position. If this gives a naked appearance to the upper part of the walls, tall weeds or plants can balance the lowness of the painting. A picture should have good lighting. Artificial lighting can be applied to the painting with small picture lights, but this may give a gallery appearance to the work. It is better, in the home, to place a print or painting where it can receive good light at all times.

Odds-and-Ends Furniture

One need not be too disdainful of boxes and crates as pieces of furniture in the home. There are many very odd things that can be used successfully as either furniture or ornamentation in a living space. Sears, Roebuck and Company has been offering a wonderful metal shelf unit with colorful boxes for storage, which can be used in a child's room, studio, recreation room, or office area, and can be effective and beautiful. Simple wooden boxes can be sanded, covered with sealer, and used as a pedestal for an old blackboard slate table; or a whole series of boxes of different sizes can be stacked against a wall, painted white, and look like a fascinating sculpture. Strange pieces of wood and cut-up legs of old chairs and tables can be added to the interior of the boxes for interest.

The once-rejected secondhand furniture known as the ice-cream-parlor chair has become a highly coveted item for the home, and there is little reason why the secondhand shop cannot yield many other interesting pieces of furniture that need only a coat of paint to bring them back to life. These do not have to be expensive antique pieces—simply old and cheap. Highly ornate pieces can often be cleaned down to simple lines, or they can be used with all the heavy carving as an accent or focal piece in a room. The careful buyer in a secondhand store can find many fine articles. He should try to buy pieces of furniture that are well made and have a great deal of life left in them. This is especially important if hours of hard work will be needed to bring the piece back to a reasonable appearance. If you are looking for authentic antiques, make sure you know the merchandise. Remember to make a thorough study; even then, it is best to call in an expert if large sums of money are to be spent.

The use of old furniture and makeshift objects can add interest to a room. Many expensive homes contain unusual furniture, the result of inventive thinking. Charles Eames has a ladder propped up against one wall in the

Mixing of furniture styles is correct and brings variety into the interior. A late nineteenth-century Thonet chair adds contrast to this contemporary family room. (Photo: courtesy of Eichler Homes.)

living room of his house. People immediately react to this when they see it. It at first seems out of place, and then it begins to seem appropriate.

Mixing Furniture

A feeling of creativity can be brought into the home by an interesting balance of variety. This, of course, can be achieved in many different ways. If you want to make a room more effective, throw away the old notion that all the furniture in it must fit a certain period, or be of a certain style, or be made of the same kind of wood. There are no rules or regulations which say that one room cannot contain furniture of different periods and styles. It must be realized that a vast number of different styles can be put together very beautifully, but this requires care and understanding. Remember the discussion of unity and variety in the first chapter. This will help a great deal in determining how and what you can combine successfully. A room dominated by Herman Miller or Knoll Associates furniture can be very beautiful, but it can also be very dull, not because the furniture itself is dull but because the accessories have not been chosen well. In a modern room, it is exciting to see a traditional object placed in contrast to machine-oriented furniture. The contrast adds warmth and color and variety. Again, in an Early American room, the simplicity of good Early American furniture can easily complement small simple objects of glass, ceramics, and metal, designed and made in the mid-twentieth century. An excellent instance of mixing furniture was the practice in the period of Queen Anne (c. 1702–1714) of including Chinese lacquered pieces in a setting of Queen Anne walnut and mahogany. As ships continually returned from the Far East with imported pieces of Oriental furniture, not only were these articles from a strange country combined with English furniture, but also the designing of furniture in England took on an Oriental character. If this mixing and influencing could happen during the 1700s, it is even more acceptable for our machine-age furniture to be combined with the objects and small furniture pieces of Africa, India, and South America, now that our world is so much smaller, and we are so much more easily influenced by other countries.

The simple Shaker and Pennsylvania Dutch designs are virtual brothers to today's design. Their honesty parallels the approach of our good contemporary designers. Here are some possible combinations which can be used in a room. These are certainly not the only ones.

BASIC ROOM STYLE	ACCESSORIES	SECONDARY STYLE
Danish Modern	Scandinavian	Early American
Herman Miller Modern	Pennsylvania Dutch	Swedish Modern
(Miller and Knoll)	Contemporary	Art Nouveau
Empire	Empire	Neo-Classic
Contemporary	Contemporary	Empire
Contemporary	Contemporary	Antique Greek
Contemporary	Contemporary	Antique Egyptian
Knoll Associates	Contemporary	Shaker
Contemporary	Contemporary	Biedermeier

This small list may give the reader an idea of many possible combinations. The more brave and inventive will mix many different styles together, not only two or three. It can be and is done with elegant taste.

BIBLIOGRAPHY AND SUGGESTED READINGS

The best reading sources for subjects discussed in this chapter are the various magazines such as *House Beautiful, Woman's Day, Design Quarterly,* and *Craft Horizons.* However, the best ideas will come from actual experimentation by the reader with "found" materials. See suggested readings for Chapter 9 and Chapter 10.

A good example of an eighteenth-century garden is at the Governor's Palace in Williamsburg, Virginia. Notice the careful, symmetrically balanced design. (Photo: John Crane, courtesy of Colonial Williamsburg.)

A natural garden of trees, water, and stepping-stones gives an Oriental feeling to the Alden Dow home. (Photo: Baltazar Korab, courtesy of Alden Dow, Architect.)

Chapter **13** THE OUTSIDE ENVIRONMENT

In the eighteenth century the ideal garden was one designed in a symmetrical, balanced composition. As one left the house and entered the gardens, one saw a rigidly planned group of walks and flower beds on each side of a central path. The palace of Versailles near Paris is probably one of the finest examples of this type of landscaping and gardening. Acres of forest and gardens stretch to the horizon, with fountains and sculptures, each one balanced with its counterpart, across the mall or path. In the United States, some of the finest eighteenth-century gardens are found in restored Williamsburg. Emperor tulips and grape hyacinths are clustered in little rows along the walkways, and meticulously trimmed trees and bushes are seen in diamond arrangements.

The garden of the twentieth century is much different from the rigid landscape of the eighteenth century. There is a return to the more natural 211 garden surrounding the house. As we saw in the placement of Frank L. Wright's buildings, the landscape often, in effect, enters into the living area of the house in a warm blending of the outside and the inside. We cannot and should not separate the outside of the home from the inside. Both are important in the total make-up of the contemporary American home. The home must be thought of as a complete entity and not merely as an interior space to be painted and filled with furniture.

ORGANIZATION OF OUTSIDE SPACE

As careful a study should be made of the outside space as of the space inside the home. The level of the land should be studied as well as the nature of the soil. Retaining walls may be needed to hold back the earth in some places; there are some places that may prove better than others for planting flower beds. One should decide what kind of activities will take place in the yard and throughout the landscape and should list these activities with associated needs, equipment, and costs. By making a careful plan, one can take the most important steps first and then, each year, can solve further problems of the landscape.

Protection from wind and sun is an important factor to consider in planning the living space and the garden area. Fences can be constructed to give cover from the winds that are prevalent in some parts of the country and to diminish exposure to the sun. Different parts of the country have different problems calling for different solutions. In the hot Arizona climate, overhanging trellises are needed for plants to shade the family from the sun, while in the state of Maine it is desirable to let the sun warm the living area of the yard. Large trees located next to the house offer shade for the living area in regions supporting trees as part of the natural environment. Bushes and low trees provide shelter from the late afternoon sun and the wind and also add beauty to the yard.

The materials used for ground surfaces and patios in living and service areas are varied. Textures play an important role outdoors as well as indoors. Smooth, clean, concrete patios reflect run rays and heat but are better than tar surfaces or asbestos. Gravel makes a very interesting pathway through the garden, but is difficult to use in the living area where a flat surface is probably best. Fieldstone and old brick make interesting color and textural additions to patio areas and at the same time provide hard surfaces on which to set chairs and tables.

The gardens of the Governor's Palace in Williamsburg, Virginia, with trimmed trees and meticulously tended flower beds. (Photo: John Crane, courtesy of Colonial Williamsburg.)

Yard Plan

A plan of the yard is as useful as a floor plan for the interior of the house. By using graph paper or a gridded paper, one can plan the yard logically, plotting the various ways in which the areas surrounding the house will be used. You can approach this problem just as you would the interior. With a scale drawing, you can indicate trees, shrubs, garden beds, and pathways. You may make a long-range plan, setting goals toward which to work, with fewer mistakes than might otherwise occur.

Façade, Service, and Living Areas

Three major areas usually surround the private home. These are the façade landscape, the service area, and the living area.

The Façade Landscape. The landscaping in the front of the house is what we see first. Most people work on it as soon as they move into a home.

There are many ways to approach the problem of landscaping a home; the method chosen depends primarily on the site and the placement of the home. If the home is in the middle of a large development, the treatment will be similar to that used in the landscaping around it. It would probably not be the best thing to put a wooden fence along the sidewalk in a uniform development where others have left their yards free of view-obstructing fences or bushes. This kind of situation calls for grass in the front yard and shrubs at the front of the house. This is not the most creative solution to a landscaping problem, but it may

A clean trimmed grass plot sets the stage for Philip Johnson's purist glass house. The landscape is surrounded by the natural environment of the woods. (Photo: Ezra Stoller.)

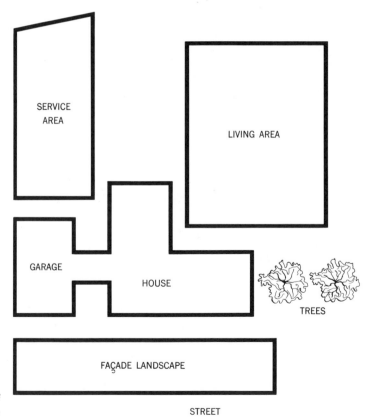

An over-all plan of the house and landscape shows how the yard is divided into different areas.

well be the best way to become an accepted part of the community.

In another kind of situation, the house and front yard can be secluded by fences and shrubbery if a private entrance is desired. Interesting results can be achieved in this way, with an intimate, mysterious approach as the façade of the house.

In another landscaping device, one can let a house remain surrounded by the natural environment in which it was built, perhaps enriching the environment somewhat. This is not always possible to do when a house is in a subdivision, but the addition of groups of trees can give the appearance of a wooded area. If one acquires property

that already has plenty of trees, the landscaping is there, and little has to be done to bring the façade landscape into order. The best approach may well be to leave the environment exactly as it was found and to let the house peek through the trees and undergrowth.

Service Area. One should give thought to the service area, when planning the landscape of a home. This area should be designed to provide outside laundry facilities, garbage and refuse can space, storage for tools and yard equipment, and, perhaps, if there are young children, play areas with sandbox, swings, and slides. A small vegetable garden might also be included. Because many of these things are more practical than handsome, it is better to isolate them from the façade as well as from the living area of the back yard. This can be done by wooden fencing with gateways, tall bushes, or a natural space within the structure of the house that would be especially feasible in some of the HUTLE floor plans. The service area should be easily reached from the kitchen and garage. It should also have a path connecting it with the living area of the yard, because equipment must often be carried from one area to another.

A concrete wall acts as a fence, a retaining wall, and as the back for a seating unit in the yard. (Photo: courtesy of National Concrete Masonry Association.)

Play and service areas should open off the kitchen for the convenience of the housewife. (Photo: courtesy of Eichler Homes.)

If the play space is to be in the service area, the mother will need a fast traffic lane for reaching this area in a crisis from both the inside of the house and the living area of the back yard.

Living Area. During the summer months, the living area outdoors becomes the family living room. It should command a pleasant view of the background or gardens and should afford privacy from neighbors, if possible. It could have facilities for dining as well as comfortable seating for lounging and sunning. It should have easy access to the kitchen for transporting food and eating equipment, and it should also be accessible from the main living spaces of the interior.

This area should have adequate surfacing so that tables and chairs will sit evenly and comfortably on the ground. Concrete, bricks, and patio blocks can be used for textural interest. Additions can be made to all three as the needs of the family change.

In developments where yards are lined up, block after block, it is certainly both proper and best to cut the view so that the family can have privacy when engaged in family affairs and in entertaining guests. Although such an action might present some problems in many suburban communities where neighbors want a clear view along the back-yard fences, it is still acceptable. One should probably enclose the living area at once, if one moves into such

Privacy is obtained in this inner atrium living area. (Photo: courtesy of Eichler Homes.)

An interesting hard-surface patio contributes to good furniture placement in this outdoor living area. (Photo: courtesy of National Concrete Masonry Association.)

a neighborhood, and not wait for a few years only to find that one's action insults one's neighbors.

The furniture for the living area should be lightweight so that it can be moved easily from place to place to take advantage of shade or sun and also moved indoors easily if it cannot withstand the ravages of weather. It should provide adequate surface areas on which to place dishes without too much limitation of space in which to move freely. You might try to plan this space much as you would plan a living room inside the home. Lighting can be a problem here as well as in the interior of the home. Much depends on how one intends to use the space. A floor plan can help in designing the outdoor living room, and it might be drawn as a separate plan from the plans for the total landscape development.

The Natural Landscape

In utilizing the natural landscape as an asset of one's home, one keeps the features of the land as intact as possible. One builds the house with a great consideration for the trees and other natural enrichment. This does not mean that changes cannot take place during the planning and landscaping of the property, but effort is made to keep the area as closely related to nature as possible. The Japanese have used this approach to landscaping for hundreds of years, and American homeowners have been practicing this art recently with varying degrees of authenticity.

In the natural landscape color is relatively monochromatic in character, unlike the bright splashy colors of the European gardens where many hues are found. The flowers found in the natural garden are quiet and natural in their environment.

An outdoor living area utilizes both hard and soft ground surfaces. Architects A. Quincy Jones and Frederick E. Emmoms in Cedar Rapids, Iowa. (Photo: Julius Shulman, courtesy of Westinghouse.)

A simple fence blocks off the view from neighbors and encloses this small concrete block patio. (Photo: courtesy National Concrete Masonry Association.)

The natural growth around this house provides the landscaping. (Photo: courtesy of Techbuilt.)

Rigid arrangements of flower beds and concrete paths do not belong here, but, instead, soft flowing lines and undulating ·pathways are the important elements. Natural groupings of rocks are found in corners of the property, looking as though they had always been there. Growing through the crevices of these piles of rocks are soft grasses and wild flowers. Rocks can also be left bare and exposed in the middle of the yard, for interest and height. Instead of grass, moss can be used as a ground cover, the type varying according to region; this will blend with the landscape, and, at the same time, will cut the maintenance a great deal.

Rocks may also be used for the pathways through the garden. The paths need not be lined up in straight rows but can move with soft rhythm across the yard, leading into small wooded areas. Small pools can be placed next to the paths, or perhaps a path can lead across small pools with steppingstones. In larger gardens, hillocks and waterfalls can be built with streams that disappear under rocks and stone bridges. This, of course, takes a good deal of work and money, but the results are fascinating and inviting.

Crafts and Fine Arts in the Landscape

Enrichment in the garden and back yard can be introduced by devices other than flowers, shrubs, trees, and rocks. Sculptures and craft objects, so important in bringing character to the interior of the home, play the same role in the exterior spaces, especially in the gardens and natural landscapes that are seemingly unplanned. In the natural Japanese garden, the viewer will find many stone lanterns and small sculptures hidden in the most surprising places. Metal, stone, and cement sculptures bring interest and sophistication into an otherwise ordinary and dull back yard. These can be placed in very open spaces in the living area or can be put into corners, to be discovered only when approached through the paths of the gardens. Small stone paths can lead one toward various sculptures throughout the garden. Even a small garden in a housing development can thus become alive and active.

Wooden sculptures as well as those of metal and

A ceramic sculpture titled Cairne, *by Betty Feves, placed in the corner of a yard, adds character and interest to the landscape. (Photo: Bus Howdyshell, courtesy of the artist.)*

A ceramic fountain by Robert Sperry. Notice the interesting natural arrangement of stones around the little pool. (Photo: courtesy of Robert Sperry.)

A garden path of ceramic tiles designed by Stan Bitters. The tiles are fascinating in design, yet simple in character. (Photo: courtesy of Hans Sumpf Co.)

Birdhouses of ceramic can be hung from trees in the yard for beauty and interest as well as to attract birds into the garden. (Photo: courtesy of the artist, Virginia Wysel.)

A backyard living area is transformed into a reflecting pool with Stan Bitters tiles and ceramic sculptures. Notice how the fence provides privacy from neighbors. (Photo: courtesy of Hans Sumpf Co.)

220

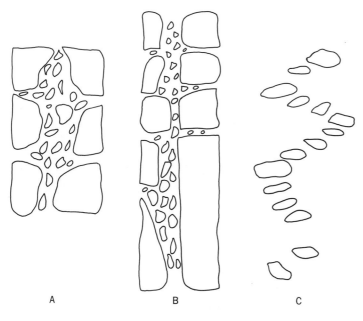

A   B   C

Traditional arrangements of stones in a Japanese garden path. "A" is a more regular grouping, with large stones on the outside and small stones set in the center of the path. "B" has a variety of stones lining the border. "C" shows how stones are arranged in a traditional manner so that they seem to wander through the garden in a rhythmic pattern.

stone can be used effectively. Wood that is left outdoors during the winter months will age beautifully and fit well into a natural landscape. Of course, sealers can be used to preserve the wood, but a more interesting patina will result from leaving it unfinished.

Ceramic pots can be placed on the walls surrounding the patio or can be set on the floor surface of the living area. Many types of pottery must be kept indoors during the winter to prevent destruction by ice and snow, but during the summer a high-fired piece of stoneware can stand outdoors without danger of damage. The pots may have plants and flowers in them, or they can be used empty just for decoration; in either case they add enrichment to the area.

Mosaic walls could surround the living area, or interesting textured concrete walls might be placed in the garden as wind barriers. The exterior of the house, facing the living area, could well be given some ornamentation that would bring color to a place where many hours are spent during the warm weather.

BIBLIOGRAPHY AND SUGGESTED READINGS

Church, Thomas D., *Gardens Are For People*, Reinhold, New York, 1955.
Dustan, Alice L., *Landscaping Your Own Home*, The Macmillan Co., New York, 1955.
Eckbo, Garrett, *The Art of Home Landscaping*, F. W. Dodge, Inc., New York, 1956.
Eckbo, Garrett, *Landscaping For Living*, Duell, Sloan, and Pearce, New York, 1950.
Korbobo, Raymond, *Complete Home Landscaping and Garden Guide*, Wise and Co., New York, 1959.
Lees, Carlton B., *Budget Landscaping*, Henry Holt and Co., New York, 1960.
Rose, James C., *Creative Gardens*, Reinhold, New York, 1958.
Tange, Kenzo and Yasuhiro Ishimoto, *Katsura, Tradition and Creation in Japanese Architecture*, Yale University Press, New Haven, 1960.
Yoshida, Tetsuro, *The Japanese House and Garden*, Frederick A. Praeger, Inc., New York, 1955.

This U-shaped kitchen was designed in cooperation with the Ladies Home Journal *for a big, bustling family. The mother could prepare dinner inside the counter while her teen-age children were cooking afternoon snacks on the two-burner cooking unit in the foreground. A sewing machine is mounted on a turntable that has a typewriter on the other side; this corner can be an area of activity and efficiency. (Photo: courtesy of General Electric.)*

An interesting and colorful family room opens to the patio. (Photo: courtesy of Eichler Homes.)

Chapter 14 SYNTHESIS: INTERIOR SPACES

The total house is composed of many elements, and each one is important in some way to the integration of a successful living space for whatever sort or size of family it will hold. In the completed home there will be paintings, craftwork, furniture, and objects of varying kinds, and all will add textures, color, and pattern to the whole scene. The problems of lighting, ventilation, traffic lanes, and space will have been considered, as well as sound barriers, maintenance, cost, and many other factors. The synthesis of all elements produces a well-planned interior responsive to the individual needs of the family members.

Since each space within the total house presents problems related particularly to the function and activities of that room, each type of room should be considered separately. For example, the things that are accomplished in the living room are different from those that concern the bed-

223

room, bath, or kitchen. It is therefore necessary to examine each room by itself in order to recognize the various individual room elements that combine to make the total house.

THE KITCHEN

It is always difficult to decide which room plays the most important role in the home, but a room that inevitably draws a great deal of activity is the kitchen. In many homes this room is the core of family life. Here the food is prepared, and the housewife spends many hours. In this room, close to 1,000 meals a year are prepared for the family. This means the housewife spends *at least* 1,000 hours in this room annually. The other members of the family make frequent visits to this room for many reasons, not all of them necessarily associated with food. The kitchen becomes a family conference area, a playground for children, and a planning center for the mother. For these reasons alone, the room must be adequately organized to accommodate a great many activities. It is a serious mistake to think that the kitchen is the part of the house solely reserved for food preparation.

Types of Kitchens

The Pullman or Strip Kitchen. The strip kitchen is the simplest type of kitchen. It is generally found in small apartments or small houses in which there is little space for a kitchen. Because the strip kitchen is on one wall only with the components placed in row fashion, there is usually more movement from one end of it to the other when food is being prepared. Its chief convenience is that the complete kitchen can be hidden behind folding doors or draperies when the cooking is finished.

The Corridor Kitchen. The corridor kitchen is similar to the strip kitchen, except that it has two sides instead of one. This is usually a more workable kitchen, because two of the major working units (range and refrigerator) are on one side, and one unit (sink) is on the other. The major drawback of this kitchen is that it often becomes a passage-

way for family members on their way from one part of the house to another, and at mealtime this traffic interferes with the food preparation. However, the corridor kitchen does give the housewife a good working situation in that most of the storage and other components are closely located within a few feet of each other; this factor eliminates many unnecessary steps during her time in the kitchen.

U-Shaped Kitchen. The U-shaped kitchen is probably the best of all the kitchen plans, for it does not become a thoroughfare for family members, and it does offer a great deal of continuous counter space. The three major units are arranged with one on each side and the sink generally at the end of the U. Storage space, as in the corridor kitchen, is located conveniently for the housewife, and most shelves can be reached without difficulty.

L-Shaped Kitchen. The L-shaped kitchen is a common type and a good one. It is not quite as successful as the U-shaped kitchen but still has most of the same advantages. The L-shaped kitchen leaves two walls empty for windows and doors; often the corner not utilized by the work space is occupied by a small, free-standing or built-in dining area.

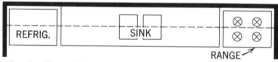

The "pullman" or strip kitchen.

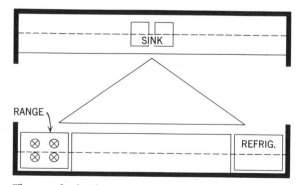

The corridor kitchen.

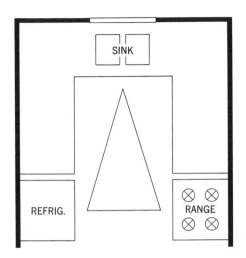

The U-Shaped kitchen.

Food Preparation. It is important to have adequate counter space or table space for the preparation of food. If possible, a wooden inset in the counter top should be provided as a cutting and slicing surface. A place to wash fruits and vegetables should be considered, as well as a place for mixing various foods. Storage space for utensils should be conveniently near the counter space where they will be used.

The three major units in the kitchen ideally should be in a triangular arrangement; this would help to eliminate many steps. If this is not possible, then other arrangements of the range, sink, and refrigerator should be planned for minimizing the steps the housewife must take when preparing food.

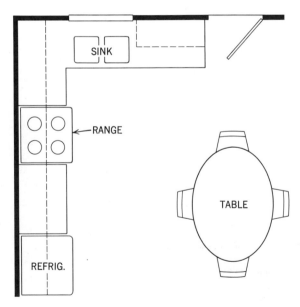

The L-Shaped kitchen.

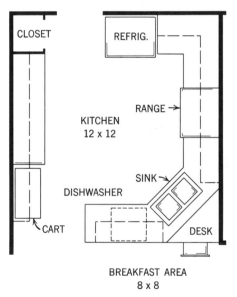

Notice the arrangement of the major units in this kitchen floor plan. Cart and desk have been included for convenience. Everything is within close reach. Small breakfast and laundry areas are also included. (Photo: courtesy of Better Homes and Gardens.)

A well-planned kitchen facilitates preparation of food. The oven is at a convenient level, good lighting is provided, and the range is low for good cooking control. (Photo: courtesy of Better Homes and Gardens.*)*

Cleaning up after the meal is an important operation to be considered also in planning the location of facilities. Garbage disposals and waste paper containers should be easy to reach. If shelves are out of reach from the sink, a small tea wagon can be used for pushing dishes and utensils to the storage space. Drain boards and double sinks are useful in the task of washing up after the meal. Counter space on both sides of the sink is convenient for stacking dishes.

Planning Area. Although it is not always possible to set aside a planning area, it helps the housewife to have some space in the kitchen for a small desk where she can work out her budget, meal plans, and cleaning schedule.

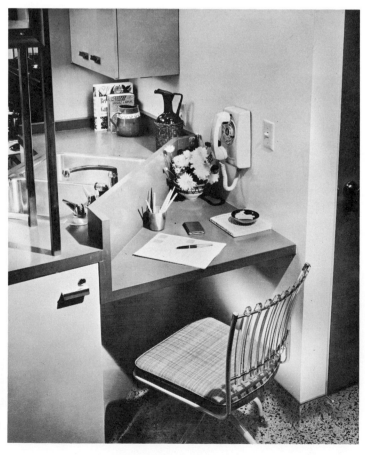

A small planning area helps the housewife organize meals and other home projects. The telephone, easily available from the other side of the counter, saves steps. (Photo: courtesy of Better Homes and Gardens.*)*

A telephone near this area is a convenience for calling the various services that might be needed by the household. Book shelves for a collection of cookbooks might well be added to the wall space beside the desk.

Multipurpose Kitchen. Many kitchens today are more than just kitchens. They often contain the laundry facilities as well as a family living room and play area for children. In this type of multipurpose room, the actual work area of the kitchen is usually off to one side and opens into the room. Generally the housewife can see easily from her work space into the family room area. This kind of kitchen usually serves as an informal dining room for the family, while another room might be set aside for more formal dinner occasions.

The Floor. The kitchen should have a sensible floor. Rugs have no place in a room where food preparation and other messy operations might make cleaning difficult. The floor surface should be smooth and maintainable with minimum effort. It can be made of colorful tiles and linoleum, which are not too hard on the feet of the housewife. When possible, splash boards should be installed for a few inches up the wall from the floor to help prevent cleaning problems. To keep the floor from being slippery, adequate friction should be provided for safety. The floor tile and linoleum should have a small textured pattern that helps to hide soiling between cleaning sessions.

There is available a great variety of tile and other covering for kitchen floors, including asphalt, vinyl, rubber, and linoleum, available in 9-inch squares.

A built-in counter range contributes to an uncluttered look and offers the housewife a clear view of the scenery and dining area. (Photo: Julius Shulman, courtesy of Douglas Fir Plywood Association.)

A modified corridor kitchen designed by the architect George Matsumoto for a "Total Electric Home" in Atlanta, Georgia. Looking away from the family room we see two ovens that are particularly good for farm families. (Photo: Julius Shulman, courtesy of Westinghouse.)

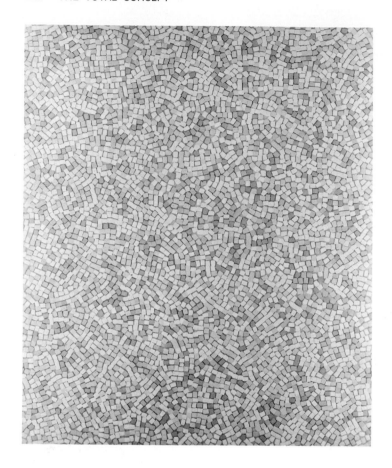

Both of these patterns are good for kitchen floor coverings. Besides being easy to maintain, they give the appearance of pattern without being too bold. (Photo: Armstrong Cork Co.)

The Walls. Like the floors, the walls should be easy to clean and maintain. The paint should be washable. Tiles of ceramic and asbestos are available as well as stainless steel squares. The tiles selected for use over the range or near the oven should be fireproof for protection. Wallpapers should have a surface finish that permits damp wipings, and any fabric applied to the wall should be coated with a protective finish. Wood in a kitchen adds warmth and color but must be used carefully lest it overpower the room.

The Ceiling. The kitchen ceiling should be simple and neat. Do not attempt to add wallpaper or fabric to the ceiling. Any pattern on a small room ceiling is likely to dominate the room and create a disturbing element. Unless the ceiling is extremely high, use light colors. Dark colors make the room oppressive.

Sound. Noisy activities occur in the kitchen. Soft textures help to reduce noises, but the best way to eliminate

noise in the kitchen is to use sound-absorbing ceiling tiles. A good ceiling can keep sounds from penetrating other areas of the house. This is especially desirable in small homes where the kitchen is close to the living area. Larger houses have less acute problems concerning the carrying of sound from the kitchen to the living area, although such problems are possible. To create a pleasant atmosphere, one can install a speaker from the record player or FM radio in the kitchen. The volume should be controllable from the kitchen as well as from the original source of the music, with volume control located near the telephone. A less expensive method would be to use a small radio or TV for diversion while performing household tasks.

A laundry center located near the kitchen. Adequate storage space is available for soaps and other needs, with a sink that can be used for rinsing delicate apparel. (Photo: Julius Shulman, courtesy of Westinghouse.)

A simple kitchen with raised counter units for easy cleaning. The small shelf provides an extra eating area for children. The over-all pattern of the floor adds interest but does not dominate the room. (Photo: courtesy of Armstrong Cork Co.)

Lighting and Wiring. Good lighting is very necessary in the kitchen. One central overhead fixture is usually not enough. Small subsidiary lights should be installed over the range and sink if the central lighting is not adequate in these places. Plenty of electrical outlets should be planned for the many electrical devices used in the modern kitchen and for the shifting of appliances from one area to another without use of extension cords. Substantial wiring is essential especially when a 220-Volt line is needed for the range and clothes dryer. It is best not to take chances in the area of wiring. One should always have a licensed electrician check the wiring system in a rented or newly purchased house. Of course, the electrical system should include adequate wiring for exhaust fans to remove undesirable odors from the kitchen. Clocks and air-conditioning units might also be considered.

The Accessories. Accessories in the kitchen should be as colorful and inviting as those in any other room. Sometimes the kitchen in an otherwise well-appointed home has been left in an unattractive or even disreputable condition, especially if the housewife does little food preparation herself. The curtains in the kitchen should be easily washable, for greases and odors penetrate them rapidly. Cottons are probably best. Half-curtains or café-style curtains permit the housewife to look out into the yard without difficulty—an absolute necessity when small children are playing outdoors and must be watched closely.

The small accessories in the kitchen should be planned with some care, so that maintenance is not too difficult. Make sure there are no complex textures that hold dirt and dust; instead, use smooth surfaces that are easier to wipe clean. Spices and interesting herbs and their containers are beautiful lined up on a shelf where they add to the decoration and are also within easy reach for use.

The aesthetic environment in the kitchen should be considered as carefully as that in any other part of the house. Attractive objects and craftwork can bring warmth and enrichment to this room as well as to the living room. There is no reason why the cooking utensils should not be well-designed items that provide the housewife with aesthetic enjoyment.

Ventilation. A hood over the range or a fan set into the wall near the cooking area will help reduce strong odors and will remove warm air during meal preparation. If such an arrangement is not possible, facilities of another nature can provide for ventilation of the kitchen. During the summer months, doors and windows can be opened, although this is not comfortable in winter. If a hood is used, it should not interfere with visibility. Lighting under the hood can illuminate the food being cooked.

Color. Color is especially important in the kitchen because the wrong colors in this room may create a feeling of more warmth than is wanted. Intense warm colors should be avoided; hues on the cool side of the color wheel should be employed. Lighter colors generally give the impression of more space; darker colors seem to close in on the room with a confining effect. Colored patterns should not be busy. If patterns on the walls and curtains are used, they should be small and quiet. Busy patterns and color create a sense of confusion.

Storage. Storage in the kitchen is very important because the placement of equipment and utensils makes or breaks the efficiency of the room's function. Unfortunately, most architects neglect to provide the adequate storage arrangements in the kitchen that would promote flexibility, accessibility, and convenience.

Shelves within cupboards should be designed as movable units so that the housewife can utilize the space as needed. As additions to glassware and dinnerware are made, the shelves can be moved up or down, eliminating much of the unused and wasted space so often found in kitchen storage. Drawers should have movable dividers that can be changed to solve new storage problems as they arise.

All equipment should be placed conveniently for use. Perhaps all pans and pots would not be stored in one place but instead would be placed close to the areas where they would be used most. Mixers should be stored near the baking equipment, while vegetable cleaning tools should be near the sink. All things that are used daily should be on the lower shelves; in kitchens where there are many high shelves, seasonal objects and tools may be stored.

THE DINING ROOM

Dining rooms vary a great deal in type, depending on the size and design of the houses where they are located. Many small houses today have only a small dining alcove or "L" off one end of the living room; such an area must be decorated and considered as an integral part of the whole living area. However, there has been a recent trend toward return to use of the separate dining room. In a smaller house, the dining room is probably used for many purposes. Besides being used for evening meals, it may be used also for lunch and breakfast. This occurs especially when the kitchen is too small to accommodate either a breakfast bar or a table-and-chair set. The dining room may also be used by the teen-agers as a place to study, by the mother as a place to sew, and by the father as a place to work on bills. It is essential to investigate all the family

A unique solution to the problem of dining space is this wall unit designed by George Nelson. It could double as a desk. Soft lighting is provided for mealtime, and interesting objects add character to the area. (Photo: By Scott Hyde, courtesy of George Nelson.)

Adequate storage space is always needed in the home. This house has a pantry off the kitchen, and it is easy to reach without many steps. (Photo: courtesy of Eichler Homes.)

activities that will take place in the dining room before doing too much expensive work.

In the larger house, the dining room may be used only for formal dining at dinner parties and Sunday meals. Even then, the room may be dually designed so that one end is used as a TV room or library. Whatever the activities, each one should be integrated logically as a functioning part of the total room.

The placement of the table is important in the dining room, so that adequate space will be provided for chairs and for free movement to clear away dishes between courses and at the end of the meal. There should be at least a two-foot clearance around chairs, to permit serving; thus, the total space needed for comfort would be between three and four feet from table to wall. Less space than this will not allow for a good traffic lane around the table and will create problems when people are preparing to sit down for meals. The chairs should not be too heavy; diners should be able to move them without effort. If the table is placed directly in the middle of the room, it might interfere with traffic passing through the dining room. Sometimes it might be better to pull the table off-center to provide a convenient passageway to other parts of the house. The table should be placed so that the hostess can easily move from dining room to kitchen without disturbing guests. It would be best for her to have space next to her seat where a tea wagon could be placed, enabling her to remove dishes between courses without leaving the table.

The Floor

In the formal dining room where little children seldom eat, carpeting of many kinds can be used. If children use the eating place as much as adults, an easily cleanable surface should be used on the floor. Although wall-to-wall carpeting is desired by many people, a removable carpet or area rug might be more practical in the dining room. It could be sent to the cleaners without difficulties. Don't, however, imagine that all adults are spotlessly clean in their eating habits; many are worse than children. Carpeting or an area rug may prevent the diner from easily moving his chair, especially if the texture of the carpet or rug is heavy and thick. The smoother the carpet, the easier it is to push and pull chairs on it, but at the same time the easier it is to see soiled places. The more texture there is on the floor, the better spotted and soiled areas are disguised.

A dining room table near the window takes full advantage of the view. Here is another example of mixing of furniture styles. (Photo: courtesy of Pittsburgh Plate Glass Co.)

Color

The dining room should employ colors that are pleasant to view during meals. They can be cheery and bright, or, for more atmospheric effect, dark and quiet. But remember that when food is being eaten in a room, the psychological effects of color and pattern play a very important role.

The Walls

The walls of a separate dining room can be covered with any type of covering—paint, paper, or wood paneling. If the area is part of the living room, the walls can have the same color or treatment as the living room, in order to help unite the two areas. Often, however, the end wall of an alcove dining area is given a contrasting color in paint or wallpaper, in order to set off the area. If wallpaper is used, one should be sure the pattern is not offensive. Remember that some designs might not be conducive to good dining. Except for some special design problem in the room, the paper should be quiet and soft so that it does not dominate the eating area and the living area.

Storage

To facilitate preparation for dining, good storage space for table linens and silverware should be near the table area. Try to eliminate unnecessary steps. A good arrangement for storing china is the kind of cupboard that opens into the kitchen, so that washed dishes can be reached directly from the dining area when the table is being set. In addition, special storage areas could provide places for flower containers or display materials, to be used throughout the house.

The Lighting

The lighting is especially important if the dining area is used for activities other than dining. This is not meant to minimize the need for good lighting for dining. Various types of lighting probably will be desired for the various uses of the room. Don't make the mistake of having inadequate lighting during a dinner party. Although romantic candlelight is not to be rejected, there are certain times and some kinds of meals when better illumination should be available. Pull-down hanging light fixtures are good for dining areas that are used for family games, studying, and hobby work. An especially good arrangement is an overhead light that can be dimmed or brightened as desired.

The Furniture

The furniture in the dining room should be substantial, if children are to be using it for most meals; the chairs

(Photo: courtesy of Fritz Hansen Inc.)

Interesting and startling mixture of furniture styles is the keynote of this dining room. Notice there is plenty of space behind the chairs for serving. (Photo: Scott Hyde, courtesy of Techbuilt.)

An unusual dining corner with a table that slides out to a full eight-foot length for use and slides back into the kitchen for clearing. Designer—John Yeon. (Photo: Maynard Parker, courtesy of Douglas Fir Plywood Association.)

must also be comfortable for adults during dinner parties when the conversation might last for a long period of time after the meal. Nothing is more unpleasant than sitting around a dinner table for several hours in a chair that is ill fitting or at a table that is too low to allow one to cross one's legs. The table should be designed so that it can seat everyone comfortably without requiring two or three people to straddle the center legs. When purchasing a table, one should check the apron to see whether it will cause inconvenience. The surface of the table should not be too delicate to be used for sewing, crafts, and other hobby work.

It is not necessary to have matched sets of furniture

in the dining room. The table can be of a style different from that of the chairs, and the grouping can still work well as a unit. The table could be formica, for example, with chairs of walnut. In a small and simple room like the dining room, it is better not to introduce too many different styles and woods, but more interest will be created if at least one of the major pieces differs from the rest.

Ventilation

Ventilation is important in the dining room as well as in the kitchen but not to the same extent. Because the dining room often retains odors from food, there should be a method of removing odors after the meal. This can be done by opening a window or by some mechanical means at that time. Strong cross-ventilation during the meal might not be very satisfactory, especially if it cools the food too rapidly.

Curtains and Draperies

Curtains and draperies often retain odors from food and cigar smoke after dinner parties. It is, perhaps, advisable to have these as washable as those in the kitchen. In a dining area off the living room, however, the draperies or curtains should be of the same fabric and design as those of the living room, for unity. With great care, one can use different colors and patterns, but one is likely to have difficulty in bringing together the two areas.

THE BEDROOM

The bedroom is the place for real design experimentation, because so little time is spent in this room; therefore, unusual wallpapers, bright colors, and unique design will not be as trying as in a room where they are seen more often. The bedroom should be more individualized than the family living area where many personalities are considered. The bedroom should say something about the person who uses that particular room. Here the special individual is considered. Try not to dictate too much the colors and décor of the child's room. Give the child two or three selections from which to choose. Let him help with

the designing and decorating. He will then find the room more acceptable and will feel that he has contributed to the general aesthetic conditions of the home. One might also remember that a child could use a large room even better than the parents. If a larger room is provided for the child, he will probably use it more frequently as his base of operations.

A bedroom with both a private place to study and enclosed patio for sun bathing. (Photo: Frank Lotz Miller, courtesy of Douglas Fir Plywood Association.)

A simply appointed bedroom for a child. Probably the framed butterfly pictures should be removed. The birds provide plenty of ornamentation, and the pictures detract from the movement of the birds. (Photo: courtesy of Eichler Homes.)

Ventilation

The bedroom presents many problems, as does any room in the home. Ventilation is a necessity for the bedroom. The room can be ventilated with air conditioners, as is often done in warm climates. In cooler climates, where air conditioners are not so prominent, windows should be placed so that cross-ventilation can air the room during the night and, when wished, during the day. Control of air is essential for health. It is not always possible to rent or buy a house with the proper number of windows in the correct places, but it is important to have two windows in every bedroom. One should not place a bed under the windows but should locate it against a wall where air will not circulate directly on a person who is asleep. Curtains and draperies should open and close easily, in order to allow good ventilation.

Along with ventilation, good control of the heating system should be planned. People often like bedrooms at a different temperature level from that of other rooms throughout the house.

Sound

The bedroom should be free from the noises of other parts of the house. This is why it is recommended that living and sleeping areas be separated by halls or other spaces. Sounds in the bedroom can be muffled by the use of carpeting, heavy draperies, and other textured materials, which absorb sounds. Closets between rooms cut down a considerable amount of noise that would travel from one room to another. If possible, bedrooms should be away from the street, in order to avoid the noises of night traffic and daytime distractions.

Space

For efficient maintenance, the bed should be free on three sides. This is not always feasible in smaller homes and rooms, but, when possible, it does make bedmaking a simpler task for the housewife. Storage space for bed linens should be nearby; perhaps linens can be stored in the hall, accessible from all rooms without too many steps; or perhaps linens can be stored for individual use in the various bedrooms.

Furniture

The furniture in the bedroom should be not only comfortable but interesting. Sets (or suites) are very unimaginative. Don't buy headboards, chests, vanity, and chairs all of the same wood and design. Variety is as important in the bedroom as in the living room. The structure and comfort of the mattress are extremely important for healthy sleeping. Adequate storage space in chests and closets for the clothing of all family members is also important. The more space that is available, the easier it is to keep clothing organized and neat in appearance.

Furniture Placement

To eliminate extra steps while dressing in the morning, one should keep one's chest of drawers close to the closets that will be used. One should also have a chair near the bed to hold a robe during the night and to sit on while dressing in the morning. This chair could be used when necessary in the living room, if it has been carefully selected, or it could be used as a desk or dining chair. The bedroom chair should be designed as a dual-purpose piece of furniture. The chair can be used in the bedroom when

A boy's room incorporating India fabrics for draperies and bedspread. The chest is attached to the wall, so that legs are unnecessary, and the room is simplified. (Photo: Ernest Braum, courtesy of Eichler Homes.)

A giant-sized bed dominates this bedroom. Over the corner desk is a nice solution to the problem of displaying family pictures. There is adequate storage space for clothing and other objects. (Photo: courtesy of Techbuilt.)

friends are visiting sick persons confined to bed. If two quite comfortable chairs are included in the master bedroom, they can be used by the parents as a refuge during teen-age parties when the mother and father wish to be out of sight but not out of hearing.

Lighting

Good lighting should be included in the bedroom, especially for people who wish to read in bed. Pull-down lamps can be used over the bed, or lamps with sufficient height to throw a soft light across the head portion of the bed can be employed. Lighting should be available in the place where the woman puts on her make-up; it should be soft and lacking in harsh shadows. If a reading or study corner is included in the bedroom, separate lighting from

the lighting over the bed and dressing table should be provided. Avoid introducing too many lamps, however, for too many lamps will cause confusion in a small room. Study the lighting needs carefully. Often the bedroom is designed for artificial lighting only, for the room will be used only in the evening.

THE BATHROOM

The bathroom is often overlooked during the decorating of a home. Generally, the back of the toilet looks like a jungle of old combs and curlers. Towels seldom seem to match other colors in the room, and frequently there is little storage space available for the multitude of items that must be kept in this room. The main thing to remember about the bathroom is that it should be kept simple and plain. It is usually too small for rich textures and patterns.

Storage

One should attempt to have adequate storage for the various types of small equipment used in the bathroom. Things like brushes, combs, and pancake make-up seldom add much beauty to the general scheme of things. A large medicine cabinet is essential for even the smallest of families. Here many of the necessities can be put out of view of guests. Don't make the mistake of putting all the old (or new) medicines here if you have small children. Find

A simple bedroom with just enough pattern to bring interest into the room. (Photo: courtesy of Eichler Homes.)

An easy chair and table in the corner of a bedroom provide a quiet refuge for a parent during teen-age parties. (Photo: courtesy of Fritz Hansen Inc.)

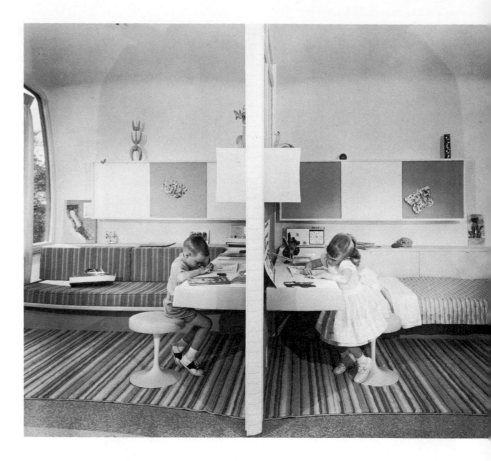

In the Monsanto Company's "Plastic Home of the Future," two children's rooms can open into one indoor play space or can be closed for privacy. (Photo: courtesy of Monsanto Chemical Company.)

a very safe, out-of-reach place for these. Even a small bathroom can be redesigned to relieve the storage situation. It is nice to have towels and other bath linens stored in the bathroom where guests can easily find them if they have not been put in the open. Such storage makes fewer steps for the housewife when she is changing linens. And there are those times when a bather might have forgotten towels and is unable to obtain them if they are not stored in the bathroom.

Sound and Ventilation

The bathroom should be as soundproof as possible and should have good ventilation. The travel of sound to other parts of the house can be reduced by the use of air-space walls. Of course, heavy textures on the floor, walls, and ceilings will also help, but too many textures might overwhelm a small room. Good acoustical ceilings are the best device if soundproofing is inadvisable for the walls. Much noise can be eliminated by the selection of the plumbing equipment. Some toilet bowls are practically noiseless; however, they are much more expensive.

A good fan should be set in the bathroom to remove steam and noncirculated air from the room. This is essential in bathrooms that do not have windows and do not open to an outside wall. In fact, building permits are usually not approved if good air circulation has not been provided.

A simple bathroom with space for storage. Tiled wall and floor make maintenance easy. Because pattern and ornamentation are limited, the effect of more space is given. (Photo: courtesy of Kohler Co.)

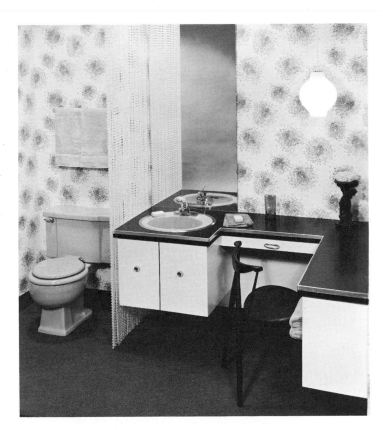

A convenient make-up corner has been placed in this bathroom. (Photo: courtesy of Kohler Co.)

A nicely planned bathroom with small ceramic tiles on the wall. Towels are stored so as to be easily reached from the basin and tub. Notice the safety handle in the tub. (Photo: courtesy of Kohler Co.)

Avoid large pattern in the bathroom. The floor dominates this room. Notice that the mirror is in three parts, giving good vision to the user. (Photo: courtesy of Kohler Co.)

Lighting

Good light should be supplied in the bathroom, especially over the mirror where shaving and make-up activities take place. Many newly designed homes have natural light from skylights. These give a soft light, but there is often a need for direct light on the face. Light-colored surroundings and smooth textures help project and reflect light to the face for better illumination.

Floors and Walls

The bathroom floor should be easy to clean and maintain. Simple tile, such as that in the kitchen, or ceramic tiles can be used. Ceramic tiles are cold to the feet, so probably a good nonslipping mat would be needed near the tub and shower.

The walls should have a surface that cannot be damaged by steam from the shower. Ceramic tile is best and easiest to clean, but plastic tiles are less expensive. If wallpaper is used, one should make sure it will not be difficult to clean and that its pattern will not dominate the

Endless space and spaciousness are the impression brought about by the limited pieces of furniture and their placement. Even the large sculpture fits into this one-room glass house without overpowering the other elements. (Photo: Ezra Stoller.)

room. A room with a neutral wall surface can be made bright and gay by the colorful towels and linens hanging on the towel racks.

THE LIVING ROOM

The living room is, of course, one of the most important spaces. This room has to answer many individual problems for the different people in the family. Their activities will be numerous and varied. The living room exists primarily as a place for conversation, but also it is the site of television viewing, parties, reading, listening to music, and hobby participation. Father might work here on his stamp collection, mother might sew here, and the children might have manifold projects in mind for this room.

The living room reflects the various individuals of the family. The visitor, as he steps into the house, can tell a great deal about the family from the type of living room he sees. The family interested in art will have paintings of unusual character on the walls, and the woman of the family involved in collecting antiques will have had a significant influence on this room.

Second only to the kitchen, this is the core of the home. It is here that the family gathers on Sunday afternoons for visiting with relatives and friends, and it may be here that the family gathers after dinner to watch favorite television programs. The smaller the house, the more important is the living room. When other rooms offer space for activities such as studying, hobbies, television viewing, book storage, and games, the use of the living room can be reduced to the entertaining of guests. Like any other part of the home, the living room must answer the problems of the family using it. There are, however, some basic con-

A living room opens conveniently to the outdoor living area. A wooden fence provides privacy for both the outdoor and the interior living space. (Photo: courtesy of Eichler Homes.)

A barrel-vaulted ceiling of plywood provides graceful design in this small Florida home. The structure of the framing is carefully articulated as part of the visual scheme of the house design by architect Paul Rudolf. (Photo: Ezra Stoller, courtesy of Douglas Fir Plywood Association.)

siderations that should be planned for in any size or type of living room.

Conversation

Since conversation is one of the main things for which the living room exists, the furniture should be nicely planned to encourage it. Whenever feasible, noisy activities should be diverted to other rooms. Television, radio, and musical instruments should, when possible, be kept out of the living room, in order to insure quiet and uninterrupted conversation. The furniture should be arranged so that traffic lanes do not cut into the conversation group or cause clashes with other members of the household. The major pieces of furniture should be placed at the side of the room when possible, so that a unit of chairs and sofa can be apart from the normal or main artery through the living room. If it is necessary to include television in the same room, then one should try to place it in a corner where it will interfere as little as possible with the area set aside for talking and reading.

Surface Space. The conversation area should provide adequate surfaces for ash trays and snack dishes. These surfaces can be on small tables or shelves that stand free and can be moved around, or they can be built into the walls.

Comfort. Adequate space for each person should be planned. Coffee tables should not be placed too close to sofas and chairs; their placement should allow plenty of space for legs and freedom of movement. On the other hand, they should be within easy reach of seating units. After the furniture has been placed according to plan, one should try each seating unit for leg and reaching comfort. A person wishing to stretch out his legs needs up to five feet.

The furniture itself should be comfortable for sitting. Make sure springs and construction parts of the furniture are not in such disrepair that guests will be ill at ease. Several styles of seating units should be available for the many kinds of people who will be using them. An older person might find it difficult to get in and out of an African

camp chair, while a larger person might find it difficult to fit comfortably in a dainty little chair.

Lighting. Because of the diversified functions of this room, the lighting must be planned carefully so that it also will function in various ways. For evening conversation, only soft, quiet light is necessary; when the room is full of

A well-planned area for conversation is the center of this house. Adequate surfaces have been provided as well as space for movement between pieces of furniture. The wood walls and ceiling add a feeling of warmth to this large airy room. (Photo: Robert C. Cleveland, courtesy of Douglas Fir Plywood Association.)

many people playing cards, more light must reach more people. Indirect lighting is warm and adequate for conversation, but probably a more direct light will be desired for reading. Like so many things in the home, lighting is a personal thing. Some people want to read under a diffused light, while others like the brightness of a light thrown directly on the page of the book. Some people find it difficult to read by a hanging light, and others cannot read in comfort by a lamp placed on a table next to the sofa. Lamps with opaque shades are good for unusual lighting effects but are generally not very effective as soft reading lights. They do not diffuse light throughout the room but project the light straight down or directly up to the ceiling. On the other hand, Japanese paper lamps are good for unusual lighting effects and also offer good, soft diffused lighting for reading corners.

Furniture Arrangement and Traffic

Arrangement of furniture should help to separate the various activities that take place in the living room. Obviously, not all living rooms are big enough to include many small individual areas for different uses; however, as much as possible, grouping should be planned. If a desk is to be used in the living room, it should be away from the conversational area and in an isolated corner. A screen or wall hanging could be used to help as a divider. TV areas should be off to one side, so that persons watching TV would not interfere with any conversation going on in the room. It is best if the television can be placed in another room. A small den, basement recreation room, or even a small corner of a large dining room might be converted to a TV viewing area, so as to remove this activity from the

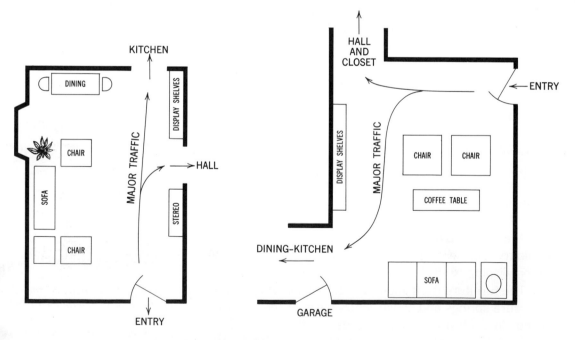

Possible arrangement of furniture in living rooms. Traffic lanes have been major considerations.

The elegance of the glass window in this room is destroyed by the placement of the furniture. The two chairs should be removed from the front of the window. There are too many textures and patterns in the room, which do not work well together. There is unnecessary ornamentation of the table lamp. The room is heavy and awkward. (Photo: courtesy of Pittsburgh Plate Glass Co.)

A living room creatively designed by Charles Eames. Floating weeds from the ceiling, interesting wall textures, the feeling of endless space and individuality are the characteristics that make this room outstanding. (Photo: Julius Shulman, courtesy of Herman Miller Inc.)

A view into a Techbuilt house shows dining area and the family area centering around the same fireplace. Simple paper lanterns furnish soft light for both rooms. (Photo: Louis Reens, courtesy of Techbuilt.)

247

A living room centered around a fireplace utilizes lots of space and furnishes the occupants with a beautiful view. (Photo: Louis Reens, courtesy of Techbuilt.)

living room. It is irritating to have television going on when guests are trying to conduct a conversation. As for music, if a separate music room is not available, one corner of the living room can be arranged for the piano or music stand.

If a fireplace is located in the living room, furniture should be placed so that everyone can take advantage of the fire. At the same time, one should be careful not to place seating units too close to the fire, thereby causing considerable discomfort to visitors who might be reticent about moving away from the heat. Place furniture so as to allow plenty of space for safe movement around the front of the fire.

The purpose of large "picture" windows or ceiling-to-floor-length windows is to provide a view of the outdoors. Furniture with its back to the window is illogically placed.

Also, one should not place a lamp directly in the center of a window where it blocks the view and represents a very trite solution to the space problem. If a lamp must be placed near to or in front of the window, one could at least use some degree of originality by an off-center placement. One should take advantage of the view, if it is interesting and can add to the beauty of the room. If there is little to enjoy outside, then draperies might just as well cover the complete window and provide the room with more wall space.

Sound

The living room should have adequate sound control, as should all other rooms in the house. People should be able to hear conversation without being unduly distracted

Although this room has many textures and many objects of enrichment, it is still simple. (Photo: courtesy of Eichler Homes.)

In this living room a limited number of objects has been carefully arranged. Notice that the painting on the fireplace wall was not placed directly over the opening of the fireplace, but was put off center for a more interesting arrangement. A handwoven divider separates the living room and dining room slightly. (Photo: courtesy of Eichler Homes.)

A dramatic home designed by Ulrich Franzen features space, clean lines, adequate lighting, and unusual placement of furniture. (Photo: Ezra Stoller, courtesy of Douglas Fir Plywood Association.)

A futuristic living room from the Monsanto plastic house. Notice how music center, life-size television and movie screen, and desk and sofa are all built in as one unit. (Photo: courtesy of Monsanto Chemical Co.)

by noises from other parts of the house. Yet, doors and passageways should not be so completely blocked that the evening sounds of children, after they have been put to bed, do not travel to adults in other parts of the house. Bathroom noises should be completely eliminated, as should sounds from the kitchen, and other unpleasing noises. Acoustical ceilings, along with carpeting and draperies, take care of this to some extent. Hi-Fi sets should be arranged so that they can be controlled easily, should the volume become too great. It is all well and good to be a fanatic about high fidelity, but don't make your guests and other family members uncomfortable.

Floors

The floor in the living room can be covered with materials ranging from terra-cotta tile to plush carpeting. The smoother the surface, the easier it is to maintain. A tile floor can easily be cleaned with wet-mop technique, while a carpeted floor will need vacuuming and yearly dry-cleaning. Although some circles associate great status with wall-to-wall carpeting throughout living room, hallway, and dining room, other materials can be just as effective. Complete carpeting can help to unify several rooms, but area rugs are usually much more interesting and give more

Tile floors can be used in a living room as well as carpeting. A clean, spacious effect is usually the result and generally is easier to maintain. (Photo: courtesy of Armstrong Cork Co.)

Area rugs and carpets can bring interest into the living room. This one was designed as a tribute to the Bauhaus. Such rugs are effective but must be placed carefully. (Photo: Wunda Weve Carpet Co.)

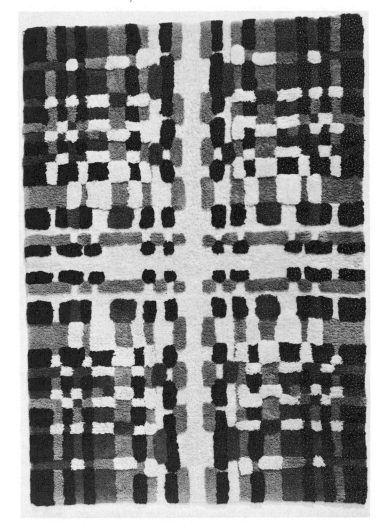

character to the living room.

Rugs. Area rugs may be hand-hooked, woven, cut from carpeting, or braided. While these are the major types of rugs, there are several other kinds that can be used effectively, such as knitted and crocheted rugs. If an area rug is used, it is desirable to have fairly neutral backgrounds and walls. Area rugs generally have more color and pattern than carpeting, and thus bring more emphasis to the floor. (See Chapter 9 for illustrations of hand-crafted rugs.) Decide if the room needs this attention to the floor through rugs. Don't overpower the room with highly colorful paintings, and at the same time detract from them with a unique rug. Rugs with deep pile, such as is found in many hand-hooked rugs, are more difficult to keep clean. Although cotton rugs are less expensive, wool flossa and rya rugs do not mat as much; they spring back much better. A hand-woven flossa or hooked rug can easily be repaired by the owner, if the rug is damaged by cigarette burns or liquids.

Carpeting. The biggest drawbacks of complete carpeting are the initial expense and the difficulty of repairing damaged areas. However, there are many very beautiful carpets that are relatively inexpensive and easy to clean, and that add warmth and color to the living room. The new man-made fibers used in carpets today reduce the possibility of permanent soiling from which it was hard to protect the wool and cotton rugs of a few years ago. Several types of carpets are sold on the market today. The standard ones are Wilton, Axminster, Velvet, and Chenille. Of these, the Wilton is considered the best and the strongest; the backing is of cotton and the cut pile is of wool. The Axminster is generally less expensive, for less wool is used in its construction, and it is therefore a very popular type of carpeting; in the Axminster, the small tuffs are inserted individually into a jute background. The Velvet is not of very good quality, is usually much cheaper than other types of carpeting, and generally does not wear as well, but with very careful buying, one can at times get one's money's worth. The Chenille is usually the most expensive type of carpeting because of the difficult manufacturing techniques used to make the wool and the carpeting; it is a rich and luxurious carpeting.

When considering the purchase of new carpeting or rugs, one should first decide whether the room in question needs complete or partial covering. If part of the floor is to be left bare, the size of the room enters into calculations to determine the coverage area of the rug or partial carpet. If the room is small (nine by twelve feet to fourteen by sixteen feet), the rug can come up to six or eight inches from the wall, but if the room is large (twenty by fifteen feet and up), at least twelve inches should be left between wall and

carpeting. A rug that is too small will look out of place in the room and will not work well with the furniture. More space can be left uncovered where a traffic lane runs alongside a conversation area, but one should never have the rug end in the middle of the traffic lane. Also, it is best not to have the rug end under a piece of furniture. When this happens, the piece of furniture is neither a part of the uncarpeted area, nor does it belong to the area that is covered.

After the size of the coverage area is determined, a simple rule for learning the amount of yardage can be followed. The width multiplied by the length (in feet), and then divided by nine, will show the total square yards needed for the room. (Otherwise, one can multiply the width by the length in yards.) The number of square yards is then multiplied by the price of the carpet per square yard to ascertain the cost.

When purchasing carpeting or rugs that are to be cut down to the size desired, one can use the cuttings for small throw rugs in various places in the house. But one should remember that throw rugs can be dangerous and must be carefully considered before being placed in traffic lanes.

Oriental and Persian rugs are regarded as the kings of floor coverings. They are sufficiently well constructed to wear for a great length of time. Traditional patterns are used and executed in very complicated knotting techniques. There are several types of knots, which differ according to the region where the rug is made. The wool is soft and extremely fine. If you plan to buy such a rug, do not make your final purchase until you have called in an expert to look at the rug, unless you are very sure that the company with which you are dealing is reputable. The prices of Oriental and Persian rugs vary from a few hundreds to many thousands of dollars.

Stone, Tile, and Other Hard Surfaces. The hard-surface floor coverings available today give the homeowner a huge range of selection. While the rug or carpet usually contributes a warm feeling to the living room, the hard-surfaced floor is colder and more sterile but often more beautiful.

Floors of marble are luxurious and expensive and can give a more regal look than any rug—hand-made or Oriental. Be sure that the tile or flooring purchased is easy to clean and that it is not too slippery and not too hard for comfortable walking. Some tiles are more appropriate to a kitchen than to a living room, and such suitability should be considered as well as the upkeep that will be required. Wood is always acceptable; it is foolish to cover the beautiful floor of a newly built house. If carpeting is planned, why should one make a surface of expensive flooring that necessitates sanding and other expenses?

Fieldstone and polished slate are beautiful flooring materials that give texture and character to a room and create a more casual and informal atmosphere. The entrance can be of fieldstone and the living room of carpeting, if one desires. There is no reason why all the floor need be covered with the same material.

The Walls

The walls of the living room should be neutral in character. Wallpapers, mural and other dominating types of wall treatments overpower the room, unless very carefully planned. Large, floral wallpaper patterns are very limiting; few, if any, paintings or pictures show up well on them. To make a room versatile, one should use simple wall covering such as paint or plain paper (if one must have paper). Whites, off-whites, light browns, greys, and slightly tinted walls give rooms an airy and spacious feeling. The more neutral one keeps the walls, the more colors one can use in accessories and furniture. The draperies and curtains can either blend into the background or contrast with the walls. Try to avoid dark draperies that give the appearance of large holes in the walls. Neutral draperies make a better background for displaying lovely objects in the living room.

Wood paneling can be used and does add warmth to a room; it tends to be more masculine than feminine in character. If the wood is too dark, it will reduce the feeling of space, but, on the other hand, dark wood can produce a very cozy room. Wood wall paneling is especially nice in study and music rooms. Brick and stone bring other characteristics into the room. If fieldstone is used, it produces an informal atmosphere, while carefully laid bricks give a cooler effect to the room.

AUXILIARY SPACES

Hallways. Hallways are important in that they are traffic lanes from one part of the house to another. For this reason, they should be left as free of unnecessary furniture as possible; unless they are large and wide, do not place in them pieces of furniture that might present hazards. Make hallways light and spacious by reducing pattern as much as possible, unless you can absolutely justify the need for pattern. The lighter its color, the more spacious the hallway appears. Some white paint, a few small pictures, and adequate lighting will make a long passageway an interesting place rather than a dull, dark hole.

In the entrance hall, space should be available for the

Hallways should be free and uncluttered to allow easy passage from one part of the house to another. (Photo: Eichler Homes.)

removal of coats, boots, and rubbers; a small bench will make this an easier task for you and your guests. Storage space for coats and boots should be near. Have plenty of good lighting so that you can see the arriving or departing guest. A telephone in the entrance hallway is likely to be inconvenient, especially if conversation can be overheard from the living room or by guests who are standing in the entrance. A good cleanable floor covering should be placed here; a carpet that shows dirt quickly and needs frequent cleaning is a senseless addition to an entrance hall. The entrance hall should be large enough to admit several people who may arrive at the same time. Make it an inviting place, one that is warm and friendly and yet does not give a complete view of the living room or other parts of the house.

STUDY AND MUSIC ROOMS AND LIBRARIES

The room designed especially for music or study is generally found in larger homes where adequate space is available for such luxuries. Such a room should be isolated from other parts of the house. It should be well sound-proofed so that noise stays either in or out, according to the

One room can serve many purposes, with wall units such as these designed by George Nelson. This living room is study, dining area, library, and music room, all in one. (Photo: Scott Hyde, courtesy of George Nelson.)

An upstairs room or attic can become a beautiful one-room apartment, if one does some careful planning. (Photo: courtesy of Armstrong Cork Co.)

purpose of the room. Good lighting is of utmost importance in rooms where reading and writing are the major activities. Adequate storage space is needed for books or musical equipment. Such rooms are highly personalized and specialized, but many of the same things we have discussed need to be considered, to enable a room to function most effectively. The individual who is to use this kind of room the most should be consulted about its functions, so that it will fit his personal needs.

A spare room used for television, reading, and other activities. Built-in wall units provide storage space for TV and phonograph, for books and art objects. (Photo: courtesy of Armstrong Cork Co.)

A studio in Copenhagen doubles as a living room or bedroom. "Swan" chairs contribute beautiful form and shape to the room, enhanced by the interesting texture of the rug. (Photo: courtesy of Fritz Hansen Inc.)

An upstairs study can be used by parents and other members of the family while activities not involving them take place downstairs. Comfort and quiet should be a prerequisite here. (Photo: courtesy of Techbuilt.)

RECREATION ROOMS

The recreation room should be studied and developed much as is a living room, but the major consideration will probably be durability and sturdiness of the furniture. If this is the area where teen-agers have their parties, everything should be easily maintainable and very efficient. It can be a colorful room—daring and bold. If it is in the basement, airiness and lighting are very important considerations. Space should be available for dancing; at least, the furniture should be easy to move to provide such space when needed.

THREE HOUSES

The total house is a building that should be directly related to the people who dwell in it. If it has been designed for specific people, it should fit them as a new dress fits the contours of the person who has purchased the garment. No house is perfect, however. As a family begins to live in its selected home, various members find areas that could be improved to facilitate their activities and interests. There are architects who have managed to reduce this problem by their sincere and imaginative interest in the family and its comfort. They understand the needs and meet them creatively and inventively with solutions that are eminently functional and workable. On the other hand, some architects and designers are constantly working on innovations merely for the sake of innovating, with results that are often unworkable, overly expensive, and even bizarre. The following three houses are illustrative of successful organization of ideas and space.

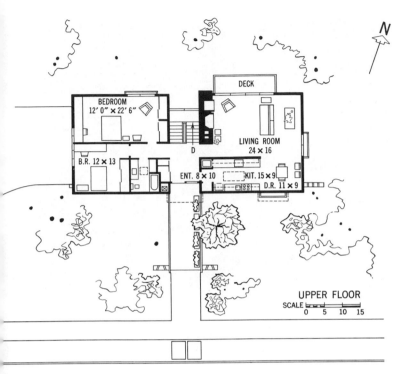

Dr. Hazel Hatcher's residence, designed by the architects Salmon and Salmon. This is the upper floor. (Floor plans: courtesy of architects.)

Dr. Hazel M. Hatcher Residence

The Hatcher house was designed by the architects Salmon and Salmon, a husband and wife team. It was built on a site that most other people had rejected as unusable because of its great slope from the street. The slope, starting at the sidewalk and descending steeply into a wooded area, presented difficulties as to foundations and house level. This called for an ingenious plan. The house was built on what appears from the front to be a blank brick wall but really is the front of the lower level; a bridge spans the slope and leads into the simple, plain façade. It is a house that might be classified in the group we previously identified as modern eclectic but with a heavy tendency toward the purist style. The way in which the house is presented to public view results in a great deal of privacy for its occupants. Little foundation was needed for the house, because the only excavated area is the area where the heating unit was established. The first floor, or lower level, is directly on the ground. This level has a small but compact guest studio, with kitchen, large bath, separate

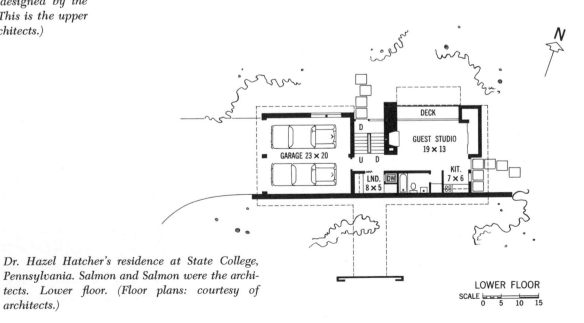

Dr. Hazel Hatcher's residence at State College, Pennsylvania. Salmon and Salmon were the architects. Lower floor. (Floor plans: courtesy of architects.)

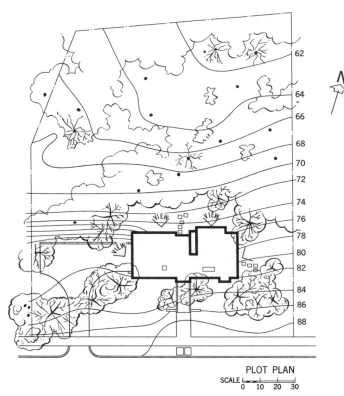

PLOT PLAN
SCALE |—————|
0 10 20 30

This is the plot plan of Dr. Hazel Hatcher's house, State College, Pennsylvania. (Plan: courtesy of architects.)

Front façade of Hatcher house. Notice the bridge leading to the front entry. Landscaping has been kept natural. (Photo: Ed Leos, courtesy of Dr. Hatcher.)

Rear of Hatcher house. Balconies overlook the woods; the lower balcony provides a place for firewood storage. (Photo: Ed Leos, courtesy of Dr. Hatcher.)

Notice the floors and the ceiling materials used in this living room. Simple objects are placed throughout the house for color and interest. Although no piece of furniture is duplicated, there is great unity in the living room. (Photo: Ed Leos, courtesy of Dr. Hatcher.)

The entryway is plain and uncluttered. Plenty of space is provided for movement through the house. (Photo: Ed Leos, courtesy of Dr. Hatcher.)

entrance, and fireplace. The laundry facilities are on this level, as well as the two-car garage. Each level has an adequate and secluded balcony from which the wooded area at the back of the house may be viewed.

The upper level is designed for efficient management. The floors are of brick-colored terra-cotta tiles, which reduce housework and introduce a new texture. The ceilings are composed of a light yellow metal, which adds interest to the ceiling and is an important part of the ceiling structure. The living area is completely separated from the sleeping area by a large foyer that was kept extremely simple. The entry way can be reached easily from the corridor kitchen. This house has many devices that were designed by the architect and the owners for convenience and simplicity. A dumbwaiter goes from the kitchen to the lower level, reducing the carrying of laundry, firewood, and other items from storage up the stairs. Skylights aid in the illumination of the kitchen and baths where there are no outside windows. The closets throughout the house are designed with enough depth to allow all drawer units to be out of sight, thus providing a more spacious feeling for the bedrooms.

Throughout the Hatcher house, the furnishing has been kept simple and uncluttered. There is no unnecessary item that fills space merely because the space is there. There is no pretense—every object is honest and answers the needs of the household. The dining room at the end of the corridor kitchen has only a small table with folding chairs to fill the space. While one would generally not

A skylight provides illumination for this corridor kitchen. Two sinks furnish adequate space for food preparation and cleaning. Often large branches of Pennsylvania rhododendron ornament the bare spots throughout the house. (Photo: Ed Leos, courtesy of Dr. Hatcher.)

accept such an arrangement in a beautifully designed house, these provisional pieces of furniture represent the planning of the homeowner to find the exactly right permanent pieces of furniture before adding any to the house. In this way, the over-all plan will hold together well when completed.

Enrichment is minimal. In the living room there are a few small, interesting objects in various places, such as on the floor, on the ridge of the fireplace, and in the corners. In several parts of the house handwoven South American belts hang in corners and over doors, adding just a touch of color and interesting native pattern.

All windows in the house are of floor-to-ceiling height, with the exception of the side bedroom windows. These high windows throughout the house not only provide adequate lighting during the day but also contribute to an airy, open quality.

It is a well-thought-out house; the architects kept in mind that minimum housekeeping was desired and developed interesting solutions. The house is unquestionably designed expressly for the needs of a certain type of person, but careful examination will reveal that many types of people could live in the Hatcher house and have their personal housing needs answered satisfactorily. Thus it is a unique but adaptable house.

Dr. Ruth Pike Residence

The Pike house, also designed by Salmon and Salmon, is completely different in character from the Hatcher house. The contrast makes one immediately aware of the versatility of the architects. Instead of being in a wooded area, it overlooks a valley of farms. The pitch of the roof actually echoes the soft contours of Nittany Mountain in the background. The whole feeling of this house is one of open spaces, airiness, and freedom of spirit. In the back, a terrace and deck overlook the land, and yet these are private and secluded from the street. The house itself has a rectangular plan as does the Hatcher house, but the addition of a separate garage and covered walkway minimizes

A simple façade faces the street. Its design echoes the lines of the mountain behind it. (Photo: Ed Leos, courtesy of Dr. Pike.)

Dr. Ruth Pike's residence, State College, Pennsylvania, was designed by the architects Salmon and Salmon. Upper floor. (Floor plan: courtesy of the architects.)

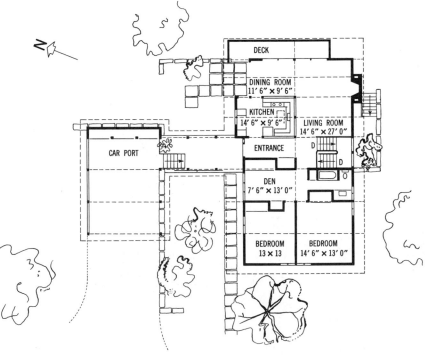

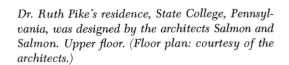

DECK

DINING ROOM
11' 6" × 9' 6"

KITCHEN
14' 6" × 9' 6"

LIVING ROOM
14' 6" × 27' 0"

ENTRANCE

CAR PORT

DEN
7' 6" × 13' 0"

BEDROOM
13 × 13

BEDROOM
14' 6" × 13' 0"

UPPER FLOOR
SCALE 0 5 10 15

The rear of the Pike house faces the mountains. Deck and patio areas provide places where one may enjoy the open view of the valley. Living area, dining area, and kitchen all open onto the outdoor living area. (Photo: Ed Leos, courtesy of Dr. Pike.)

A bench, horizontal lighting, and a wall relief by Ruth Ratico of ceramic, plaster, and walnut lead the visitor into the Pike home. (Photo: Ed Leos, courtesy of Dr. Pike.)

The stairwell to the lower floor is enclosed with opaque glass to provide privacy. (Photo: Ed Leos, courtesy of Dr. Pike.)

The dining area of the Pike house is so placed that guests can view the scenery. (Photo: Ed Leos, courtesy of Dr. Pike.)

Enrichment in the Pike house adds to its character. A wall hanging by Sybil Emerson is the focal point in this room. Delicate floral arrangements, ceramics, and mobiles also contribute interest. A slate fireplace ledge provides additional seating space for large groups of people. (Photo: Ed Leos, courtesy of Dr. Pike.)

the rectangular effect of the Pike house. There is a definite separation of the living and sleeping area, as in the Hatcher house. An interesting room in the Pike house is the small den placed in front of the bath and two bedrooms. This open area is a cozy study and reading place where the occupant does her writing. Throughout the Pike house lovely craft objects are exhibited and used as part of the appointments. One instantly realizes that the person living in this house has a great interest in contemporary American crafts.

One can recognize the entirely different feelings of the living rooms in the Hatcher house and the Pike house. In one, the floor is tile-covered and the ceiling is flat; in the other, the floor is carpeted and the ceiling is of the studio type.

In both houses you can go through the house without entering the living area. In the Pike house the hallway ends

George Nelson's and Gordon Chadwick's experimental house is made of twelve-foot-square boxes on piers. (Photo: courtesy of George Nelson and Co.)

in a stairwell, which has opaque glass to permit plenty of light to enter and yet provide privacy from a neighboring house.

Only the area under the living room of the Pike house has been excavated. A workroom, an extra bedroom with bath, and a closet that is completely cedar lined for storage of clothing have been included here.

Lighting for the kitchen in the Pike house comes from ribbon windows opening into the living room area. Since they are high and at the ceiling peak in the living area, one is hardly aware that they are there. The kitchen, which is U-shaped, has a small, built-in dining area for breakfasts, as well as many other special features designed for the occupant.

Nelson and Chadwick Experimental House

The third house is the result of an experimental study started several years ago in Grand Rapids, Michigan, by George Nelson and Gordon Chadwick. Their particular interest was the utilization of mass-production, industrial methods in the design of a private shell. Before they

View of the Nelson and Chadwick experimental house shows use of extension units with basic box. (Photo: courtesy of George Nelson and Co.)

Overhead view of the experimental model. Notice the patios that act as sound buffers. (Photo: courtesy of George Nelson and Co.)

Two views of the interior of the experimental house by Nelson and Chadwick. It is easy to see how the extension boxes are added to enlarge rooms and add variety to the interior space. (Photo: courtesy of George Nelson and Co.)

started on this project, they established the following limitations and rules:

1. No originality, because the problem is not one of invention but of assimilation.

2. No personal expression, for the industrial product is anonymous.

3. No consideration of cost, since this is a research and development study.

4. No consideration of market acceptance, because this is not relevant to the research.

5. No natural materials, because the design is for production and not romance.

6. A minimum inventory, because this keeps the project simpler for production.

7. Flexibility, because this allows for maximum consumer choice.

These were the basic governing factors that dictated the results of this study.

The house design was based on a box or cage twelve feet square in horizontal dimensions, with variable vertical measurements. There was to be as little foundation as possible, so the boxes were set on piers. This also meant that the site need not be changed to fit the house; instead, the various box structures could be placed on different levels with ease and convenience, adapting the piers to the slope of the land if necessary.

Service areas within the house, such as the bath and kitchen, were planned as packaged units to be attached to the basic twelve-foot-square cage. The hall and connecting units were also planned as extension packages. Each service area could be added at the place desired for most efficient use for the family.

Sound was eliminated by means of the decentralization of the house, which produced space between sound-producing areas. The result, of course, was similar to the court or atrium type of plan. Illumination was provided through a double plastic shell with controllable liquid levels between the two shells; the amount of liquid in the shell could determine the quantity of light that was brought into the room.

BIBLIOGRAPHY AND SUGGESTED READINGS

Ball, Victoria Kloss, *The Art of Interior Design*, The Macmillan Co., New York, 1960.

Bevlin, Marjorie Elliott, *Design Through Discovery*, Holt, Rhinehart, and Winston, New York, 1963.

Faulkner, Ray, *Inside Today's Home*, Holt, Rinehart, and Winston, New York, revised edition, 1960.

Goldstein, Harriet and Vetta, *Art in Everyday Life*, The Macmillan Co., New York, revised edition, 1954.

Graves, Maitland, *The Art of Color and Design*, McGraw-Hill Book Co., New York, 1941.

Hatje, Gerd and Ursula, *Design For Modern Living*, Harry N. Abrams, Inc., New York, 1962.

Obst, Frances, *Art and Design in Home Living*, The Macmillan Co., New York, 1963.

Praz, Mario, *An Illustrated History of Furnishing*, George Braziller, New York, 1964.

Rutt, Anna Hong, *Home Furnishing*, John Wiley and Sons, New York, second edition, 1961.

Stepat-De Van, Dorothy, *Introduction to Home Furnishings*, The Macmillan Co., New York, 1964.

The Treasuries of Contemporary Houses, F. W. Dodge Corp., New York, 1959.

Whiton, Sherrill, *Elements of Interior Design and Decoration*, J. B. Lippincott Co., Philadelphia, 1963 Edition.

PART FOUR: COMMENTS

The completed house is the total synthesis of all the elements we have studied. Each step in the designing of a home is important both for the family and for the designer who is working out the problems with which he is faced. The smallest detail or object is considered with almost the same intensity as that devoted to the over-all plan of the building. The end product is a home that makes living an enjoyable experience for the occupants of the house.

Individuality is one of the hallmarks of a well-developed interior. It is through selection of craft work and art objects, and the use of creative ideas carried out by the family that the spaces within the home portray the character of the people who reside here. A statement of uniqueness is found throughout the house; it says that there is only one home such as this. The personalities of the occupants will be deeply embedded in the whole attitude the house presents to visitors.

But individuality alone is not enough. In addition, the home must express beauty. This is an element that most people wish to have around them, but it is not a commodity that comes easily. One must work for it. Most societies are interested in beauty and have been since the beginning of time. To surround ourselves with things of beauty is one of the basic motivations in our struggle with our environment.

The functional operation of the home is another end product of designing a house. A well-designed home will have not only originality and beauty but also efficient living to which both of these elements will and should contribute. The more easily a home operates, the more time there is for appreciating the beauty that has been placed within it. The whole house, from floor plan to the smallest drinking vessel, should be made to meet the specific needs of comfort, maintenance, workability, and aesthetic enjoyment.

Appendix ■ FURNISHING COSTS AND BUDGETS

The breakdown of costs for furnishing a home is important for the home-maker. It must be stressed that costs for furniture and accessories are very flexible and the range is tremendously large in various parts of the country and in different communities. Probably no single home or room could be termed completely "high cost" or "low cost," for the furnishings of each room would probably represent various levels of costs. In attempting to classify budget areas, we might use four groups. Although two of these groups are low cost, each has different objectives and needs. The four groups are Student Low Cost, General Low Cost, Moderate, and High Cost. The first two groups are separated because the student group is generally composed of very inventive people who, through imagination and discovery, can manage to furnish a small apartment with the barest of essentials and still have an attractive environment for living; the general low-cost group probably includes people who are more concerned with appearances and stereotyped solutions to family space problems in the small home or apartment. The third group has moved along into a moderate income and can begin to purchase furnishings that are relatively more expensive than those bought by the low-cost groups. The last group has funds adequate for almost any type of furnishings or at least places a high value on expensive furniture; these people are, therefore, willing to invest a greater percentage of their earnings in making their surroundings aesthetically pleasing. Within these goups there are many fluctuations. They are not stable by any means, but the following price ranges may indicate how these groups might spend money on furnishings for the home.

LIVING ROOM	STUDENT	LOW COST	MODERATE	HIGH COST
Sofa	$ 10–$ 50	$100–$175	$200–$ 275	$ 500–$1500
Chair	$ 8–$ 15	$ 35–$ 50	$ 75–$ 90	$ 200–$ 800
Chair	$ 2–$ 10	$ 20–$ 35	$ 50–$ 75	$ 150–$ 300
Coffee table	$ 7–$ 10	$ 20–$ 50	$ 50–$ 100	$ 125–$ 350
Draperies	$ 12–$ 20	$ 20–$ 50	$ 50–$ 200	$ 200–$ 400
Rug or carpet	$ 10–$ 20	$ 25–$ 75	$175–$ 300	$ 500–up
Lamp	$ 2–$ 10	$ 10–$ 20	$ 20–$ 40	$ 40–$ 75
Accessories	see accessories budget breakdown			

DINING ROOM				
Table	$ 5–$ 10	$ 25–$ 75	$100–$ 200	$ 200–$ 500
4 Chairs	$ 8–$ 15	$ 25–$ 80	$ 80–$ 200	$ 200–$ 600
Storage unit	$ 10–$ 20	$ 20–$ 75	$100–$ 175	$ 200–$1000
Draperies	see living room			
Accessories	see accessories budget breakdown			

BEDROOM				
Bed	$ 30–$100	$ 60–$100	$100–$ 150	$ 150–$ 175
Headboards	$ 2–$ 15	$ 9–$ 50	$ 75–$ 200	$ 200–$1000
Chest	$ 5–$ 15	$ 35–$ 75	$100–$ 275	$ 300–$ 800
Chairs	see living room and dining room			
Draperies	see living room			

Total expenditures would be (without accessories):

	STUDENT	LOW COST	MODERATE	HIGH COST
LIVING ROOM	$ 51–$135	$230–$455	$620–$1085	$1715–$3425
DINING ROOM (without draperies)	$ 23–$ 45	$ 70–$230	$280–$ 575	$ 600–$2100
BEDROOM (without draperies and chairs, but with high-cost, $150, bed)	$157–$180	$194–$275	$325–$ 625	$ 650–$1950

BREAKDOWN OF ACCESSORIES

Fine Arts

Paintings (oil and water color, originals)	$5–unlimited
Reproductions (paintings)	$1–$50
Prints	$5–$1000
Sculptures (originals)	$5–unlimited
Reproductions (sculptures)	$5–$100

Crafts

Ceramics (bowls, etc.)	$2–$400
Glass (vases and sculpture)	$10–$2500
Wood (trays and bowls)	$3–$50
Wall hangings	$10–$500

Commercial Accessories

Glassware (glasses and goblets)	$.10–$5
Dinnerware (per five-piece place setting)	
Plastic	$1.50–$10
Earthenware	$1.25–$15
Bone china	$2.50–$45
Stoneware	$5.00–$15
Porcelain	$15.00–$50
Silverware (per place setting)	
Stainless	$.50–$25
Silver plate	$2.50–$20
Sterling silver	$20.00–$75
Table Coverings	
Place mats	$.20–$6
Table cloths	$1.00–$75

FABRICS

Burlap (per yard)	$.59–$1.50
Cotton	$.29–$15.00
Linen	$1.50–$20.00
Heavy upholstery fabrics (wool, rayons, nylons, and combinations)	$2.00–$45.00
Fiberglas	$1.50–$5.00

When the breakdown of furnishings is computed in percentages spent for each room, there is a great variance, but generally it could look like this:

Living Room	35–45%
Dining Room	20–25%
Bedroom (master)	15–20%
Bedroom (second)	10–15%
Kitchen	20–25%

There is no perfect budget. Each family must make a careful study of personal finances to determine what can be afforded for investment in furnishings.

■ INDEX